Creating Writers

Creating Writers

A creative writing manual for schools

James Carter

First published 2001
by RoutledgeFalmer
11 New Fetter Lane, London EC4P 4EE

Simultaneously published in the USA and Canada
by RoutledgeFalmer
29 West 35th Street, New York, NY 10001

RoutledgeFalmer is an imprint of the Taylor & Francis Group

Typeset in Sabon and Bell Gothic by Keystroke, Jacaranda Lodge, Wolverhampton
Printed and bound in Great Britain by TJ International Ltd, Padstow, Cornwall

British Library Cataloguing in Publication Data
A catalogue record for this book is available from the British Library

Library of Congress Cataloguing in Publication Data
Carter, James, 1959–
        Creating writers : a creative writing manual for schools / James Carter.
            p. cm.
        Includes bibliographical references and index.
        1. English language—Composition and exercises—Study and teaching
(Elementary) 2. Creative writing (Elementary education) 3. English language—
Composition and exercises—Study and teaching (Middle school) 4. Creative writing
(Middle school) I. Title.

LB1576 .C3179 2000
88′.042′071—dc21   00–032214

ISBN 0–415–21691–5

For our daughter Lauren, with infinite love.
Thank you for bringing so much happiness.

Contents

Figures

Acknowledgements

We are most grateful for permission given to reproduce extracts, illustrations or materials from the following.

PETER ABBS AND JOHN RICHARDSON
The Forms of Narrative – reproduced by permission of Cambridge University Press.

DAVID ALMOND
Skellig – reproduced by permission of Hodder & Stoughton Limited.

NICK ARNOLD
Bulging Brains (Scholastic)

PETER BAILEY
Rough illustration for Philip Pullman's *Clockwork* (Transworld)
Illustration of Green Man from Tony Mitton's *Plum* (Scholastic)

IAN BECK
Illustration © Ian Beck 1993. Taken from *Tom and the Island of Dinosaurs* by Ian Beck, published by Doubleday, a division of Transworld Publishers. All rights reserved.

MALORIE BLACKMAN
© Oneta Malorie Blackman 1997. Extracted from *Pig-heart Boy* by Malorie Blackman, published by Doubleday, a division of Transworld Publishers. All rights reserved.
© Oneta Malorie Blackman 1999. Extracted from *Dangerous Reality* by Malorie Blackman, published by Doubleday, a division of Transworld Publishers. All rights reserved.
© Oneta Malorie Blackman 1995. Extracted from *Thief!* by Malorie Blackman, published by Doubleday, a division of Transworld Publishers. All rights reserved.

MELVIN BURGESS
Cry of the Wolf by Melvin Burgess – first published by Andersen Press.
Also published by Puffin.

JAMES CARTER
'Tear' – first published by Hodder Wayland.
'The River' – first published by Heinemann.
'Electric Guitars' – first published by Macmillan.

HELEN CRESSWELL
The Bongleweed by permission of Oxford University Press.
The Piemakers by permission of Oxford University Press.

The Night-Watchmen and *Snatchers* – reproduced by permission of Hodder & Stoughton Limited.

GILLIAN CROSS
The Demon Headmaster by permission of Oxford University Press.
Wolf by permission of Oxford University Press.

JAN DEAN
'Angels' from *A Mean Fish Smile: Sandwich Poets Volume 4* (Macmillan)

TERRY DEARY
Mad Millennium – play script (Scholastic)
The Woeful Second World War (Scholastic)
The Lady of Fire and Tears (Orion Children's Books)

BERLIE DOHERTY
Dear Nobody (Hamish Hamilton, 1991) reproduced by permission of Penguin Books Ltd.

JOHN FOSTER
'My Front Tooth'
'Goran'
'The Snow Monster'
'Grandma'
from *Making Waves* (Oxford University Press)
First three lines of 'Mrs. Nugent's Budgie' from *Standing on the Sidelines* (Oxford University Press)
All reproduced by permission of Oxford University Press.

JAMILA GAVIN
Out of India (Pavilion)

MORRIS GLEITZMAN
Bumface (Penguin Books Australia Ltd)
Water Wings (Macmillan)

JANNI HOWKER
Extract from *Badger on the Barge* © 1984 Janni Howker. Reproduced by permission of the publisher Walker Books Ltd, London.

ROGER MCGOUGH
'The Cats' Protection League' from *Bad, Bad Cats* (Puffin)
'Rabbit in Mixer Survives' from *Selected Poems 1967–1987* (Jonathan Cape)

ANTHONY MASTERS
From the book *Dark Side of the Brain* by Anthony Masters (published by Bloomsbury 1997)
Ghost Blades (Egmont)

TONY MITTON
'Little Red Rap' from *Big Bad Raps* (Orchard)
'Green Man Lane', 'Rainforest Song', 'Nits' from *Plum* (Scholastic)
'Bathroom'

BRIAN MOSES
'Letter from a Soldier' from *Stories from the Past* – compiled by Brian Moses (Scholastic)
'Lost Magic' from *Barking Back at Dogs!* (Macmillan)

ANDREW FUSEK PETERS
'When I Come to the Dark Country' from *The Weather's Getting Verse* (Sherbourne Publications)
'Unevensong' from *Poems with Attitude* (Hodder Wayland)
'Fire at Night'

CELIA REES
Blood Sinister (Scholastic)

MICHAEL ROSEN
'Down Behind the Dustbin' from *You Tell Me* by Michael Rosen and Roger McGough, published by Puffin. Reproduced by permission of Peters, Frazer & Dunlop literary agency.

NICK SHARRATT
Cover illustration © Nick Sharratt. Taken from *The Dare Game* by Jacqueline Wilson, published by Doubleday, a division of Transworld Publishers.

NORMAN SILVER
'Snap, Crackle, Pop' from *The Walkmen Have Landed* (Faber & Faber)

ROB VINCENT
Three photographs in 'Fiction' chapter.

JILLY WILKINSON
Artwork for Norman Silver's *The Blue Horse* (Faber & Faber)

BENJAMIN ZEPHANIAH
'I Luv Me Mudder'

Every effort has been made to trace all copyright holders. In the event of any queries please contact RoutledgeFalmer, London.

Introduction
Where *do* ideas come from?

When the children's author Philippa Pearce went to Buckingham Palace to collect her OBE, the Queen asked her, 'Where do you get your ideas from?' – to which the author replied, 'Harrods, Ma'am'. Whether this anecdote – borrowed from Philip Pullman – is entirely true or not hardly matters for it delightfully proves that it is an impossible question to respond to with any certainty, except perhaps with the answer:

Anywhere and everywhere.

Above all else, it is the aim of this book to empower children to discover this very answer for themselves.

Many authors feel that, to an extent, ideas are the easy part. It is what you do with them that counts. So this book sets out to show what popular and established children's writers do with their ideas and how they grow and develop them into fully fledged poems, stories, novels, plays and information books.

The material in *Creating Writers* comes from a variety of sources. Some of the author quotes stem from interviews conducted especially for this book; some material comes from public talks, performances or writing workshops. Other quotes derive from my book of interviews, *Talking Books* (Routledge). In all cases, full permission has been granted to use the material.

The main part of *Creating Writers* is a Creative Writing Manual, and covers poetry, fiction and non-fiction. The ideas, advice, activities and models of writing featured are provided by a variety of contemporary children's authors, and offer teachers contexts and opportunities in which they can help enable young writers to

- enjoy and explore their own creativity
- express themselves in a range of literary forms and genres and for many purposes and audiences
- reflect upon the craft and process of writing
- engage with and respond imaginatively to the text of others
- consider the elements of narrative, such as dialogue, characterisation, place and plot
- consider the elements of poetry, such as rhythm and rhyme, alliteration and assonance
- perceive themselves as members of a writing community.

The authors represented here were chosen because they each had something invaluable to contribute in terms of passing on advice about creative writing to young people, in terms of sharing their writing methods and of talking about the wealth of experience they have had in schools as writing workshop leaders. Extracts are taken from their texts that are not only relevant and accessible to Key Stage 3/Upper Key Stage 2 but also prevalent and popular resources in primary and secondary schools. It is for these reasons that there are two Scholastic

'Horrible' series (*Horrible Histories* by Terry Deary and *Horrible Science* by Nick Arnold) in the 'Non-fiction' chapter. These award-winning series serve as useful models from which young writers can produce their own non-fiction text.

The Creative Writing Manual part of *Creating Writers* could be used in one of two ways – either as an entire creative writing course to be followed through from start to finish or alternatively as an 'off the shelf' source book for ad hoc writing activities. The manual has been written, where possible, in accessible, everyday language in order that it can be used with Key Stage 3 and Upper Key Stage 2 pupils. Teachers will observe that the majority of the material is pitched directly at – and could be read aloud to – the pupils.

None of the workshop activities presented in this book are set in stone. Teachers are encouraged to view these resources as starting points to be adopted and adapted according to the varying needs of classes, writing environments and individuals. Indeed, a number of the workshop ideas that appear in this book have been used with adults as well as primary and secondary age children, and have been adjusted to suit the ages, ability levels and interests of the writers.

The Author Visit Guide, the second part of this book, features 'Author case studies' of visits conducted by six children's writers – Malorie Blackman, Anthony Masters, Brian Moses, Andrew Fusek Peters, Celia Rees and Jacqueline Wilson. In each case study, one visit is reported in detail. In some of the case studies, the authors reflect upon visiting schools and libraries, performing their work, conducting workshops and meeting their readers. Workshop activities reported and discussed in this section could serve as further starting points for classroom literacy activities and workshops.

In the 'Arranging an author visit' chapter, detailed advice is given on initiating and organising author events. Examples are also provided of the wide range of literacy-based activities that can be undertaken before and after author visits.

Acknowledgements

Creating Writers has been a most exciting and rewarding project in which I have met many generous and inspirational people who were only too willing to give up so much of their precious time. I wish to thank all of them for helping me to assemble this book. I am most grateful to all of the authors for inviting me into their homes and offices, for talking with me, for digging up old manuscripts and for revising the interview transcripts. Please refer to 'Selected current titles' (pp. 243–62) for lists of children's books available by these authors.

I wish to thank the illustrators Peter Bailey and Jilly Wilkinson for once again allowing me to reproduce their artwork. Ian Beck deserves a very special word of thanks – for his unfailing commitment to this project, his warm and congenial support and the truly excellent artwork he has provided for the cover. Thanks must also go to Rob Vincent for his wonderful photographs and to Ken Bentley for his technical wizardry in designing the word wheels.

I thank Malorie Blackman, Anthony Masters, Brian Moses, Andrew Fusek Peters and Celia Rees for allowing me to shadow them during their visits to schools and also Jacqueline Wilson for taking time out of her hectic schedule to visit my own writing class at Reading University; a transcript of Jacqueline's talk is reproduced in the Author Visit Guide. Thanks must also go to the staff at all of the schools I visited – and especially Anne Newman (Farmor's School), Maggie Moorhouse (Stoke Park School), Graham Macarthur (St John's Church of England School), Angie Burroughs (The Weald School) and Vicky Fox (Bedfordshire Libraries) – for their overwhelming help and interest. I am most grateful to the pupils from these schools for allowing me to reproduce their workshop ideas, poems and stories. I must highlight the fact that all of the material in this text – from child or adult, professional or otherwise – has been donated without charge. I am genuinely touched by the generosity of each and every contributor.

Talking Books, my previous title for RoutledgeFalmer, had just one editor. For various reasons, with *Creating Writers* I have had the good fortune to have had three – Jude Bowen, Nina Stibbe and also Helen Fairlie (now formerly of Routledge) – whose adept nurturing helped me to establish and shape the project at the outset. To all three of them I extend my warmest gratitude – for their invaluable input and insight throughout the production of this book. Finally I wish to thank a few more people who have given much time and energy to this book – Michael Lockwood (Reading University), Alice McLaren (formerly of Puffin), Naomi Cooper and Kate Giles (Transworld), Nancy Cooper (Hodder), Nyree Jagger (Scholastic) – and also my brilliant wife, Sarah, for all her love and understanding and for bringing us our wonderful daughter, Lauren.

James Carter

Part One
Creative Writing
Manual

1 Write from the start

Ways to approach creative writing and writing workshops

A positive writing environment

In practice, a positive writing environment can mean many things to many people, but it is surely one in which each and every person in a writing workshop feels that their ideas and contributions are valid and valued. The writing environment is very much the responsibility of the teacher or the workshop leader. A healthy and positive workshop ethos can be achieved in a number of ways, including

- listening with genuine interest when pupils make contributions or read their work aloud
- writing alongside the pupils on a regular basis, and sharing writing with the group
- publishing work on a regular basis (see 'Publishing' section on pp. 11–12)
- making supportive and sensitive but critical comments on students' drafts
- allowing pupils to work at their own pace and to spend time thinking about their writing (see 'Time to think' on p. 4)
- keeping an open mind on the length of a piece, as creativity should ideally not be quantified
- asking only volunteers to read aloud a first draft; there can be set times when all pupils can prepare for a reading of their pieces
- taking time to read pupils' drafts on an ongoing basis
- being flexible as regards the content of workshop activities – at times allowing pupils to take their writing in directions of their own
- recognising and accepting that some activities will inevitably work better with one group as opposed to another
- encouraging pupils to be supportive and attentive to each other
- organising the group into 'feedback partners' or small groups on an ongoing basis (see 'Feedback partners')
- above all, generating real enthusiasm for writing.

Feedback partners

Feedback partners work together on a regular basis to read each other's work and to offer useful support, advice and criticism. When a piece of your own writing is still fresh, it is hard to be objective and to distance yourself from the piece – so having a feedback partner is ideal. When you are giving feedback to a partner, it is important to be sensitive and polite at all times. As Brian Moses suggests, it is best to start with a positive comment first and then make a suggestion for developing the piece – for example, 'Your main character seems quite interesting, but do we know enough about her yet?' or 'This poem has a lovely rhythm, but I'm not sure about the last line – do you think it has too many words?'

Make sure that you read your partner's work slowly and carefully. You could even ask whether your partner minds if you make notes in the margin in pencil. And you may choose to discuss your ideas for a new piece with your partner before you begin writing. Sometimes you could ask your partner to read your piece to you, as this may highlight anything that is not right and enable you to find what needs to be done next.

The 'Poetry checklist' in the 'Poetry' chapter (p. 76) and the 'Fiction checklist' in the 'Fiction' chapter (p. 152) provide a range of issues to consider when reading your own and your partner's writing; these can also be used by teachers when commenting or responding to pupils' pieces. (See 'Drafting and editing', pp. 5–7.)

Time to think

We all need time to mull over and explore our ideas, to ponder over how we are going to start or even develop our writing. Thinking and daydreaming are vital to creativity, as Celia Rees emphasises:

> **CELIA REES:** It took me a long time to realise that writing is not just about sitting at a word processor or a pad of paper and getting things down. Writing is everything: reading, going to the library, visiting places, researching, taking photos and even thinking – thinking is an inherent and very important part of the writing process.

Yet thinking too hard and for too long can often lead to a blank sheet of paper or computer screen. Many authors say that their best writing occurs when they have stopped thinking intently and the piece just seems to write itself, as Malorie Blackman believes:

> **MALORIE BLACKMAN:** When you sit down and begin to write, don't think too hard about it. If I think too hard about what I'm going to write, I get really stuck. When I just sit down and do it, even if I eventually chuck away ninety-nine per cent of what I've done, at least I've got something to work on. If you get to a difficult bit, just do it – you just write through it. There have been times when I've written a whole chapter and later I've deleted all of it and only kept a page, but at least I know where I want to go once I've done that.

Freewriting

Many people find it hard to go into a writing activity cold. Freewriting allows pupils time to adjust to the creative demands of a workshop. Tony Mitton has used this method himself:

> **TONY MITTON:** I used to do freewriting exercises – which involved sitting down and writing for ten minutes per day. The intention of the exercise was to keep writing non-stop for ten minutes. It didn't matter if you got stuck, or if you wrote rubbish, just so long as you were writing something, anything, and the words were coming out. I discovered by doing that what a torrent of creativity the human brain is.

It is best to avoid going straight into a workshop activity. Even a couple of minutes of freewriting will help pupils to focus and allow ideas to start flowing.

Workshop structure

A workshop ideally needs a coherent structure, something along the lines of:

- freewriting
- informing the students as to what they will be writing later
- discussing the writing activity or reading a text as a model
- doing the writing activity
- sharing the writing – with partners, small groups or the whole class
- concluding – where to take writing next – discussion of developing, revising, drafting and editing.

As Cliff Yates recommends in his book *Jumpstart: Poetry Writing in the Secondary School* (Poetry Society), it can be most worthwhile informing the students at the start of a session what they will be writing. This, as Cliff has discovered, allows the mind time to work subconsciously on the activity some time before the actual writing begins.

As regards the forms of writing to be covered over a period of time, balance and variety are important. Interspersing different genres will also serve to highlight the similarities between the various literary forms. Some workshops need to be 'free choice', allowing pupils the opportunity either to develop drafts produced in previous workshops or to explore areas of interest.

The workshop leader will need to have a good supply of appropriate texts that can serve as models to show to the class. Changing text models from year to year will help to keep workshop activities fresh. There can also be times when pupils source their own books or poems as models.

Drafting and editing

Drafting is the process of producing different versions of a text so that it develops and improves. Sometimes you may do a number of different versions of a piece – either handwritten or typed out – or you may work on one single sheet of paper and keep making changes on that one sheet. Pupils regularly ask how many drafts it takes to produce a successful and final version. Yet there can be no set answer: a piece will need to be reworked until it is right, however many drafts it takes.

Whether you are writing prose, poetry or non-fiction, it is vital to take time to read aloud work in progress. All forms of writing take on a new life when read out loud. Clearly, it might not be possible to do this in a classroom or a workshop context, but you can read through your text in your head, and hear it in your mind's ear, as many writers do. Ensure that you read as carefully as you can, looking for anything that could be developed further or improved upon. For areas to consider when reading through your drafts see the 'Fiction checklist' and 'Poetry checklist' worksheets.

As you are reading your text you will no doubt need to make various changes. You will make notes in the margins, add extra text, delete words, phrases or sentences – or even change the order of passages of text. This is all perfectly normal and is exactly what professional authors do, and it is evidence that you are crafting your piece of writing. See how David Almond has changed his text on a manuscript page for his novel *Skellig* (Figure 1.1).

In your first couple of drafts you do not need to be concerned about the presentation of the piece – that is, the spelling, handwriting, grammar, punctuation – as this type of work, known as 'editing', can be done at a later stage. As these authors believe, in the early drafts of a piece of writing you should be concentrating on getting your ideas down:

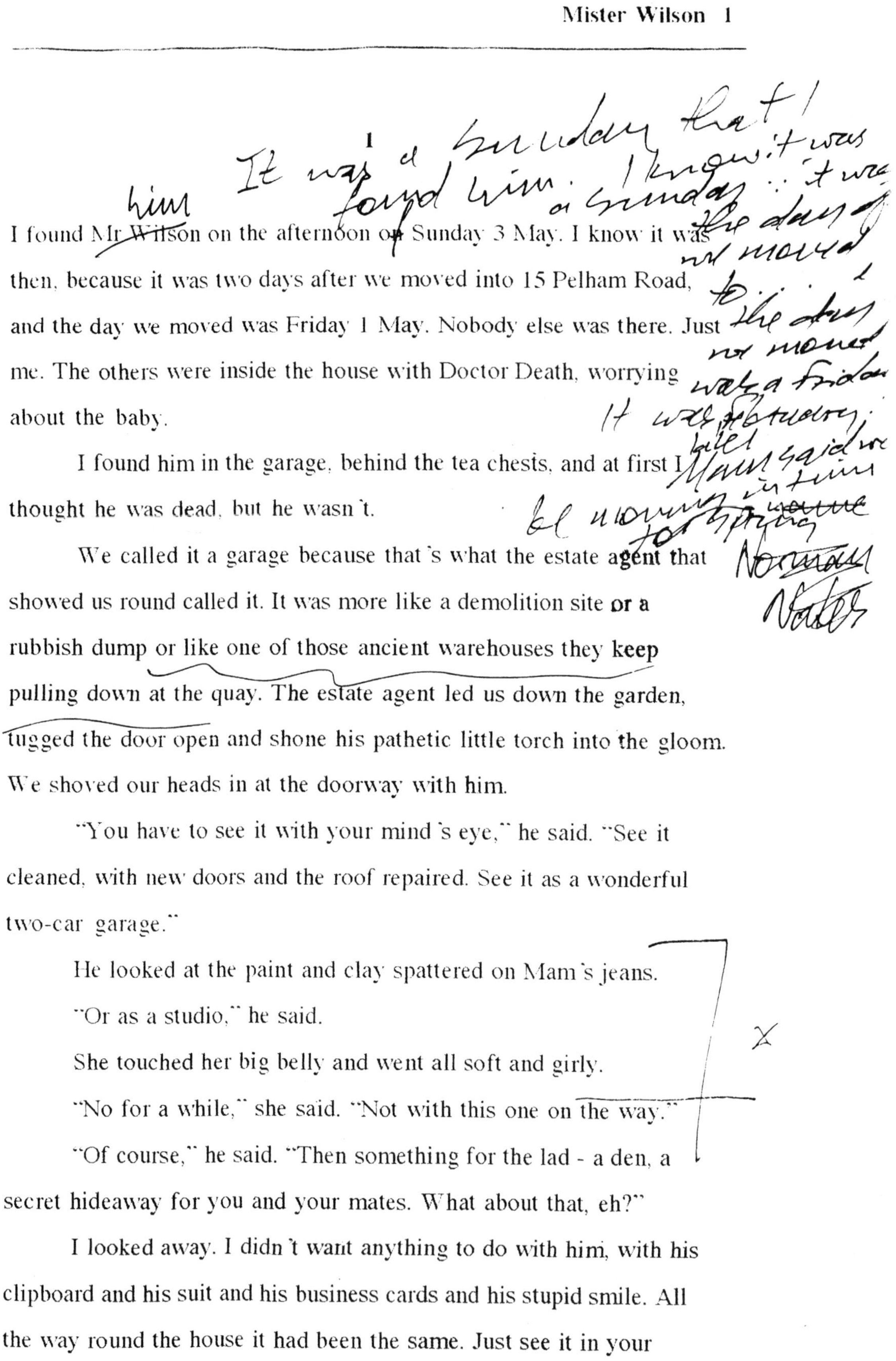

Mister Wilson 1

I found Mr Wilson on the afternoon of Sunday 3 May. I know it was

then, because it was two days after we moved into 15 Pelham Road,

and the day we moved was Friday 1 May. Nobody else was there. Just

me. The others were inside the house with Doctor Death, worrying

about the baby.

I found him in the garage, behind the tea chests, and at first I

thought he was dead, but he wasn't.

We called it a garage because that's what the estate agent that

showed us round called it. It was more like a demolition site or a

rubbish dump or like one of those ancient warehouses they keep

pulling down at the quay. The estate agent led us down the garden,

tugged the door open and shone his pathetic little torch into the gloom.

We shoved our heads in at the doorway with him.

"You have to see it with your mind's eye," he said. "See it

cleaned, with new doors and the roof repaired. See it as a wonderful

two-car garage."

He looked at the paint and clay spattered on Mam's jeans.

"Or as a studio," he said.

She touched her big belly and went all soft and girly.

"No for a while," she said. "Not with this one on the way."

"Of course," he said. "Then something for the lad - a den, a

secret hideaway for you and your mates. What about that, eh?"

I looked away. I didn't want anything to do with him, with his

clipboard and his suit and his business cards and his stupid smile. All

the way round the house it had been the same. Just see it in your

Figure 1.1 Manuscript page for David Almond's novel *Skellig*, with working title *Mister Wilson*

ANTHONY MASTERS: You mustn't ever worry about spelling and grammar when you're creating, or you'll ruin the flow of your ideas.

JACQUELINE WILSON: Surely it's best to write the story and to imagine it as hard as you can first, and then you can go back and do an exercise on how to punctuate it.

Gillian Cross focuses upon the story first and later goes back to work on the phrasing:

GILLIAN CROSS: I tend to concentrate on my language more when I've got the shape of the story right. The hang up I used to have as a child and teenage writer was that you had to get the language right first time. That was something that made it difficult for me. I know some people will correct chapter 1 until it's right and then go on to chapter 2, but I'd be on chapter 1 for ever!

Philip Pullman has his own view of drafts:

PHILIP PULLMAN: I don't agree with the emphasis that teachers lay on drafting. I never write drafts – I write final versions. I might write a dozen final versions of the same story, but with each one I set out to write it as a final version. If you set out to write a draft you'll take it less seriously than you should.

As the authors in the 'Poetry', 'Fiction' and 'Non-fiction' chapters of this book demonstrate when discussing their books and poems, a polished and successful piece of writing does not come about in one sitting. A piece of writing takes time to craft. Therefore, pupils will need time to draft their work over a number of workshops.

To demonstrate the drafting process to young writers, teachers can produce displays of work in progress by professional authors, and the manuscript page from David Almond's *Skellig* reproduced in this chapter (Figure 1.1) could be used for this very purpose.

Realistic expectations of the first draft

The first version of any text is rarely, if ever, the last version. You cannot expect your first draft to be the only one you will do. Most of the poems, plays, information books, short stories or novels that you read will have been drafted, redrafted and revised numerous times. Once you have worked on a piece and you cannot do any more to it, leave it for a while. Let it breathe. When you come back to it in a few days, you will see more clearly what needs to be done next. Do not worry if you find yourself making quite a few changes – this is often a sign that you are viewing your work analytically and objectively. The author Ernest Hemingway was keen on redrafting – he rewrote the first paragraph of his novel *Fiesta* forty times! And this paragraph has itself been reworked some five or six times.

Young writers can have unrealistic expectations of a first draft, and can feel that it has got to be perfect in every way. You are expecting the impossible if this is how you feel. Here is some useful advice from Tony Mitton on writing poetry – but the principle could be applied to prose as well:

TONY MITTON: When you're writing poetry you have to be prepared to write rubbish as you go along, rubbish that you can get rid of later. You just have to keep going until you write something that you like. It's a bit like trudging through a desert until you find your oasis, finding a place where you want to be.

Melvin Burgess adopts a very similar attitude to Tony Mitton:

MELVIN BURGESS: The first draft is like ad-libbing on to paper. You take out the rubbish afterwards. I spend a couple of days on the ad-libbing, then I go over it again pulling out the bits I don't want. Then, when I've finished the whole thing, I'll go through it again, checking as a reader to find the bits that I'm doubtful about, bits which don't work. Then I drop into the manuscript at random to check various things, so the whole thing gets re-read a lot.

You may even choose to think of your first draft as just experimenting with ideas. Roger McGough and Alan Garner both use the word 'doodling' to describe this process of exploring early ideas.

JACQUELINE WILSON: Don't fuss too much about how you start off, because you can always go back and rewrite the beginning. Just think about getting yourself into the story.

RUSSELL HOBAN: Don't worry about the form, and don't worry about beginnings, middles and endings. Take hold of the thing, wherever you can, whatever of an idea presents itself to you, whether it's the foot or the elbow, grab it, and work out from there.

Most of all, do not expect too much of yourself when you start writing – simply put a few words down on the page and see what happens.

Process and product and portfolios

There has often been a preoccupation in schools with pupils having to complete each and every single piece of creative work that is started. But why?

Writers often find that some pieces of writing 'go cold' on them and, as a result, these pieces are never finished. Alternatively, some of these stories and poems may be ransacked for ideas at a later stage. With creative writing, nothing is wasted: ideas can be recycled.

Process, as many authors have said, is as important as product. For pupils to experience and experiment with writing in a wide variety of forms is arguably of greater value than completing just a few. And it is not only the finished piece that matters, but also understanding and appreciating the inherent elements of each form as well as the processes involved in creating different types of text.

What can be very useful is a portfolio – a folder or file in which pupils keep ideas, drafts, completed pieces, brainstorms, story outlines, character sketches, planning sketches and so on. By doing this, a pupil can, rather than start a new piece of writing every workshop, go back to unfinished pieces or start a piece that was simply an initial seed of an idea. Finding fresh ideas on a regular basis can be very draining, and portfolios can be an ideal way of overcoming a lack of inspiration.

Ideas and notebooks

The whole notion of creativity and of discovering ideas is a difficult one to discuss with any certainty.

TERRY DEARY: Ideas come to you out of the blue, and that's why it's sometimes hard to talk about the writing process. Inspiration is not definable. You can't bottle it, and if you could you would be a millionaire. Yes, there are moments of inspiration, where suddenly you think, that's what I've been looking for. It's very exciting!

JACQUELINE WILSON: All writers get asked where we get our ideas from. No writer can ever come up with a reasonable, convincing answer. You just don't know – an idea bobs into your head, just like that.

But once you get an idea – what are you going to do with it, and what happens if you are not writing anything at that time?

ALAN DURANT: I have a notebook in which I write various bits and pieces – ideas for titles, jokes, interesting names, descriptions of interesting faces – all kinds of things. Every now and then I go through my notebooks to see if there's any material I can use.

BRIAN MOSES: I store all my ideas in notebooks and on disc. I keep all my poetry notebooks, and most of the ideas are dated. I'll remember a poem by the place I wrote it in. And I can usually remember quite accurately the year and time I would have written it. Sometimes I'll go through the notebooks, taking out ideas I want to use.

JACQUELINE WILSON: Keeping a notebook gives you the feeling that there's always something to work on. As a fiction writer, it's frightening – you do literally have to conjure things up out of nothing. Even half a page of jottings in a book can be a big help.

Most writers keep notebooks and regularly use them to jot down ideas. But what can you write in a notebook? Here are a few suggestions:

- interesting names that you come across
- something that might serve as a good title
- words, phrases or descriptions that you come across in conversation, in magazines, books, newspapers, on TV or in a film
- details on a character or plot you might be working on
- a line for a poem
- in fact, anything that might serve as a potential idea!

Ideas come in all shapes and sizes – but, unfortunately, one shape and size they do not come in is that of a finished story or poem, as Ian Beck comments:

IAN BECK: An idea never arrives perfectly formed. It has to be built upon. It will arrive as a nudge saying, 'You think about that'. And your instinct just tells you that this idea is worth thinking about.

Sometimes one idea needs another to connect up with.

RUSSELL HOBAN: Things circulate in my skull waiting for other things to hook up with them.

CELIA REES: Often I'll get an idea, but it won't be complete. I may have a story or a plot, but it will need more. Then I have to wait until there is something else to add to it to make it whole.

Within reason, nearly any idea is good – in the right place. But do not spend too long trying to fit a square peg in a round hole. If something is not quite working, leave it, and come back to it later when you can view the piece more clearly. Just because a poem or a short story might not seem to work the first time you write it, do not throw it away. You may find yourself redrafting it at a later stage, or using some of the ideas for another piece. Sometimes, you may find that a piece contains too many ideas. Do not be too precious about deleting whole chunks of text. It is what is best for that piece that counts.

Ideas and good habits to get into

The more you get into the habit of writing, that is writing on a regular if not daily basis, the more ideas will come to you, and the more you will experience and observe many things that will serve as potential ideas for writing.

> **RUSSELL HOBAN:** Do something every day. Let the ideas develop as they will – don't require of yourself that you do a whole story or a whole novel, just do whatever you can, every day.

> **PHILIP PULLMAN:** I believe that success in writing, as with any other enterprise, is due to three things: talent, hard work and luck. Of those, the only one you have any control over is the hard work. You can't decide to be talented; nor can you say 'I'm going to my room to be lucky for two hours'. But you can say: 'I'm going to write a page every day', and you can go on doing it. It soon mounts up. After a few months, you'll have written the equivalent of a book. You might want to change most of it, but at least it'll be there to work on, which it won't be if you waste your time wishing you were talented or waiting for your luck to change.

Versions of one idea

Sometimes you may find that you have an idea that you think is worth exploring, but when you start to write it down it does not seem as good. If this is the case, leave what you have written and keep pondering over that original idea. Keep coming back to that idea and trying it until you have a version that you like. It could be that your earlier versions were not working for a number of reasons – perhaps the idea worked better as a poem rather than a story, or perhaps your story should have been in the first person and not the third person (see 'Fiction' chapter), or perhaps the idea needed developing or being joined together with another idea. Try not to be too precious about what you have written – keep an open mind as to how a piece should grow.

Occasionally, an idea that you are working on will want to change shape. You may be working on a short story and find that it wants to become a rhyming narrative poem, or that a free verse poem wants to be a shape poem, or whatever. If an idea such as this comes to you, go with it, and see what happens.

> **ALAN DURANT:** Ideas come in all shapes and sizes. Sometimes I know where to put an idea – if it's a novel or a short story or picture book. But ideas can change at times. One of my books, *Little Troll*, for example, started out as two different picture books. However, something wasn't quite right about them, and I rewrote them as one storybook text for younger readers.

An idea is like a lump of clay. It can be moulded into many shapes. But some clays make good coffee cups, other clays make good floor tiles. Your idea, say, could be about someone starting at a new school. That idea could be turned into a funny rhyming poem or a comic strip, a school drama story, or a more serious free verse poem or a monologue. You have to work out what that idea wants to be. It is as simple – and as difficult – as that!

Stimuli for writing

Later in this book you are encouraged to use a variety of stimuli to generate writing. These include:

- music – instrumentals from any genres and also song lyrics
- pictures – photographs, postcards, paintings – in books, magazines, on the Internet or in art galleries and museums
- artefacts – anything from presentation boxes to musical instruments to objects from other countries or cultures to historical objects
- clips from films, documentaries or TV dramas (ideally with the sound turned off)
- walks, school trips and visits
- an original story or poem – to spark off a poem adopting either the same form, character(s), structure, theme or point of view.

Dictionaries and thesauruses

It is always useful to have a collection of dictionaries and thesauruses to hand. Do not be afraid to use either of these two books. A writer needs to have access to a wide vocabulary, to know the meanings of many words, and to be able to think of alternative words and phrases. When used in the right way, a dictionary and a thesaurus can be an extension of one's own knowledge and word store.

Other texts that might prove useful are a rhyming dictionary and a 'Name Your Baby' book. The latter can be very helpful when choosing fictional characters' names.

Publishing

Publishing needs to occur on a regular basis and gives writing a sense of purpose. If pupils are actively involved with publishing themselves, it can be a source of motivation. Publishing takes many shapes and forms, such as:

- class or year group anthologies
- school magazines
- local community magazines or local newspapers
- displays in classes, corridors and school halls
- school websites
- performances in class, assemblies or parents' evenings
- magazines such as *Young Writer* – contact Kate Jones, Glebe House, Weobley, Herefordshire HR4 8SD, tel: 01544-318901, website: http://www.mystworld.com/young writer
  and also the *Times Educational Supplement*
- websites such as 'Poetryzone': http://www.poetryzone.ndirect.co.uk.

- for details of poetry competitions contact the Poetry Society, tel: 020-7420-9880 website: http://www.poetrysoc.com
- for details of other competitions see the appendix at the end of this book.

Using word processors

Most writers agree that computers are a great asset to creative writing.

MALORIE BLACKMAN: I write straight on to my computer, but I always edit and rework my stories on paper. I can't imagine writing the first draft on anything but a computer. I like to chop and change and play about with sentences, paragraphs, pages and sometimes whole chapters. On a computer it's a doddle. I'd go crazy if I had to use a typewriter and type each page again every time I changed even a word.

ROGER MCGOUGH: The thing about the word processor is that you can work too quickly. The poem looks too professional – and too good too soon – on the screen.

CELIA REES: Word processors have changed the whole concept of drafting in that it's not quite the same process as when people wrote by hand or used a typewriter. Then you would have to do numerous individual redrafts to get the final draft. Now, I draft as I go along, as I'm writing.

John Foster has the following advice for writing poetry on a computer:

JOHN FOSTER: I suggest to children that if they use a computer they should do lots of printouts. I recommend that they don't use the 'delete' button too often and I advise that they type out all the different versions as they go along so that they can keep all of their ideas. I write my poems by hand, and I do all my drafts on one single sheet of paper. This enables me to use words or phrases or lines that I might have crossed out in an earlier draft of a poem. This way, I don't ever lose any of my ideas. More of my poems are written by hand than on a computer – but that's because the idea will come when I'm away from the screen. I don't find sitting in front of the screen conducive to finding ideas for poems.

One major disadvantage in using computers for writing is that the majority of them are not portable – only a few people have laptop computers. But a notepad can be taken anywhere – and can save you having to write on bus tickets and envelopes when you are feeling inspired! Some writers – although they may write directly on to a computer – choose to do a printout on rough or recycled paper in order that they can do a penultimate draft by hand. You might wish to try this yourself. Some classes will use a word processor for typing up final drafts prior to publication. Another instance in which a computer can be a very useful tool is when creating shape poetry (see 'Poetry' workshops, pp. 68–72).

Talking points

Many children's writers begin their workshops by discussing various ideas and issues surrounding the writing process. You may wish to discuss some of the following:

- Why do we read and write?
- What happens when we read and write?

- Could society survive without language or stories?
- What are the similarities and differences between oral and written language?
- Do we develop as readers after teenage?
- Why is reading essential to writing?
- When did storytelling begin? How has it changed in the past 200 years?
- Have computers affected how we write and also read and work?
- Can you think of a different book that you have read in each year of your life after the age of 4? Make a list.
- What would your three 'desert island' books be?

A fun and interactive way to explore storytelling is to work in pairs or small groups and to tell a story of your own, something either amusing or interesting that has happened to you.

Writing for the reader in you

Both Alan Durant and Melvin Burgess stress how important it is to entertain yourself as you write:

ALAN DURANT: To be a writer, you've got to be a reader. You write first for yourself as a reader.

MELVIN BURGESS: Write for yourself – but make it so that it's accessible for your audience.

Enjoy yourself!

This has to be the most important aspect of writing – because if you do not enjoy what you write, how can you expect others to?!

2 **Poetry**

MATTHEW SWEENEY: As Robert Frost said,
poetry is a fresh look and a fresh listen.

A new way of seeing: some thoughts on writing poetry

The quote from Matthew Sweeney and Robert Frost that opens this chapter – 'Poetry is a fresh look and a fresh listen' – can be adopted as a very useful approach to writing poetry. It can encourage us to aim for something new and 'fresh' when creating a poem, not only 'fresh' in terms of what we are writing about, for example a new way of thinking about a subject, but also 'fresh' in terms of *how* the poem is expressed – in terms of the language and the imagery that we use. Colin Macfarlane expresses very much the same thing when he says that in poetry 'a good description gives a new way of seeing'.

Some people feel that poetry is easier to write than other forms of fiction or non-fiction. Indeed, a short poem can come about fairly quickly. However, even the shortest poem may need revisiting a number of times to rework, amend or even add to: perhaps the rhyme in the fourth line is not quite right, or the adjective in the opening line does not precisely capture the mood or image you want it to. There is always something that can be done to develop or improve a piece. Yet it can be difficult to know when to stop making alterations, as Brian Moses reflects:

> **BRIAN MOSES:** What I enjoy about poetry is that you can create a poem quickly and it's there and you feel good that you've done something that day – but a poem can take anything from five minutes to a year to write. An average poem will initially take an hour or two – but I'm always tinkering away at it afterwards. Then I'll perform it and modify it. And then maybe perform it to a different audience and modify it again. Performances can help me to see if there are any flat points. Sometimes I'll start to write a poem, put it away for a couple of months, and then go back to it, and do a bit more to it – and it might take a year to get written. I don't think I ever quite know when a poem is finished. The only time I'll finally leave it alone is when it's published in a book.

In one sense, poetry writing requires a lot of patience – perhaps more so than writing fiction or non-fiction – as more time is spent concentrating on the smaller details. With a poem you are focusing upon individual words and phrases or the ordering of the lines and the stanzas, or even the combination of word sounds or the number of beats in a particular line. The writing of poetry requires a fascination with language, and the desire to spend a great deal of time experimenting with it, moulding it and shaping it:

> **TONY MITTON:** If you want to write well you need to become an expert with words and language. You need to be as skilful with words as a painter is with paints or a composer is with sounds. You've got to care about every word, every pause, every last detail of what you put.

One of the many things that poetry can offer is a space for writing about our experiences and memories. In this way, poetry can help to preserve, explore and make sense of our experiences as well as to share them with other people. As Michael Rosen recommends in his influential book *Did I Hear You Write?*, young writers must be encouraged to use their own voices – their own everyday, colloquial speech – in poetry, particularly when writing autobiographically. (See John Foster's discussion of 'My Front Tooth' and the accompanying workshop activity later in this chapter for further comments on colloquial language and autobiographical writing.)

As fiction and non-fiction have genres, poetry has its many forms, from modern to classical, oral to literary. So Benjamin Zephaniah's image of poetry – that of a tree – is most apt:

BENJAMIN ZEPHANIAH: I see poetry as this big tree that has many branches. You can get introduced to the tree by climbing up one of the branches, but it doesn't mean to say that you can't explore other parts of the tree. I got on to the tree via oral poetry, but I've gone on to love all kinds – from nonsense verse to classical poetry like Shelley – and I love them all equally.

This chapter considers a number of the most popular contemporary styles of poetry – including free verse, rhyme, rap, ballad, haiku and shape poetry. As many poets advocate, pupils should begin by writing mainly free verse and non-rhyming forms as rhyme is a challenging discipline for those who do not have the extended vocabulary of older, more experienced writers. Advice on rhyme and free verse is provided in this chapter.

Once you have read the poets' definitions of poetry in the next section you could give thought to the following issues yourself, remembering that when talking about these ideas, there are rarely right or wrong answers:

- How would you personally define poetry?
- How do you feel about poetry? Why?
- What do you think is the difference between poetry and prose?
- When is an idea best served as a poem or as prose?
- Can you write poetry using sign language?
- What can a poem do that other forms of writing cannot do?
- Why do more people read prose and non-fiction than poetry?

(For further discussion points see 'Talking points', pp. 12–13.)

What's poetry good for? Poets share their personal definitions of poetry

Every poet has their own interpretation of what poetry is. Here are a few contemporary poets responding to the question 'What is poetry and what is it good for?'

JAN DEAN: A poem is to wake you up. It's to make you connect more vividly with the world and to be more alive in how you see and respond to everything around you. One of the many things that a poem needs to do is to create a tension between recognition – 'Oh yes, it is like that' – and strangeness – 'I never thought of it like that before'. Recognition and strangeness are like opposite poles of a magnet, and they give a poem its energy.

JOHN FOSTER: I'm often asked what poetry is and the only definition that I can come up with that actually works is that poetry is words patterned on a page. Also, poetry can be about any subject matter – for example, Michael Rosen has written a poem about a tube of toothpaste!

Poetry can explore anything that writing can explore. What distinguishes it from prose is that it doesn't have to have a narrative element and it's patterned differently.

ROGER MCGOUGH: I don't really want to add to the list of definitions – though most reading is for information or for entertainment, and poetry is neither of these two. Poetry is something that is coded and it seems to come from another way of thinking. When I first discovered poetry it seemed almost secretive in that it worked in a way that I couldn't define. What's it good for? It's good for tapping into something unconscious. Most writing is to carry information from A to B, whereas poetry is the wandering off, it's the looking at things from a different angle or in close-up.

TONY MITTON: Poetry is patterned language. The patterning of free verse may be very elusive, but even free verse patterns language. Though it could be said that, to an extent, all writing patterns language. Certainly I know that well-written prose is not easy to write – and is just as crafted as poetry. Then you might say how do you distinguish poetry from prose? I would say that prose tends to be more narrative-sequential linked, whereas poetry is much more varied. It can be more theme-based. As a teenager I got very excited when I read T.S. Eliot's comment that poetry is the 'dance of the intellect'. I don't necessarily agree with that, but I do certainly think that poetry is the dance of the language, and that poetry dances more than prose does. If I had to sum it up in one sentence, I'd say that poetry is language dancing.

BRIAN MOSES: I suppose because I'm attracted so much to music and the rhythms of music, I'm attracted to the rhythms of poetry and language. I love words and how poetry allows you to string words together in a variety of ways. For me, a poem is a snapshot giving you a brief glimpse, but a glimpse that is often so powerful that it can stay with you forever. It enables you to look at the world in a different way.

ANDREW FUSEK PETERS: It's working with words in a way that can make people think about the world they live in, in terms of politics, in terms of emotions, in terms of getting people in touch with things they avoid, in terms of entertainment. Poetry is also a craft, something to be worked at.

BENJAMIN ZEPHANIAH: What's poetry good for? It's good for capturing big emotions in a small, concise way, or for taking little teeny things and stretching them out. It's good because Ted Hughes can do it, Bob Geldof can do it, Benjamin Zephaniah can do it – but also Mr Brown at the allotment can do it. It's the most democratic art form you can get. All you need is a pen and a piece of paper, and when it comes to oral poetry, you don't even need a pen and paper. When someone comes to me and says that they're a poet, then they're a poet. I don't know if they're a genius, a mad person or what. If they've written a couple of lines, if they've had some imaginative thoughts, then they're a poet. I often tell people that publishing poetry is not the be-all and end-all. I tell them to perform it, because audiences will tell you what's good and what's bad. It's a very simple philosophy, and it's always rung true for me until this day. Another thing that poetry's good for is spreading the message of peace, love and unity.

How do poems begin? Poets examine the ways in which their poems evolve

As with fiction, an idea for a poem can come from almost anywhere. In this section, poets reflect upon some of the ways in which their own poems come about.

JAN DEAN: Ideas for poems are like little gifts. Sometimes I'll see something interesting, and that may well end up as an image in one of my poems. But most of my poems begin with a phrase that just comes into my head.

JOHN FOSTER: An idea for a poem often comes from something I see or hear. One of the things I've discovered as I've written more and more poetry is that I'm often trying to find something that is a common experience. What I try to do is to write in a way that kids will connect with that common experience. One example might be the experience of waking up in a strange room and wondering for a split second where you are, or the experience of being afraid of the dark. Or, alternatively, there might be something specific that I read about or I see on the television that will spark a poem off. Or, when I'm editing poems I might come across a form of poetry that I want to imitate. One example would be a piece by Tony Mitton called 'Ten Things You Never Thought To Ask About Elephants'. I thought that was so funny that I then wrote 'Ten Things You Never Thought To Ask About Hippopotamuses', with lines like: 'What do you call a young female hippo? A hippopota-miss!' So, you can get ideas for poems from other people's structures.

This goes to the heart of my philosophy as an English teacher. As teachers we should present poems as models. I believe the way to develop people as writers is to present them with a text and to analyse it, to look at what the writer is doing and the techniques that the writer is employing in that particular text. Then, the children can have a go at writing in the same way – not using the same content, but the techniques and the appropriate form. Then comes the stage that so often is missed, which is for the children to analyse where they have succeeded or not. This is not for the teacher to do, but for the children – and for them to look objectively at their own work. Until you start to evaluate your writing critically you can't begin to develop or improve as a writer.

ROGER MCGOUGH: Well, if I don't have anything specific to write about, doodling with words and phrases usually sets me off. Words themselves lead me on to an idea often. Of course, it can often be a concrete or a visual idea that will spark a poem off. In the way that an illustrator will draw a line, and a line will become a circle, and a circle will become a face, and so on – I just frequently start doodling with a few words. And as with drawings, you don't know what the poem is going to be about until you've finished it.

As Gertrude Stein once said, 'Poetry is a process of discovery' – it's not a process of describing the known. But people still seem to think that with poetry you have an idea and with it the whole poem just comes into your head in a shape, and that's it. It's very rare that it happens like that. The exciting thing for me is discovering what a new poem is about. Then part of the trick is knowing when to step away from the creative process and to let the poem that's emerging have its own life.

BENJAMIN ZEPHANIAH: Most of my poems start in my head with a rhythm:

I *luv* me mudder and me *mudder* luvs me

It can be just that for a while. Then I might go on:

We *cum* so far from *over* de sea.

And I'll pace up and down the room as I'm saying it, and sometimes I'm actually kind of dancing. I think a lot of oral poets do that. I remember hearing a story about Dylan Thomas building a shed at the bottom of his garden. It was his daughter telling the story, and she said she could hear him in there at night chanting his poems out.

For me, one of the most important things about poems is *how* they're said. When they roll off my tongue nicely, that's when I know that they're ready for writing down. Sometimes I just create the whole thing in my head. But it really varies. One thing I don't want is a technique – I like to do it all different ways. I've got a recording studio downstairs and sometimes I'll write in there and perform to a drum machine rhythm. Other times, I'll record a poem on to a little tape recorder or dictaphone. But if I'm doing free verse, I'll do it on paper.

I sometimes feel that I'm writing all the time, that I'm always collecting ideas, whatever I'm doing. There's a difference between creating a poem and writing a poem. I create poems anywhere and everywhere – like when I'm jogging – but the actual writing happens here in the office.

Masterclass: poets respond to questions often asked about writing poetry

What is the right beginning for a poem?

JAN DEAN: It's the one that allows you to write the next line. Until I've got the right first line – and I'm happy with the sound and feel of it – I can't move on to the second line. Sometimes you can be stuck on a first line that won't let you carry on, and maybe that's because it's not meant to be a beginning and it should be somewhere else. You only realise that when you leave a poem for a few days or weeks and then come back to it. Only then can you see that there should be other lines in front of your original first line.

BRIAN MOSES: The first few lines are what hooks the reader, so the opening has got to make an impact and to encourage the reader to want to read on. It's like the first page of a novel – you want to read on because you've been intrigued somehow by what you've read. And a good ending can be one of many things. It can be a good idea that you saved till last to round off the poem, or something that sums up the poem in some way or a joke or even something unexpected.

What is the right form for a poem?

JOHN FOSTER: The form develops from and is suggested by what you think of or write down initially. So, if you wrote something like –

> There are four chairs round the table
> Where we sit down for our tea

you know that's going to be a rhythmical, rhyming poem. But if you wrote –

> Yesterday,
> Our neighbour Mrs. Nugent
> Accidently sat on the budgie

[from 'Mrs. Nugent's Budgie' in *Standing on the Sidelines*: Oxford University Press]

you know that's going to be a non-rhyming poem. When starting a new poem, a poet will experiment with the form until they find one that is right. In the same way, novelists will experiment with the voice or point of view of a narrative until they find one that suits the story that they have to tell.

Can poems ever change from one form to another?

ANDREW FUSEK PETERS: Yes. Recently I started writing a long poem in free verse, and I suddenly thought, no, this needs to be a sonnet. I had to edit, edit, edit to change from one to the other. Form is interesting like that. However the final result was just as powerful – emotionally – as the free verse – but, in one sense, it was more powerful because it was contained within that envelope of the sonnet. Form does help to channel things, to make things sharper, and more direct. But there are no real rules about which subject matters are better expressed in certain forms of poetry.

How does the rhythm of a poem become established?

COLIN MACFARLANE: If you've written a first line or two, or even a short verse, say it over and over in your head so that the rhythm is fixed and you know the feel of it well – then carry on – with that first verse in the back of your mind. Don't forget to keep doing this throughout the poem.

JAN DEAN: Once you have a rhythm you have to keep it up for the whole poem. It can be very disturbing if you set up a strong rhythm at the beginning and then you break out into a different rhythm. You really do need to stick with it. If you do change the rhythm, there has to be a reason for it in the meaning of the poem.

TONY MITTON: I try to establish the rhythm from the first stanza. I also consider in that first verse if I've found a rhythm I can satisfactorily work throughout a poem or whether I'm going to have to move away from it. As sometimes I do step from free verse into a tighter and more rhymed pattern, like in my 'Forbidden Poem'.

What advice do you have on writing free verse?

BRIAN MOSES: Free verse isn't just prose that's been chopped up on the page. In my workshops I say that a free verse poem must look like a poem on the page right from the start because then it makes it much easier to inject a rhythm into it. Whatever type of poem it is, it must have a rhythm. Rhythm often comes from the rhyme, but in free verse, the rhythm has to come in some other way – such as the repetition of certain lines or phrases.

(See Jan Dean's discussion of 'Angels', Brian Moses' discussion of 'Lost Magic' or John Foster's discussion of 'My Front Tooth' later in this chapter for examples of free verse.)

How can I write good rhymes?

JAN DEAN: If you start using rhyme at the beginning of a poem, you must use it for the whole piece. But it's perfectly reasonable to have a non-rhyming poem that ends with rhyme, and it can finish a poem off quite nicely. And that can give a poem a bit of extra colour and extra music at the end. I really like using internal rhymes and playing around with rhymes, and putting them in irregular places.

JOHN FOSTER: Young children do enjoy rhyme and like writing their own rhymes. Many children come to poetry through nursery rhymes and rhyming stories. But rhyming is difficult. In my workshops I'll tell children that if they want to rhyme, then fine, but they'll find it much harder than free verse.

In one workshop I did recently I asked the class if they knew the golden rule of writing rhyme. One very bright child put his hand up and said 'Don't give up!' I thought that was great! My golden rule is that if you are going to rhyme, then the rhyme must fit the sense and the meaning of the poem. Therefore, children need to be given tips on how to find more rhyming possibilities than the ones they can immediately think of. My first tip is to brainstorm through the alphabet, not just using initial letters, but using common letter strings too. So, if they come to 's' in the alphabet, they can also do 'sc', 'sh', 'sl', 'st', 'str' and so on. So, for example, if the word they want to rhyme with is 'tall', they put all the letters of the alphabet at the front of the word until they get a word that fits the poem that they're writing: 'a-all', 'b-all', 'c-all' and through to 'z'. But you must also bear in mind that the spelling of the '-all' sound may vary, because it could be '-awl' or '-aul'.

What I learnt from the children's poet Eric Finney is that you can dip in and out of rhyme in poems and it can work. Just so long as you don't start with rhyme, you can move in and out of it through the poem, and that's fine. The other way – starting with rhyme and then not using it – would sound wrong. So if you start with a strict rhyming and rhythmical pattern you must stick with it. Eric Finney does this very well in his work.

(See John Foster's discussion of 'My Front Tooth' later in this section.)

ROGER MCGOUGH: Usually the best rhyme isn't the first one that pops into your head because that's usually a rather obvious one. Listening to the poem can make ideas for rhymes come because rhymes are part of the music of what you are writing.

TONY MITTON: One very good way of learning to rhyme is a way that Michael Rosen has shown in his 'Down Behind the Dustbin' poem – in that you take a nonsense or humorous form in which it doesn't really matter what you say. If it's pathetic, if it's funny, it doesn't matter. The dangerous thing to do is to write a really serious thing in rhyme when you're not experienced, as you might trip up and you might write something unintentionally comic in rhyme without realising it, while you actually intend to be serious.

So, a good way to learn to use rhyme is through comedy, nonsense rhyme, doggerel or limerick. Or, as I've said, you can take a poem like 'Down Behind the Dustbin' and use it as a model poem and make up your own verses:

> Down behind the dustbin
> I met a dog called – Nell
> I thought she was a cat –
> But who can tell?

If what you come up with is slightly nonsensical, but it doesn't matter in that context. The important thing is that you're learning to work the rhythms and rhymes.

ANDREW FUSEK PETERS: What makes a good rhyme? Something unexpected, a word you wouldn't expect to rhyme with the word at the end of the previous line. My advice with rhyme is that it has to flow, it has to be transparent, and you mustn't make it seem as if you're desperate to make a rhyme. It must make sense. You can't just say, 'The sun is yellow as a daffodil / Yesterday I went to see Bill'!

What stages can a poem go through?

TONY MITTON: I do a first draft or two of a poem in my notebook. Then I'll type it up onto the computer and print it out and work on it manually again. Then, I'll go back and rework the poem on the screen. I like that late stage of working with the poem on the computer as by then I'm feeling that the poem is pretty much finished. At that late stage I might make some crucial changes – such as moving verses about or adding new lines. I tend to spot any weaknesses in a poem at that stage.

BRIAN MOSES: My first draft is done either by hand or by dictaphone. I take a dictaphone around with me everywhere I go. If I'm in the car and I get an idea, I'll speak it into the machine. I always do a lot of work with a poem on paper first. Then there arrives a time that it just needs to go on to the computer. Then I jigsaw the lines around until it's finished.

BENJAMIN ZEPHANIAH: When I work on the page I write it out really rough and then I type it out immediately. Then I'll see whether I like it or not. What I do next is to perform it, and I'll actually say to the audience, 'This is brand new. I don't know if you're going to like it or not.' I'll see by their responses what they think of it. Some poems will end up being scrapped. When I've had some half-hearted responses to new work, I can usually tell why, and I'll know that I've used the wrong ending or I should have put another verse at the end, or that I need to change a certain word or whatever.

When is a poem finished?

JOHN FOSTER: This is a very difficult question! – but I would say that a poem is finished when every word counts and when every word sounds right. Even if I'm writing a non-rhyming poem, I'll read it aloud or at least say it through in my head to see if it is sounding right and every word is doing the job it should be doing.

ROGER MCGOUGH: The rhyming will be working well and the tone will be just right. I test out a poem by reading it out softly to myself, I'll be mouthing the words and I'll run it through many times. The words have got to fit in the mouth well.

What makes a good title?

JOHN FOSTER: Most of my titles will signal to the reader what the poem is all about. Other titles can be more clever. The title for my poem 'Everything's Fine' is ironic, as the poem is all about a family going on holiday and everything goes wrong. Sometimes I'll use both a title and a subtitle – as with 'Market Forces (The arms dealer's defence)' – so, even before the poem begins there have been two pieces of information. With this type of title, the title becomes an integral and important part of the poem. At other times, when it's difficult to find one, I'll use the first phrase or the first line of the first verse, which is what I did with my poem 'It Hurts', which is the phrase that begins each stanza, – and it also sums up the poem. I'll usually wait until I've finished a poem to give it a title. I leave the top of the page blank until I get the right title.

TONY MITTON: Usually, it's the last thing to come. I'm not usually very interested in titles. I sometimes regard them as an unfortunate necessity. What counts is the poem. With the title I usually go for something simple and direct, though if it's a wordplay poem, I might go for a wordplay title. And I do like assonance and alliteration in a title – like in 'Freak Cat Flea' or 'Puzzled Pea'.

My advice on titles? If it's a serious poem and you want to title it, then try and look clearly at the poem and see what title suggests itself. If nothing comes, just be logical and say 'What is this poem about?' Say it was about Stonehenge, then why not call it 'Stonehenge'? Also, you might want to think about your reader and the fact that you are giving your title as a doorway into that poem for the reader, and that it helps to inform them what the poem is all about. If you were writing a metaphorical or playful poem about some rocks you might not actually say in the piece what it is about, so you might need a title like 'The Rocks' or 'Seashore' to tell the reader what it really is about. It's like with an abstract or figurative painting – you have to look at the title to fully understand the piece.

Is there a difference between a performance and a page poem?

ANDREW FUSEK PETERS: There's a huge difference. One of the poems in my collection *Poems with Attitude* – 'Unevensong' – is about bullying. It works well as a performance poem, but it doesn't quite work on the page, to stand alone and read. However, the form is tight and fits with 'What shall we do with the drunken sailor?'. So, in that sense, it's a crafted piece of writing, but it's not a page poem. Here's the chorus and the first verse:

> *Unevensong (sung by the stupid)*
>
> [To the tune of 'What shall we do with the drunken sailor?']

> What shall we do with Duncan Taylor
> Now he's become a stinking wailer?
> This is the life of a teenage jailer
> Early in the morning!

> *Hoo-ray and up he rises!*
> *Life is full of cruel surprises!*
> *And we're several sizes*
> *Bigger than him this morning!*

And, like this, a performance poem really needs a strong rhythm.

ROGER MCGOUGH: People often ask me if I write poems for performance or for the page. I think the two are one. It seems a strange question to me! I don't think you can put words down on the page unless they really work well verbally.

Do you ever say your poems out loud as you are writing them?

JAN DEAN: Yes! It's very, very important to me to hear a poem out loud as I'm writing it. I can sound it out it in my head – and the more you write, the more you're able to do that. When you get the idea that will spark the poem off, you hear that in your mind's ear. But how you hear something in your mind's ear can be very different to how the mouth will actually say it. When I go into schools I tell children to trust their ears and to test their poems by reading them out loud. Something might look right on the page, but if you say it, it might not sound right.

What advice do you have on using words in a poem?

JAN DEAN: When you are writing a first draft of a poem you tend to use familiar words. But the most familiar word is not necessarily the best one. I like to approach things sideways, and poetry is all about approaching things from different angles. So, you might want to choose a word that is almost familiar, but not quite. So if you're describing an action you might think of something obvious. And then when you read it back later you realise that it's not quite the word that is needed as it doesn't describe your subject as well as it could.

JOHN FOSTER: Every single word, even down to the last pronoun, counts. It matters in a poem whether you use, for example, 'a' or 'the'. I spend a lot of time just improving single words to find the best one for the job. A message I spread to children is that you can actually spend up to half an hour working on just one single word.

COLIN MACFARLANE: Be highly descriptive but beware of using too many adjectives or adverbs. Instead, find exactly the right adjective that you need. Also, if you are using adverbs too often it may mean that your verbs are weak and not expressive enough.

BRIAN MOSES: Each word is very important. There's that old adage by the poet Coleridge – 'Prose is words in the best order, poetry is the best words in the best order.'

How do I write about images?

VALERIE BLOOM: You need to 'show' and not 'tell'. By this I mean that you need to actually 'show' your reader things, not simply 'tell' them about them. And you need to let your reader experience things in your poem – that is, seeing or hearing or feeling something. These are what I refer to as 'sense words'. Take the sentence 'He was a very fat man.' This is 'telling'. It is not very imaginative and does not conjure up much of an image. If we want to really 'show' what the man is like we could say, 'His stomach bulged over the waist of his trousers.' – and then we understand he's fat. Likewise, 'He was very upset' might be better expressed as 'Tears streamed down his face.' This way you are providing your reader with a clear visual image.

What general advice do you have on writing poetry?

JAN DEAN: The process of writing a poem involves the three s's:

> SEE IT – using the words to describe an image or feeling
> SORT IT – drafting the poem as the first version is rarely the last
> SOUND IT – anything that doesn't sound right, won't do.

Trust your ears. Always sound a poem out loud as you are writing it. Don't just say it, but actually sound out the words of the poem. By this I mean listen to the music of the poem – the rhythm, the sounds of the words, the combinations of the words.

JOHN FOSTER: Become a word-hoarder. Collect words and play with them – juggle with them, try out unusual combinations – stretch them and twist them until they say whatever you want them to say.

TONY MITTON: Look at lots of poetry and try to find how many things a poem can be. Poems come in many shapes and sizes, many types and forms. If you find a poet or a kind of poetry you really like, get to know that poetry well. You may like to try writing like that yourself. It's all right, especially early on, to copy other writers occasionally. And the more you write, the more you'll develop a voice of your own.

ANDREW FUSEK PETERS: Find out about all the different forms you can write in. Practice. Read other poets – past and present.

MATTHEW SWEENEY: The big enemy in poetry is vagueness, the other cliché.

Be like spies – keep your eyes and ears open for anything you see and hear that's interesting or different.

GROWING POEMS

In this section, poets talk about the evolution and crafting of specific poems. They reveal the origins, the themes and the ideas behind each piece. At the end of each discussion there are related poetry workshop activities. The form of the poem and the literary devices used by the poet in each piece are highlighted in bold at the start of each discussion.

Jan Dean

Angels
We are made from light.
Called into being we burn
Brighter than the silver-white
Of hot magnesium.
More sudden than yellow phosphorus.
We are the fire of heaven;
Blue flames and golden ether.

We are from stars.
Spinning beyond the farthest galaxy
In an instant gathered to this point
We shine, speak our messages then go,
Back to the brilliance.
We are not separate, not individual,
We are what we are made of. Only
Shaped sometimes into tall-winged warriors,
Our faces solemn as swords,
Our voices joy.

The skies are cold;
Suns do not warm us;
Fire does not burn itself.
Only once we touched you

And felt a human heat.
Once, in the brightness of the frost.
Above the hills, in glittering starlight,
Once, we sang.

(from *A Mean Fish Smile: Sandwich Poets Volume 4*: Macmillan)

'Angels' is a **free verse** poem. Here, Jan Dean talks about the writing of the poem and discusses **drafts, imagery, language, line breaks, monologue, repetition, rhyme** and **internal rhyme, rhythm, simile** and **titles**.

JAN DEAN: This poem was written back in 1993 and came about as a result of writing my other Christmas poem, a jokey piece called 'Heart Stuff'. The last line of that poem is:

I keep remembering a marvellous baby in the shining snow

I'd been thinking about that line and an image came to me. It was an image of the first Christmas, of the shepherds on the hillside outside Bethlehem. Suddenly, the whole sky was lit up with these angels singing to the shepherds. I began thinking about the angels – how they could appear so quickly and how they could transform from one form and shape into another. The first line of the poem is 'We are made from light'. I wanted to get across the idea that these angels were made of a special substance, light – light that had changed its shape. I was trying to think of the brightest thing I could think of, like a cold silvery light. I remembered one science lesson at secondary school and seeing magnesium burn. That memory brought together the scientific and the spiritual for me – the fact that angels are mystical, spiritual beings yet are as bright as a scientific element. Generally speaking, I'm very interested in science and the history of science.

In the poem I say 'hot magnesium'. I used the word 'hot' and not 'burning' as I prefer the sound of the word 'hot'. I like the breathiness of the word. And I wanted a contrast between the heat of magnesium and the fact that angels are actually cold – they're not alive, in the same way as human beings are alive. I wanted to give a sense of their alien-ness, to put across the idea that they are very different to us, and that's why I used the scientific imagery with magnesium and phosphorus. I have the reference to 'yellow phosphorus' because I remembered, again from those science lessons, that when phosphorus comes into contact with water it shoots around wildly. This echoes the fact that the angels in this poem also move about swiftly and effortlessly. So, the magnesium depicts the angels' colour, and the phosphorus tells of their speed of movement.

By having 'Angels' as the title, it meant that I didn't have to use the word again in the poem. If I hadn't had such a straightforward title, people might not have known what it was about. In fact, my original first line was 'Angels are made from light'. When I came to actually write it down I changed it to 'We are made from light' and 'Angels' then became the title. It's one of those titles that lets you know what the poem is about before you start reading it.

The poem took about five drafts, which is about average for me. Though it didn't change a lot over the drafts. And I was lucky with this poem because once I started writing, most of it happened quite instantly, in one sitting. The original version was one block, one long stanza. In the redrafting I removed quite a bit of material. I have a tendency to repeat myself in my early drafts. I'll often say the same thing but in two different phrases.

In this poem I'm trying to express something seriously, solemnly and precisely. The angels all speak as one voice, as 'we', as in a sense, they are one being, hence the line:

We are not separate, not individual,

The original draft also made reference to the angels carrying swords, but I changed it so that 'swords' became a simile to describe their faces:

Our faces solemn as swords,

And this gives the idea that their faces are metallic and steely. In the next line I could have said that their voices are 'joyful', but I wanted to put across that their voices are actually the essence of joy. So there's the contrast between 'solemn' and 'joy' – but in spiritual terms, those terms are not incompatible.

In the third stanza, there's a paradox, a contradiction – that these angels are made of fire and light yet they are cold. They are made of fire, yet they do not burn or warm themselves, as it is a spiritual fire. All those words – like 'brightness' and 'frost' and 'glittering' and 'starlight' – are there to give a hardness, a sharp edge to those lines. There's no softness to the sounds of these words.

For me, this is a magical poem about Christmas. I wanted to put across the idea that the birth of Christ was something so amazing, so special that it affected the whole of creation – and not just humanity. Angels, as spiritual beings, are usually above emotion, but the birth of Christ, of God becoming human, is such a wondrous thing that even the angels are moved too. Yet I felt that for these angels there was a sense of longing – that this was a once-only event – it would never happen again, and this would be the closest they would ever feel to humanity. As I said before, any repetitions in my first draft I usually take out. But here I kept them in for effect. Three lines begin with 'Once', which emphasises the uniqueness of the event for the angels.

This is a free verse poem. There are rhymes at the start of the first verse, but you don't really notice them as they are incidental. I like using rhymes in this way. Overall, the sound of the poem was important for me, as it was about these strange, serious beings talking about themselves in a monologue. Therefore, it couldn't sound too ordinary and everyday. So the language needed to sound slightly odd and other-wordly – but not frightening. I had to find the right voice, the right language to convey this sense of otherness. Take the phrases such as 'We are made from light' and 'we are from stars'. We more commonly say 'made *of* light' and 'from *the* stars' – so not only am I saying something unusual – that the angels are actually made from light and stars – but the phrasing is unusual too. Also, in the line 'Only/Shaped sometimes into tall-winged warriors/' the word order is deliberately unusual too. Usually, a word such as 'sometimes' would come at the start of the sentence.

Children in schools often ask me about line endings in free verse. In a rhyming poem it's obvious where the lines should end, but this is not so with free verse. Sometimes the line breaks are determined by the picture that the poem creates – and each line can give a separate picture. At other times it's do with creating possibilities. You can leave a possibility open at the end of a line just for a split second, even if the next line then shuts down those possibilities, and the sentence takes one meaning. This is why I placed 'Only' at the end of the line in the second verse. By having the word here I am giving emphasis to the idea of only-ness. Also, line breaks can be determined by the rhythm – the line will end where the rhythm naturally pauses. So a line can be a unit of sense as well as sound.

When I write either poetry or fiction I imagine what I'm writing as scenes in my mind. I'm quite a visual person. I imagined all of 'Angels' visually, like a short film in my head as I was writing it, and I can recall all of those original images now. When I get these images I then have to find the right words to make the reader see the images as well. One of the nicest compliments I've had about this poem was somebody saying that it made them shiver. I like that! In all, I'm very pleased with this piece, and I think this is one of my best poems.

Workshop activities: free verse

AN ANGEL ON EARTH

Write your own poem in free verse about an angel (or a group of angels) which has come to earth, either to witness and celebrate a special event or to help someone at a difficult or challenging time in their life. If you decide that your poem is to be about a group of angels, perhaps you could begin your piece – or even every stanza – with 'We are . . .'. Think about what Jan Dean has said about trying to make the angels' language slightly unusual. Consider how an angel might speak. Also, think about where you will put your line breaks.

A GUARDIAN ANGEL

Would you like a guardian angel? What could it do for you? Or would you want a guardian angel for someone you know? Write a free verse poem – either fun or serious – in which you explore this idea.

John Foster

My Front Tooth

When my front tooth came out,
Miss wrapped it in tissue paper
And looked after it for me
Until hometime.

When I got home,
I took it out and put it down
On the carpet to examine it.
Just then, Samson, our dog
Came bounding in.
Before I could stop him,
He'd gobbled up the tooth
And swallowed it.

'Serves you right
For not looking after it properly,'
Said my sister.
'Now you won't get anything
From the tooth fairy.'

'I will, won't I, Mum?' I said.
But all she said was,
'Wait and see.'

That night,
I put a note under my pillow
Explaining what had happened.

In the morning, it had gone.

But there was no sign
Of any money.

Feeling fed up, I went downstairs
To let Samson out.
Propped against his basket
Was an envelope addressed to
The Owner of the Lost Tooth.

I tore it open.
Inside there was a note
From the tooth fairy, which said:
Although your tooth cannot be found,
The dog's to blame,
So here's your pound.

(from Making Waves: Oxford University Press)

'The Tooth Fairy' is a **free verse poem**. Here, John Foster talks about the writing of the poem and discusses **assonance, colloquial language, drafting, dramatic monologues, ideas for poems, narrative, narration, rhyme** and **stanzas**.

JOHN FOSTER: This poem came to me after a school visit. I'd performed a poem by Susan Stranks called *The Tooth Exthpert*. It's a humorous poem all about lisping when you've lost your two front teeth. I'd also performed my own poem called *When Ali Had a Front Tooth* as well. One boy, Peter, put his hand up afterwards and said 'When my front tooth came out, the dog ate it!' And I just knew I had to write a poem about this. If a child gives me an idea for a poem, I will often try to work their name into the piece and I send them a copy of the poem when I've finished it.

Before I started the poem I had the idea of writing the letter to put under the pillow. As I began writing I realised that the way to make this story really work was not to have the money under the pillow, but to have an answer from the tooth fairy and for the money to be beside the dog's basket. That's an example of an idea coming actually as you write the poem. The whole story – and the way the story was going to be told – came out in that first sitting.

Right from the start this poem was always going to be a first person dramatic monologue – a non-rhyming story poem in the style of Michael Rosen. When you draft a poem like this you have to make sure that you use the voice of the child. So, the language had to be that of a junior school age child – and also colloquial and not literary.

I often use this poem as a model with children. I use it in response to that question they always ask – 'Where do you get your ideas from?' My answer is that you get ideas in three ways – from your own experience, from observation and from imagination. This poem has elements of all three. Many people, including me, have lost a tooth and have written to the tooth fairy – so that's the writing from my own experience; the observation comes from hearing Peter tell me the story; the imagination is the way that I chose to shape, tell and conclude the poem. I had to use my imagination with naming the dog, for example. I called it Samson because the name makes you think of a dog the size of a retriever or a labrador. And the phrase 'Samson our dog came bounding in' conveys the size of the dog without actually saying it.

The poem didn't need much rewriting, just a bit of tidying up. A free verse poem like this can be easier to write because you're not having to think about a rhyme or a strict rhythm. Some of my poems have taken as long as six months to finish because I'd got locked into a particular rhythm and rhyme scheme that was working in the first two verses, and the third verse took ages to get right.

Was I aware of the assonance – all the t's – in the first verse? No! Sometimes a poet may achieve an effect like this without even being aware of it. As I was writing it I would have been especially aware of the narrative and the rhythm – and I would have been saying it through to myself to ensure that it flowed well.

At the end of the piece I use rhyme in the tooth fairy's note. It helps to round off the poem –

> Although your tooth cannot be found,
> The dog's to blame,
> So here's your pound.

Sometimes, like with this poem, it just feels right to do this. What it also highlights is the fact that it's another voice coming into the poem. You can do this type of thing in a first person narrative poem.

What determines the length of each stanza? Well, this poem is written in what I call 'verse paragraphs'. They are paragraphs within the story. Each paragraph is a little event that contributes to the story as a whole. What's interesting is that in one sense this poem could have been written as a short story, however I don't think it would have worked very well. Judith Nicholls does this workshop exercise in which she tells the story of Jack and Jill, but not as a poem, as a story – and it becomes far too long-winded. Poems often have narratives though they do not have enough of a story to make them work as a narrative in their own right. This is the case with 'The Tooth Fairy' too. It's told as an anecdote – a short, personal story – and it works best as a poem. If I'd written it as a short story in prose I'm sure it would have lost a lot of its appeal. The poem creates its impact by working very swiftly through the narrative. Yet it could possibly work as a subplot in a novel, as just one of a number of minor incidents that take place in a longer narrative. 'My Front Tooth' is a poem that I often do in schools. I think it works well in performance.

Children often ask me why I write poetry. I say that there are two reasons. One is to entertain children, and secondly to make children think. There are certain things that I want children to think about. I'm writing poetry for more serious reasons than might be apparent in some of the poems that I write. Words are fun so I want children to enjoy words. And there is certainly a teacherly and serious side of me that wants children to read about certain issues. So, I write about the contemporary family and the contemporary world situation in a way that I hope will help children to understand the world in which they live. I'm not claiming that I write the world's best poetry, but I write poetry that I hope is accessible to children and that I think they ought to be reading. I began writing poetry for children when I started compiling anthologies. And since then, the audience, the child I'm writing for, has been foremost in my mind.

Workshop activity: an amusing event

Write a poem about something amusing that has happened to you – perhaps recently or when you were younger. It might even be about a tooth coming out or writing to the tooth fairy. If you can't think of anything that has happened to you (see below), think of something that has happened to a friend or a member of your family. Brainstorm some ideas first. Before you begin writing, look at how 'The

Tooth Fairy' is laid out, and how the poet has arranged his 'verse paragraphs'. Write your poem in your own voice. Use rhyme only if you think the poem really needs it. If you want to read some more poems to give you further ideas, take a look at some of the non-rhyming poems by Michael Rosen, many of which are written about his own childhood experiences.

Here are some topics you could consider writing about:

- a misunderstanding
- a row
- a favourite moment on holiday
- something that once annoyed you that you now think is funny
- something that you used to be afraid of.

John Foster

The Snow Monster

When the Snow Monster sneezes,
Flurries of snow swirl and whirl,
Twisting round trees, curling into crevices,
Brushing the ground a brilliant white.

When the Snow Monster bellows,
Blizzards blot out the sky,
Piling up drifts, blocking roads,
Burying the landscape in a white grave.

When the Snow Monster cries,
Soft flakes slip and slide gently down
Into the hands of waiting children
Who test their taste with their tongues.

When the Snow Monster sleeps,
The air crackles with children's laughter
As they throw snowballs, build snowmen
And whizz downhill on their sledges.

(from *Making Waves*: Oxford University Press)

'The Snow Monster' is a **non-rhyming poem**. Here, John Foster talks about the writing of the poem and discusses **alliteration, assonance, drafting, imagery, rhyming, titles** and **verbs**.

JOHN FOSTER: The reason I wrote this poem was that I was editing an anthology of monster poems and it suddenly struck me that nobody had written about monsters made up of the elements – so I decided to write one poem about a snow monster and another about a fire monster.

The original first verse was as follows:

When the Snow Monster laughs
Flurries of snow swirl and whirl,

> And spread like white arms wrapping fields and trees
> Coating, crusting in a crest of dazzling white

I thought that the imagery in this first verse was very ordinary. So when I came to the rewrite I looked for something that was more expressive and less ordinary. I wanted to capture something of the movement of snow. I didn't like the word 'laughs' as it conveyed the wrong mood, so I changed it to 'sneezes'. And the next draft of the last part of that verse became:

> Scurrying to wrap fields
> Coating the ground,
> Painting the ground a brilliant white

'Painting' has become 'brushing' in the final version. By the final version, I had movement words throughout the first stanza – 'twisting', 'curling' and 'brushing' and I hope I've lost the ordinariness that I had originally.

The original second stanza began, 'When the Snow Monster bellows' and I crossed out 'bellows' and put 'roars' instead. And it went on:

> Blizzards of snow writhe and twist
> Slapping the faces of buildings
> Burying in white graves

Later on, I put the word 'bellows' back in as I was conscious that it alliterates with 'blizzards'. And there's further alliteration with the phrase 'blizzards blot' which I've got in the final version. I didn't like 'Slapping the faces of buildings' so I replaced it with 'Piling up drifts, blocking roads / Burying the landscape in a white grave /' which works better. The three verbs – 'piling', 'blocking' and 'burying' – nicely echo the three verbs in the previous stanza. Despite all the other changes, I had the structure, that of starting each verse with 'When the Snow Monster . . .' in the very first draft.

In the third and fourth verses I don't continue with the same pattern of the three verbs. This is because the children come in at this point. The first two verses were all about the snow, but as we get into the third verse the atmosphere and mood change with the arrival of the children.

It's all about awareness of audience. I was not aiming to write a poem that was purely descriptive because this poem is also about how children behave when it snows. I'm trying to be child-centred and tell the experience from their point of view, which is what I try to achieve in many of my poems. Even my more serious poems are often child-centred. I wanted the third verse to have an element of awe and wonder about it. Again, I'm trying to capture that common experience – something that we have all done. Most of us at some point have stuck our tongues out and tasted the snow! It's what children naturally do. I deliberately went for alliteration in this third stanza – with 'slip' and 'slide' – and with 'test' and 'taste' there is both alliteration and assonance.

The final word of the poem was going to be 'toboggans' – but the sound and the rhythm weren't right, so I changed it to 'sledges' which works much better and fits in with many of the other two-syllable words peppered throughout the poem. I think this poem would have been quite different if I had used rhyme. I have written rhyming poems about snow, but they've tended to be more rhythmical –

> It's snowed. It's snowed.
> It's blocked the road.
> School is closed today.

Workshop activities: weather and travels

MONSTER OF THE ELEMENTS

Invent a monster made of another element – perhaps wind, water, hail, clouds or ice. Write a poem in which – like John Foster has with 'The Snow Monster' – you describe a storm in which your monster is coming to life; your poem can be a rhyming piece or even free verse. Alternatively, write a poem in which different element monsters meet up: so, what would happen when a rain monster meets up with a wind monster? Or a fire monster with a hail monster? Before you start your poem, brainstorm all the words and phrases you can think of to describe the element(s) you are using. Be as imaginative as you possibly can, and aim for unusual and powerful descriptions.

AFTER THE STORM

Write an atmospheric poem about the aftermath of a storm. Perhaps there has been a snow storm or a flood or perhaps trees have been blown down and there is a power cut. Think: how will it affect people's lives? What will they do? Also, consider how you will convey the atmosphere (see 'Suspense and atmosphere' in the 'Fiction' chapter: pp. 142–4) – what descriptions will you include? Aim to be as original as you can in your descriptive phrases. Perhaps you could start your poem with people coming out of doors for the first time after the storm.

TRAVELLING IN SNOW

Write a piece in which you are travelling – by foot, bus or car across a town or city that is covered in snow. Perhaps you could highlight details such as icicles hanging off drain pipes or roofs, snowdrifts against houses, people clearing away the snow, ponds frozen over. Or, you could write about a train journey in which you describe the snow scenes that you pass.

WALKING IN A WOOD

Imagine you are walking through a wood at night, a wood that is covered in snow. The moon is full and enables you to see quite clearly. Write a poem about your walk – in the present tense. You could begin 'I am walking . . .'.

John Foster

Goran

At the end of science,
No one could find Goran
The new kid from Sarajevo.

Eventually, someone heard a sobbing
Coming from the cupboard
At the back of the room.

Miss opened the door
And there was Goran
Curled up inside.

Miss coaxed him out
And put her arm round him.

We filed quietly out to play
Wondering what nightmares
The flames from our Bunsen burners
Had sparked inside
His war-scarred mind.

(from *Making Waves*: Oxford University Press)

'Goran' is a **free verse poem**. Here, John Foster talks about the writing of the poem and discusses **first person narration**, **form** and **content**, **research**, **'showing and telling'**, **stanzas** and **themes**.

JOHN FOSTER: With 'Goran', although it may seem like a real event that I'm reporting, it's totally imaginary. I have read many harrowing stories about refugees in the *Guardian* and I've read *Zlata's Diary* by Zlata Filipovic, so I've got some insight into children's experience of this war. This poem is a sort of distillation, a result of all the reading and all the thinking I've done about refugees. The character Goran represents one of many Yugoslav refugees that have come over to England.

'Goran' is in the first person, and is told by one of Goran's classmates. Right from the start I wanted the poem in the voice of a child. Each stanza is a 'verse paragraph' – a little event that makes up the story as a whole.

I once read a stunning poem by Julius Lester, a black American poet. I think it was about a murder or something, and the poem achieved its effect by simply and starkly telling the story in a very understated way. I wanted to achieve that effect in 'Goran'. If you're writing about something bleak – as I am in 'Goran' – you choose a form like free verse as rhythm and rhyme will get in the way. The form will interfere with the content.

The part of this poem that is based on experience is that as a teacher I was once told a story about a very disturbed boy who spent a whole lesson inside a cupboard. I then married that thought with the idea of a refugee child in a classroom in a strange country. So my very first idea for the poem was that of a disturbed child, a child refugee from Yugoslavia that was unable to cope with the situation. Though it was one of those poems that occurred as I wrote it, I didn't have much of an idea what I was writing about until I did it. For example, the image of the Bunsen burner actually came to me as I was writing. This poem took a little while to write, but once I got going, the ideas flowed quite freely.

With the last stanza I'm leaving the reader to work out for themselves what is going on and what Goran has been through. At the same time, I'm hopefully helping children to understand the damage that Goran's experiences have done to him. We know in the way that the narrator says 'we filed quietly out to play' that the children in the class are responding in a sensitive and sympathetic way to Goran. I hope that children who read this poem will also want to be sensitive to children who they know who have problems. Really, that's what the whole poem is about for me – showing compassion.

In these poems I'm giving the reader something to think about. And it's often more effective if you understate your theme. If you say too much it can ruin the effect for your readers and stifles any chance of them thinking the issue through for themselves. It's the same as in novels, you have to 'show' not 'tell' – it's more powerful if you describe an event without telling your reader how to respond to it. I tried to present this poem in as few words as possible so that I can empower my readers and let them do the work and let them respond in their own way.

Workshop activities: verse paragraphs

NEWS ITEM

Read through some local or national newspapers and look for any news items that interest you, any events that you feel strongly about. First of all, write down how you feel about the news item, then re-tell the news item in the form of a free verse poem. Before you begin writing, look at how 'Goran' is laid out, and how the poet has arranged his 'verse paragraphs'. Try not to shape your readers' responses to what you are expressing in your poem, and let the readers make up their own minds.

A DIFFICULT TIME AT SCHOOL

Everyone at some point has a difficult experience. As John Foster says, it is important that we show compassion to those who are suffering. Write a poem in free verse in which someone is having a difficult time at school, but is shown warmth and sympathy by her or his friends. Before you begin writing, look at how 'Goran' is laid out, and how the poet has arranged his 'verse paragraphs'.

Roger McGough

Daily Telegraph: 'Rabbit in Mixer Survives'

A baby rabbit fell into a quarry's mixing machine yesterday and came out in the middle of a concrete block. But the rabbit still had the strength to dig its way free before the block set.

The tiny creature was scooped up with 30 tons of sand, then swirled and pounded through the complete mixing process. Mr. Michael Hooper, the machine operator, found the rabbit shivering on top of the solid concrete block, its coat stiff with fragments. A hole from the middle of the block and paw marks showed the route.

Mr. Reginald Denslow, manager of J.R. Pratt and Sons' quarry at Kilmington, near Axminster, Devon, said: 'This rabbit must have a lot more than nine lives to go through this machine. I just don't know how it avoided being suffocated, ground, squashed or cut in half.' With the 30 tons of sand, it was dropped into a weighing hopper and carried by conveyor to an overhead mixer where it was whirled around with gallons of water.

From there the rabbit was swept to a machine which hammers wet concrete into blocks by pressure of 100lb per square inch. The rabbit was encased in a block eighteen inches long, nine inches high and six inches thick. Finally the blocks were ejected on to the floor to dry and the dazed rabbit clawed itself free. 'We cleaned him up, dried him by the electric fire, then he hopped away,' Mr. Denslow said.

Rabbit in Mixer Survives

'Tell us a story Grandad'
The bunny rabbits implored
'About the block of concrete
Out of which you clawed.'

'Tell every gory detail
Of how you struggled free
From the teeth of the Iron Monster
And swam through a quicksand sea.'

'How you battled with the Humans
(And the part we like the most)
Your escape from the raging fire
When they held you there to roast.'

The old adventurer smiled
And waved a wrinkled paw
'All right children, settle down,
I'll tell it just once more.'

His thin nose started twitching
Near-blind eyes began to flood
As the part that doesn't age
Drifted back to bunnyhood.

When spring was king of the seasons
And days were built to last
When thunder was merely thunder
Not a distant quarry blast.

How, leaving the warren one morning
Looking for somewhere to play
He'd wandered far into the woods
And there had lost his way.

When suddenly without warning
The earth gave way, and he fell
Off the very edge of the world
Into the darkness of Hell.

Sharp as the colour of a carrot
On a new-born bunny's tongue
Was the picture he recalled
Of that day when he was young.

Trance-formed now by the memory
His voice was close to tears
But the story he was telling
Was falling on deaf ears.

There was giggling and nudging
And lots 'Sssh – he'll hear'
For it was a trick, a game they played

Grown crueller with each year.

'Poor old Grandad' they tittered
As they one by one withdrew
'He's told it all so often
He now believes it's true.'

Young rabbits need fresh carrots
And his had long grown stale
So they left the old campaigner
Imprisoned in his tale.

Petrified by memories
Haunting ever strong
Encased in a block of time
Eighteen inches long.

* * *

Alone in a field in Devon
An old rabbit is sitting, talking,
When out of the wood, at the edge of the world,
A man with a gun comes walking.

(from the collections *Waving at Trains* and *Selected Poems 1967–1987*)

'Rabbit in Mixer Survives' is a **rhyming narrative poem**. Here, Roger McGough talks about the writing of the poem and discusses **assonance, internal rhyme, lines, point of view, rhythm, titles, verses** and **wordplay**.

ROGER MCGOUGH: I remember I was doing a reading at Aston University in Birmingham. I was early and I was sitting in the bar reading the *Daily Telegraph*. There was an article entitled 'Rabbit in Mixer Survives'. As I was sitting there, I got the idea for the first verse, of the little rabbit talking to the big rabbit – 'Tell us a story Grandad' – and it just came out like that. I didn't have to think how I was going to tell it. It was instant.

If I'd been asked to write a poem about this, I would probably have sat down and written something like 'It was a sunny day and the rabbit' – I'd tell the story. But with poetry, you can adopt any point of view you like – even the concrete mixer's point of view! The gift of writing this poem for me was that I suddenly had the voices of these cheeky rabbits talking. It's a nice idea as you've got this whole world that you've created, and you can tell the whole story from their point of view. It's quite a funny idea – what with the quicksand and putting the rabbit in front of the fire to roast!

So I'd got this idea for the poem and I sat there and wrote about three or four verses in my notebook straight off. I knew that I had the idea for the poem all there, though I didn't know what was going to happen at the end – either to the rabbit or where the poem was going at that point. I couldn't wait then to get back home and see what would happen. The adventure then for me was writing it out.

I don't know what else I'd been reading at that time, or what might have helped to shape or influence the poem, but there's a sense of old age in the piece, which is what the poem's all about, really – youth and old age. Maybe it was something going on inside of me at the time, I don't know, I can't remember.

The poem came out very much as it is now, but I did spend some time rewriting various lines and getting the rhymes in. And there's a question of whether it's a child's or adult's poem. I think it's probably a poem for teenagers or adults. However, I often read it when I go into schools.

I do like some of the wordplay in the poem such as 'drifted back to bunnyhood' and also the two meanings of 'petrified'. And with the lines:

> When spring was king of the seasons
> And days were built to last
> When thunder was merely thunder
> Not a distant quarry blast.

I'm trying to picture the world as how the rabbits would see it. I don't know if I got it quite right or if it quite works, but I do like the idea of the rabbit being trapped – 'Encased in a block of time / Eighteen inches long'. Some people have one experience in their lives – such as the war – after which life is nothing, it's as if they're trapped in that time and it's all they want to talk about. I was trying to get that kind of idea in there.

Some of the words I've put in capital letters. With 'Iron Monster' – it's a bit like with Ted Hughes' 'Iron Man' – it's not just any iron monster, to that rabbit it was *the* 'Iron Monster'. 'Humans' has a capital too. It's the same issue, to that rabbit they are *the* humans – *the* enemy.

Did I consciously inject assonance into this poem? No, but there is a fair bit in this poem, such as with all the t's in the verse that begins 'Poor old Grandad'. I don't consciously look for things like that, they just happen.

In the verse before last the lines become shorter. I think it's because the music and the rhythm of the poem need to change at this point to help bring the poem to its conclusion. Perhaps also the music is changing because the film, as it were, is ending.

At the end of the poem the younger rabbits have all gone off and the old rabbit is stuck there in his time capsule. The ending brings the story back into the present tense. I do see this final part of the poem as being very much like the end of a film before the credits roll. For, suddenly in the final verse, the camera, as it were, moves out and in long distance we see the scene of the old rabbit talking to himself as the hunter now enters the picture.

When I perform this poem at my readings the audience always goes 'Ahhh!' at the end! And some girls have even written to me because they don't approve of the ending of the poem – and they ask me why the rabbit had to get shot. But really, it depends on your interpretation. There's a hunter and there's a rabbit – and it's up to the reader to decide whether the rabbit escapes or not.

Workshop activities: narrative verse

NEWSPAPER POEMS

Read through some local newspapers for interesting stories. Cut them out and spend time reading through the articles a few times. Choose one that you could adapt into a poem. You do not have to tell the whole story necessarily, you might want to take one small incident. Or, like Roger McGough, you might want to tell the story from an unusual point of view. Take, for example, the age-old story about a cat that is stuck up in a tree and the fire brigade come along to get it down; this could be told from the cat's point of view – or even the bird that is higher up in the tree. Also, you do not have to stick closely to the facts – you can merge fact and fiction together.

Or, you could invent your own humorous newspaper story about an animal – 'Tortoise Found Climbing Tree' or 'Goldfish Falls Out Of Sky' or 'Baby Rabbit Chases Rottweiler' – and then turn it into a poem.

A SEQUEL

Write a sequel to Roger McGough's poem, in which the main character is one of the old rabbit's grandchildren. What adventure could this rabbit have? And would you choose for the rabbit to tell its own story?

ANIMAL NARRATOR

Write a poem in which one animal is telling a story. It could be a cat talking to its kittens, a dog talking to all the other dogs in the neighbourhood, or a bear talking to the other animals in the forest. Write your own poem in free verse.

Roger McGough

The Cats' Protection League

Midnight. A knock at the door.
Open it? Better had.
Three heavy cats, mean and bad.

They offer protection, I ask, 'What for?'
The Boss-cat snarls, 'You know the score.
Listen man and listen good

If you wanna stay in the neighbourhood,
Pay your dues or the toms will call
And wail each night on the backyard wall.

Mangle the flowers, and as for the lawn
A smelly minefield awaits you at dawn.'
These guys meant business without a doubt

Three cans of tuna, I handed them out.
They then disappeared like bats into hell
Those bad, bad cats from the CPL.

(from *Bad, Bad Cats*: Puffin)

'The Cats' Protection League' is a **rhyming poem**. Here, Roger McGough talks about the writing of the poem and discusses **drafts, rhymes, testing poems** and **wordplay**.

ROGER MCGOUGH: This poem came about when an editor from the publisher Hutchinsons rang me and she asked if I had any poems about cats for a collection from which all the proceeds would go to the Cats Protection League charity. At that point I didn't have any cat poems, but

I told her that I would write one for her. In the mean time, she sent me some brochures with information on the organisation.

However, this poem really began before that at the time when a fox once came into our garden. It came right up and sat down in the middle of the lawn. It was in broad daylight, so the fox was being very bold. It stayed there for ages, and I just stood there in the conservatory staring at it. As a result of seeing the fox I began a poem called 'Fox in Suburban Garden', which I still haven't done anything with. These are the first few stanzas, which are really notes towards a poem:

> From the (bedroom) window, a double-take
> Hunched comfortably on the lawn
> Like a ginger sphinx, a fox
>
> Never seen a fox before
> Run downstairs and open the door
> Leading on to the garden
>
> He does not run or flinch
> But looks up almost sniffily
> And then away. Sauce-fox

'Sauce-fox' is very much a homage to Ted Hughes' 'Thought-Fox'!

> I step outside. Imagining perhaps
> He had chosen this garden
> This particular garden because
>
> Of me. Of us, the family
> Who would wish him no harm.
> Who would give him food, a place

Some time later, as I was reading the brochures on the Cats Protection League I'd been sent, I started making notes as ideas for a poem came to me, ideas which I didn't use eventually:

> I have a cat called
> Katmandu
> Do you know what my
> cat can do?

This was 25 October 1996. I always date all of my poems.

Next I remembered the fox poem, and I thought I'd change the subject of the poem to cats – so that some cats are now coming to visit me, not a fox. So that's where the idea for the first line of the poem came from, with the cats at the door. As you can see, the original draft of the first stanza was quite different:

> They are at the door
> Shall we open it? Better had.
> Five heavy cats, mean and bad.
> They offer protection. I say 'But guys,
> I live in a nice neighbourhood.'
> One says, 'Listen, and listen good,
> If you don't pay up it will end in tears.'

So I'd got the rhyming scheme for the first couple of lines, but not for the others yet. Then I rewrote the first three lines again:

> Midnight. A knock at the door
> Open it? Better had.
> Five heavy cats, mean and bad.

By this point I'd thought of the main joke of the poem, which is vital to the whole thing, which is the wordplay on 'protection'. In this poem, it's a reference to the Mafia – gangsters that run extortion rackets. They force people to pay them money, and in return they offer security and protection from others. Once I had that idea, I knew exactly what the poem would be like. In my poem, instead of calling them the Mafia, I decided to call the cats the CPL. I made notes in the margin as I was thinking about what to call them (see Figure 2.1):

> The Mob, The Mafia, The CPL
> The Feline Mafia, The CPL

I went back to the poem the following day and I almost completed it. Over the different versions, I went from having five cats down to four and finally down to three. I made other changes too. The line 'Mangle the flowers' was originally 'Trample the flowers' and then it became 'Top the flowers' but I settled on 'Mangle the flowers' as I didn't feel that the others were quite as clear or direct. Another change I made was to the three cans of tuna, which were originally three cans of Kattomeat. I'm constantly trying to improve the language in my poems in this way. I'm always looking for the best way to express my ideas. I'd say that the evolution of 'Cats' Protection League' is fairly typical of most of my poems, in that it went through about two or three drafts.

In the *Bad, Bad Cats* collection there are a few poems that could easily have gone into a collection for adult readers, such as 'The Going Pains'. I often do 'The Cats' Protection League' at performances for adults. In a sense, it's more of an adult poem as adults will appreciate the subtleties of the joke – and the wordplay on 'protection' – which might be beyond the frame of reference of some children.

The whole collection came about once I'd written 'The Cats' Protection League' and also the 'Carnival of the Animals' series of poems which was commisioned for a performance at the Barbican Centre in London. Once I'd written 'The Cats' Protection League' I decided to pursue the cat theme a little further and I then wrote all the other cat poems that appear in the book. The title *Bad, Bad Cats* was one of a number of options. Other choices included *Carnival of the Animals* and *Over to You* and *Waxing Lyrical*. The editors at Puffin wanted to call it *Big, Bad Cats*, but we finally decided upon *Bad, Bad Cats*. And the title of the poem 'The Cats' Protection League' was always just that, because of the wordplay on the mafia connection. Of all my collections for children, I probably prefer *Bad, Bad Cats* and *An Imaginary Menagerie*. I do like pursuing a theme across a whole collection as I did in *An Imaginary Menagerie*.

Workshop activities: animal poems

ANIMAL VISITOR
Imagine an animal visits your school playground (or even somewhere near where you live). You could choose a domestic creature like a dog or cat or a rabbit – or even a wild animal such as a fox or a badger or a weasel or a hedgehog – or perhaps something even more out of the ordinary. When would it come – early morning or

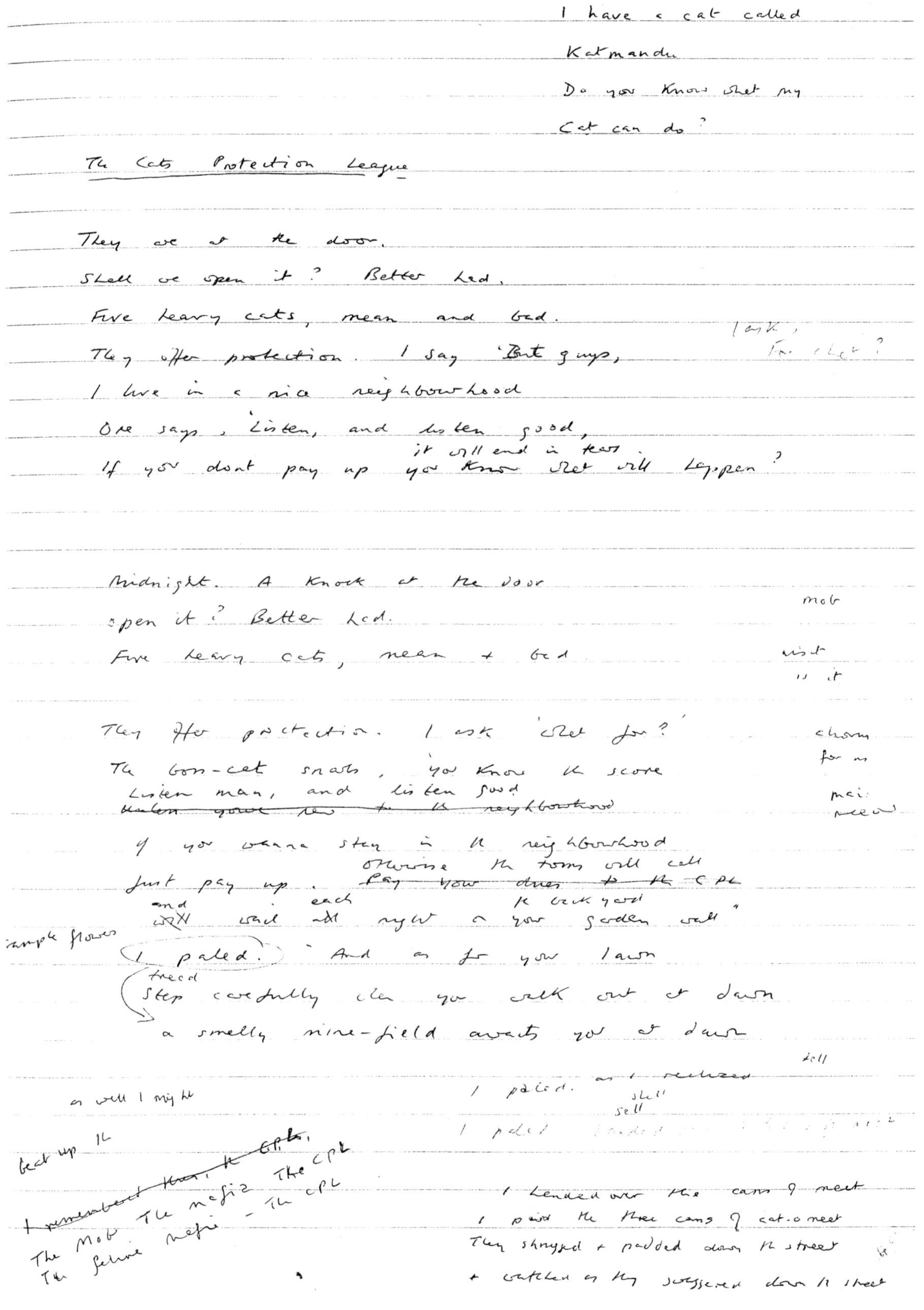
I have a cat called
Katmandu
Do you know what my
Cat can do?

The Cats Protection League

They are at the door.
Shall we open it? Better had.
Five heavy cats, mean and bad.
They offer protection. I say 'But guys,
I live in a nice neighbourhood
One says, 'Listen, and listen good,
it will end in tears.
If you dont pay up you know what will happen?

Midnight. A knock at the door
open it? Better had.
Five heavy cats, mean + bad

They offer protection. I ask 'What for?'
The boss-cat snarls, 'You know the score
Listen man, and listen good

If you wanna stay in the neighbourhood
Otherwise the toms will call
Just pay up.
each the back yard
and wail all night on your garden wall'
I paled. And as for your lawn
Step carefully when you walk out at dawn
a smelly mine-field awaits you at dawn

I paid.

I handed over the cans of meat
I paid the three cans of cat-o-meat
They shrugged + padded down the street
+ cackled as they swaggered down the street

The Mob The mafia The CPL
The feline mafia

Figure 2.1 Manuscript page for Roger McGough's poem 'The Cats' Protection League' at night or late in the afternoon? What would it be after? Think of some unusual and interesting ways of describing the creature. Perhaps you could make a list of descriptive words and phrases before you begin the poem. (For an animal description, see 'Non-fiction' workshop 'Painting animals with words', p. 185.)

ANIMALS AS HUMANS
In 'The Cats' Protection League', Roger McGough gives human qualities to animals. The term for this is 'personification'. Write your own personification poem. For example, you could imagine your school run by animals – would the staff be all one creature, or different types? Don't be too unkind in your choices! Or, how about an animal football team, pop group, team of astronauts – anything you can think of. Or, imagine your friends or family as animals. What would they be? Your poem does not have to rhyme, it could be written as free verse.

NEW ENDING
Take just the first two opening lines to Roger McGough's poem and write a new poem of your own.

Tony Mitton

Little Red Rap
Just on the edge of a deep, dark wood
lived a girl called Little Red Riding Hood.
Her grandmother lived not far away,
so Red went to pay her a visit one day.

She took some cake and she took some wine
packed up in a basket nice and fine.
And her ma said, 'Red, now just watch out,
for they say Big Bad Wolf's about.'

But Red went off with a hop and a skip.
She was feeling good, she was feeling hip.
So she took her time, she picked some flowers,
and soon the minutes had grown to hours.

And the Big Bad Wolf who knew her plan,
he turned his nose and he ran and ran.
He ran till he came to her grandmother's door.
Then he locked her up with a great big roar.

He took her place in her nice warm bed,
And he waited there for Little Miss Red.
So when Little Red she stepped inside,
that wolf, his eyes went open wide.

Says Red, 'Why, Gran,
what great big eyes!'
Says Wolf, 'I'm trying
You out for size.'

Says Red, 'Why, Gran,
You're covered in hair!'
Says Wolf, 'Now, dear,
it's rude to stare.'

Says Red, 'Why, Gran,
what great big claws,
what great big teeth,
what great big jaws!

And goodness, Gran,
what a great big grin!'
Says Wolf, 'All the better
to fit you in!'

But Little Miss Red says, 'Not so fast . . .'
And she calls to a woodcutter strolling past.
'Hey, you there, John! Can I borrow your axe?'
And she gave that Wolfie three good whacks.

'That's one from Gran and one from me
and one delivered entirely free.'
That wolf ran off with a holler and a shout
and Little Miss Red let Grandma out.

They called the woodcutter in to dine
And they all sat down to the cake and the wine.
And that's how the story ends . . .
Just fine!

(from Big Bad Raps: Orchard)

'Little Red Rap' is a **rap poem**. Here, Tony Mitton talks about the writing of the poem and discusses **alliteration, assonance, colloquial words, couplets, genre, narrative, quatrain, refrain, rhyme, rhythm** and **stanzas**.

TONY MITTON: When I was working as a part-time special needs teacher at Kings Hedges School in Cambridge, I used to visit an Infants class. I'd go and do poetry with this class during the breaktimes, just for the pleasure of it. The teacher, Edna Blake, and the children really embraced that. I used to read them my poems. In a sense – like Shakespeare at the Globe! – I had an immediate audience that I was writing for. This wasn't writing for the idea of being published, it was writing for an event, for a reading. The class even asked me to write them poems about various topics they were doing.

At that time I had a tape of a young Irish storyteller doing something called 'The Goldilocks Rap'. It was the story of *Goldilocks* told in a chanty, rappy way. I used to play it in class and the children used to join in with the choruses. They loved that tape. One project this teacher did with her class was looking at different versions of fairy tales such as *Little Red Riding Hood*. The class asked me – and it was a direct request – if I'd do a *Little Red Riding Hood* rap. I was working mornings only at that point and I went home one day and I sat down and wrote the rap in one sitting, in about one hour. It wasn't quick to do because of being a rap, but sometimes a poem such as this does come very fast and very right and very quickly. I just instinctively knew how to do it, I instinctively knew the rhythm I was going to use.

There are very few changes from the original version to the published one of 'Little Red Rap' – only a few little tweaks to the odd word or phrase. For example, the original had the word 'granny', and I changed it to 'grandmother', and I changed the word 'call' to 'visit'. What I did with 'Little Red Rap' – and with all the other raps I've written since – was to compose the rap orally in my head, and I'd get it to the point where it was working well and then I'd write it down (see Figure 2.2). I don't say my poems out loud as I'm writing them as a rule – I tend to do them in my mind's ear.

Back in the early 1980s, I used to watch a programme called *The Kenny Everett Video Show*. Kenny Everett was a comedian and he used to have various characters he would do, Sid Snot – a punk rocker, and another who was a teddy boy. In character, he'd do these raps – and they were humorous, comic raps. I can't remember the content of them. I could almost swear that I took my rhythm for raps – for all the raps I've done – from Kenny Everett!

My raps are a comic, white rap converted into humorous verse, but still keeping that rap idiom. Wherever possible I lace my raps with humour, using everyday, colloquial catchwords like 'gimme five' and 'cool dude' and 'wicked'. Occasionally I might quote a pop song. For

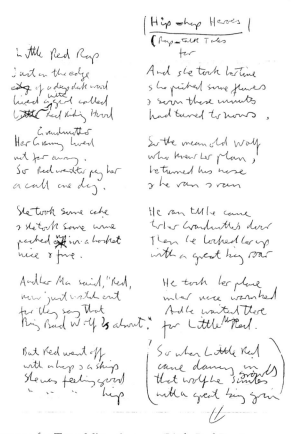

Figure 2.2 Manuscript page for Tony Mitton's poem 'Little Red Rap'

example, in 'Hairy Rap', the werewolf rap, when the character becomes a werewolf he says 'I'm bad' – quoting Michael Jackson.

In the books themselves, the raps are written as quatrains, verses with four lines. But it would be better – in terms of showing how a rap works – to lay a rap out in couplets, a verse with two lines. (I've used that pattern – that very simple recipe of ABCB rhyming in four line stanzas – for all my raps in the six books I've done now.)

I'm using rap to tell stories, so in a sense I'm rubbing two genres together. In the first two books I'm interweaving the fairy tale genre with the music of rap. And I'm sure it's been done by people in the past – I'm sure there are versions of fairy tales told in Chicago gangster language by an American author back in the 1920s. The two rap books after *Big Bad Raps* were in the the horror genre, with characters such as Dracula and Frankenstein. And as the series went on, the books went up the age range, and they became more sophisticated.

I tried to be quite true to the original stories, but in my version, Red is given a kind of feminist power – she's the one who drives the wolf away at the end, not the woodcutter as in most versions of the tale. With all the fairy tale raps I was quite careful not to alter the actual storylines too much, as other writers had done that kind of reworking of fairy tales before. I do like to keep the stories intact. For some of the raps I actually went back to the original fairy tales to re-read them, to check them out – such as *Jack and the Beanstalk, The Three Little Pigs, Little Red Riding Hood* and *The Billy Goats Gruff*, but I knew most of them well anyway.

At the beginning, they were great fun to do, when I was taking them into school and reading them. Later, they were harder to do, harder to keep fresh. I really did enjoy the process of turning rap into what I call comic lyric verse – that of writing rap tightly and rhythmically. And because it's comic verse for children I'm frequently working with – but often unconsciously – alliteration and rhyme. I like the alliteration in the line:

> And goodness, Gran,
> what a great big grin!

And with the stanza:

> 'That's one from Gran and one from me
> and one delivered entirely free.'

I'm using the sort of chanty refrain or chorus that you get in some folk tales, such as 'Fe fi fo fum I smell the blood of an English man' in *Jack and the Beanstalk*.

I use a very regular beat for my raps – four beats to each line – with a very tight, exact rhyme scheme. Occasionally I'll allow myself an extra line, such as:

> You can rap about a robber
> You can rap about a king
> You can rap about a chewed up piece of string
> Or you can rap about almost anything

When I perform these raps I do them quite dramatically, so they're very much performance pieces. I sometimes find that those children who find listening to poetry difficult will wake up and listen. One of the reasons I'm glad I've written the raps is that if I can't catch children in the audience with poems from my collection *Plum*, I'll often inspire them with the raps. It tends to be – if I can be stereotypical about it – the non-reading boys who will switch on to my performance at that point. I get 'cred' by doing rap! In fact one library recently suggested I do a reading in a burger bar for their less literary boys! A lot of libraries have said they like the raps because they can turn the less literary boys or girls on to them because they've got that popular music form and association that children can identify with. At my readings I win certain children with the raps, and having caught them I'll try and get them to listen to something like 'The Selky Bride', warning them in advance that it's a slower and sadder piece, and that like the raps, it tells a story, but in a slightly different way.

Workshop activity: rap poem

Think of all the fairy tales you've ever heard. Think of one that you could rewrite as a rap. It could be a folk tale, perhaps one from another country. Write down a summary of the plot to remind yourself of the story – just a few phrases or sentences.

Your first line could be 'Once upon a time . . .' or 'Once there lived . . .' or 'Once there was . . .'. Find the one that works best for you. Rather than worrying about getting your ideas down on paper first, work on the first few lines in your head, or even say them out loud.

You do not have to stick to all the details of the original tale. Also, you might only want to tell part of the story. Another way would be to tell the tale from a certain character's point of view – such as Cinderella from the Fairy Godmother's point of view. Try and see if you can inject some humour into your rap too.

As Tony Mitton says, you don't have to worry about getting a perfect rhyme at the end of the line, half-rhymes will do. Think more about the rhythm, and telling the story to that beat. Use a simple rhythm, and clap or tap your feet 1–2–3–4 nice and slowly. You could even use a metronome as a beat keeper – if your school has one. Set the metronome to a reasonably slow pace – somewhere between 96 and 100 beats per minute.

Another way of approaching this activity is to work in pairs, and you could write a rhyming chunk each as you go along.

Tony Mitton

Figure 2.3 Peter Bailey's Green Man illustration for Tony Mitton's book *Plum*

TONY MITTON: For those readers who have not yet met the Green Man, he is a well-known figure in British folklore. He is often thought to stand for the power of growth in nature. The Green Man's name is preserved on many pub and street signs. His image can be seen in churches all over Europe, carved in wood or stone (Figure 2.3).

Green Man Lane

As I went walking down Green Man Lane
I met a stranger there.
His clothes were all of foliage
and tangled was his hair.

He did not pause for pleasantry
nor bid me how-d'ye-do.
He only stood with eyes of wood
that pierced me sharply through.

The leaves crept close around me.
The earth pressed at my feet.
I felt the breeze upon my skin,
My heart's insistent beat.

Never a word the stranger spoke,
Though his stare was keen and clear.
But the leaves around us rustled,
And my blood ran thick with fear.

And the leaves around us shivered
as a sudden silence fell.
And I felt the life of the ragged wood
in that dark and greeny cell.

I felt the thirst of each living leaf
as it lapped at the air for breath.
And I felt the search for each striving root
as it sifted life from death.

A scent of blood and fear sprang up,
a grip of beak and jaw.
And slow things moved in rich decay
beneath the forest floor.

Then a small bird sang out sharply
as the sunlight filtered through.
So I stepped out into the meadow
beneath a sky of blue.

And I saw how the field of bearded wheat
had grown from green to gold.
Then I thought of the man in the leafy coat,
with his look so keen and bold.

But whether the sun be shining bright
or the hedge be wet with rain

I'll hesitate before I pass
along that lane again.

(from Plum: Scholastic)

'Green Man Lane' is a **rhyming poem** written in the **ballad** form. Here, Tony Mitton talks about the writing of the poem and discusses **alliteration, ballads, drafting, epiphany, fantasy, first person narration, folklore, folk song, metaphor, myth** and **rhythm.**

TONY MITTON: I'd admired a poem by Charles Causley called 'Green Man in the Garden'. It's a very haunting, sinister poem – quite understated but ghostly somehow, and unnerving. In my view Causley's poem is all about how we can't escape our natural origins and the fact that we come from nature. However much we technologise and like to separate ourselves, human beings are basically dependent upon the planet, whether we like it or not. We can't escape our links with nature – we rely on the air we breathe, the water we drink. We are our environment, we can't ignore it.

I used to take my daughter Doris to a riding lesson at the weekend at Barrington, outside Cambridge. To get there I drove through the village of Harston. On the journey back I'd always see at the bottom of the hedge a street sign that read 'Green Man Lane'. Seeing that sign used to trigger off feelings and thoughts about the character of the Green Man.

For a long time I'd known about the Green Man. He's an old pagan figure – a myth from English folklore. The Green Man is part human, part nature. He is like a metaphor for nature. In pictures or carvings, the Green Man is often shown dressed in foliage, in clothes made of leaves. It's often unclear as to what exactly he is made of, and whether he is more human or more wild. The Green Man has also been called a 'wodwo' or wildman. He's a feral person, a man that lives out in the wild. In the past, people were known to go feral – that is, live out in the wild – and perhaps this is where the myth of the Green Man stems from. Who can say?

I later discovered that the real Green Man Lane in Harston was only about twenty or thirty yards long and led to a small enclave with houses. I can only assume that before the village was built up the lane would have led down to some fields or woods. I now know there are many Green Man Lanes all over England. There's even one in London.

As I drove past the road sign week after week I found myself thinking of the line 'As I went walking down Green Man Lane'. To me that sounded like the opening line of a traditional folk song or a ballad. It's like 'As I stepped out one midsummer morning . . .' or any of the folk songs that begin 'As I went walking . . .'. And then it didn't take long until the next line – 'I met a stranger there' – came to me. I like that word 'stranger'. It's a very old-fashioned word for me. Words like 'strange' have a very Anglo-Saxon and archaic feel to them. There's a folk song I learnt once, that tells of another stranger, as many such folk songs do:

One misty moisty morning
when cloudy was the weather
I met with an old man
His clothes were all of leather
With a cap beneath his chin
Singing 'How-d'ye-do and how-d'ye-do
and how-d'ye-do again.'

I actually quote this song in the poem. I think in a lot of the old songs the old man in some way stands for death. I think in my poem I was in some way echoing that type of song. I'm quite attracted to the idea of poems about encounters in which the narrator meets a person or figure from somewhere else. Overall, in this poem I'm trying to create a zone of folk and rural language.

When I'm writing this form of tradional ballad my main concern is keeping the rhythm and the rhyme working effectively, but within that I'll allow myself to use quite strong alliteration in a slightly medieval style:

> And I saw how the field of bearded wheat
> had grown from green to gold.

Alliteration was used a great deal in medieval verse. For me, such a thing is not deliberate, it's just a stylistic habit. If anything, I have to stop myself using it too often as I over-alliterate.

'Green Man Lane' is a fantasy. I have walked down the real Green Man Lane, but the event in the poem is fiction. What I used in this poem is my own imaginary vision of what the lane used to look like. In the poem I am imagining what it would have been like coming off the main street of the village and going down this lane which led to the woods or the corn fields.

Unlike my poems 'My Hat!' or 'Little Red Rap', both of which took very little time to write and had very few changes, this poem took numerous drafts. I wrote a version of this poem in which I met the Green Man but then the vision of the man was disturbed by the sound of a lorry rumbling down the street:

> Then out in the road I heard the hum
> of a lorry rumbling by
> and the man I thought I'd seen had gone
> with barely a stir and a sigh

At that point I thought this was a very potent image – that of the traffic interfering with the vision from the past. I've actually written other poems about the Green Man figure, and about how towns seem to have wiped him out, but that actually he still exists. If you ever see a wasted industrial site, in a sense you can see the Green Man breaking through – as grass and weeds will be growing in abundance. It's a potent image of nature reclaiming its territory.

I showed versions of this poem to my wife, who felt I should remove all the references to traffic and that I should write a purer poem. There were many different drafts and versions of this piece. Writing this poem was a bit like doing an oil painting where you're wiping off the paint and painting over. This poem was worked many times before I was finally happy with it. The version published in *Plum* is probably as good as I'll ever get it. Yet I'm not quite satisfied with the last line:

> I'll hesitate before I pass
> along that lane again.

I'm not at all sure about that last line. It has too much assonance and rhyme for such a short line. I've thought of some alternatives since. When I read that last stanza at performances I have to work it orally, to force it slightly to make it flow and come across as it doesn't quite work with the rhythm of the previous verses.

For me, 'Green Man Lane' is a bit like my poem 'Dreaming the Unicorn' in that they are both poems about an encounter. The narrator in both pieces is me, the poet, in imagined form. 'Green Man Lane' uses the first person narration and I actually say 'I' and 'me' in the poem. However, I wanted this to be a universal experience, I wanted the 'me' to stand for any human being. I'm quite attracted to poems that feature encounters. It's like a dream or a dreamscape or even a fairy tale in which a character goes on a journey and encounters a magical figure. It is a narrative, but it's meant to evoke an imaginary landscape that is like the real world – the woods, the corn fields – but it's slightly idealised. This is Arcadia, the rural idyll.

The poem tries to say that whilst nature is wholesome and wonderful, it's also pretty terrifying. I'm trying to convey the idea that the force that drives nature is malignant as well as benign, and that life and death are two sides of the same coin, that life – through re-birth – is generated through pain and death. This is why I'm using that kind of language:

> A scent of blood and fear sprang up,
> A grip of beak and jaw.
> And slow things moved in rich decay
> Beneath the forest floor.

The poem tells of a realisation and is a rite of passage – an initiation into the natural world. The character in the poem is surrounded by nature:

> The leaves crept close around me.

I wanted to express the idea of being imprisoned, of being closed in. Here, it's like in those cartoons in which the trees come alive and wrap their branches around people. And you can't escape this Green Man – you're being hunted down by him – and it's an experience that you have to go through. In the Causley poem the Green Man is in the garden, but he's also waiting at the top of the stair. He's a figure you can't get away from. In the same way, humans try to avoid the issue of death, but it's impossible.

> The leaves crept close around me.
> The earth pressed at my feet.
> I felt the breeze upon my skin,
> My heart's insistent beat.

So, nature's coming at you from the outside but also the inside as well. Nature is not only on the outside as you are nature too.

When you are writing for younger readers you can't do a lot of allusion to other texts, as your young readers might not know the reference. But the line 'And slow things moved in rich decay beneath the forest floor' is an indirect reference to *The Ancient Mariner*, in which there is an image:

> Yea, shiny things did crawl with legs
> Upon the shiny sea

Also, the line 'a grip of beak and jaw' is another allusion, this time to the familiar phrase 'nature red in tooth and claw', which tells of the malignant, harmful side of the natural world, which is what I was conveying here. I could have just quoted the poem directly, but that would have been a cliché, so I changed it to 'beak' and 'jaw'. In this line I wanted to represent both the bird world, with 'beak', and the animal world, with 'jaw'.

With this poem I let myself go. This is quite a sophisticated poem in terms of both the language it uses and the ideas it deals with, and as a result is quite a challenging read. I only ever perform this poem if I've got a top Junior group whom I've got an extended session with.

Workshop activities: nature and time

A WALK INTO THE PAST

Think of a road or a street near you that you know well. Imagine what it would have been like fifty years ago. Would there have been much traffic? Would the same buildings have been there? Was it a field? Who would be walking about there? Where would they have been going? Next, imagine what it would have been like a hundred years ago. Keep going back in time until you find a time that interests you.

Your poem does not have to be a rhyming poem necessarily, for you may choose to do it in the form of free verse. Perhaps you could begin your poem with 'As I went walking down . . .', or you may have your own alternative.

NATURE RECLAIMS

How many times have you seen weeds growing through the cracks in the pavement, or a garden overgrown with weeds? Write a piece in which nature is a wild and living creature, coming to reclaim the world for itself. Try not to be too inhibited with this poem and really let your imagination go!

AS I WENT WALKING DOWN . . .

In 'Green Man Lane', Tony Mitton imagines what a lane may have been like hundreds of years ago. Take a street that you know well and describe how it is now. Like Tony Mitton's poem, begin your poem 'As I went walking down . . .'. Brainstorm all the different features of that street and think of how you can describe the street imaginatively. (Or listen to the song 'Penny Lane' that Paul McCartney wrote when he was in The Beatles. Listen to how he paints a picture of the people in words.) Write a poem or song lyric about the people in a street or road that you know well. If you are writing a song lyric, why not borrow the tune from a song that you know?

Tony Mitton

TONY MITTON: For many of the peoples of the rainforests, the forest has been their entire world, providing them with everything. It is giver and taker, material and spiritual in its nature. As the forests are hacked back by modern ways, so the ways of life of the rainforest peoples are gradually destroyed.

Rainforest Song
(for the people)
Forest, my mother,
feed me your fruit.
Forest, my father,
trace me my root.
Forest, my shelter,
spread me your shade,
as I walk in the glow
of your green forest glade.

Forest of whispers
and intricate ways,
Forest of spirits
that slip through your maze,
Forest of mystery,
subtle and deep,
you glide like a snake
through my waking and sleep.

Forest, the home
of my eye and my hand,
Forest, the meaning
I understand,
Forest, the ground
where I place my tread,
where I breathe my being
and pillow my head,

Forest, the world
I depend upon,
where will I walk
when my Forest has gone?

(from *Plum*: Scholastic)

'Rainforest Song' is a **rhyming poem**. Here, Tony Mitton talks about the writing of the poem and discusses **conclusion, drafting, improvisation, libretto, moral, rhythm** and **stanzas**.

TONY MITTON: I wrote this for St Lawrence's Primary School in Cambridge as they were doing a musical project. A composer had come to work with the school for a week, helping the children to write their own opera about the rainforest. I wrote this piece as a poem for them, and they put it to music, so it became the libretto for their rainforest opera. With the music added to the poem it sounded like a religious chant.

This earlier version demonstrates how the rhythm of a poem can change from one version to another. As I started to write the poem I was just spinning lines, just improvising:

The forest is my father
He teaches me the truth

The forest is my mother
She feeds me with her fruit

I was writing in the language of an imagined rainforest person. I heard a voice or way of speaking which you might pick up from films or documentaries on native peoples of South America. And it went on:

The forest is my shelter
It shields me with its roof

The forest is security
She grips me by the root

These lines were not quite right, but these are the sorts of things I'll do in a notebook – just improvising lines until I find something that I like. After some redrafting the lines above changed, so that I ended up with:

> Forest, my mother,
> feed me your fruit.
> Forest, my father,
> trace me my root.

With this poem I've ended up with three eight-line stanzas and a short four-line stanza to finish. In the first and third stanzas I'm looking at the physical realities of the forest, with references to food and shelter, and in the second stanza I go on to look at the mysterious and mystical aspects of the forest. Many rainforest peoples believe in the harmony of the physical and spritual worlds. And the Aboriginal people in Australia have a similar belief or mythology called the Dreaming, in which the land has a spiritual dimension. Perhaps some Westerners may find these spiritual ideas about rainforests quite unusual, but if you actually think about it, our own dreams can affect our waking lives – and in this way the spiritual and material worlds are closely connected for us too.

The final stanza talks of the tragic destruction of their forest:

> Forest, the world
> I depend upon
> where will I walk
> when my Forest has gone?

When the white people, the Westerners, took over and colonised the lands that previously belonged to the Aborigines or the native North Americans or the rainforest peoples they didn't seem to realise that they were destroying something that couldn't be replaced. The white people would say, 'You can live on a reservation, you'll have everything you need' without realising what the land meant both physically and spiritually to these people.

I did quite a few drafts of this poem, and there are a number of lines and stanzas that didn't make the final version, such as:

> Forest my shield
> from shimmering heat
> Forest the place
> where I tread my feet

Before I wrote this poem I'd been reading a book with my daughter Doris – a collection of tales, lore and legends from rainforests all over the world by Rosalind Kerven. So this poem, in one sense, is the result or distillation of reading that book. In that book it said that the people that live in the rainforests often refer to themselves as 'the people' – they see themselves as one species. So hence my dedication 'for the people'. I sort of feel that the rainforest is about all of us, and I feel that when you destroy a bit of the rainforest you destroy a bit of yourself. Those people are part of humanity as we are – we are them and they are us.

I decided to finish the poem on a question:

> Forest, the world
> I depend upon
> where will I walk
> when my Forest has gone?

Some might think that it's a cheap trick because you're raising a question but not providing an answer. My feeling is that questions are an opportunity to evoke a quite complex issue to which there isn't a simple answer. Simply asking the question, I think, is important. It's partly a rhetorical question and partly a very blunt statement: that there can be nowhere once the rainforest has gone.

Poetry can have the opportunity to be powerfully moral without necessarily being didactic or a blatant protest. 'Rainforest Song' doesn't do anything as conscious as that. But if it gets people thinking, then all well and good.

Workshop activities: poster and song

PROTEST POSTER

Design and write a poster with a poem informing people about some ecological issue – such as rainforests, pollution or global warming – whatever interests or concerns you. As Tony Mitton did with 'Rainforest Song', try not to simply say something as direct as 'Don't pull down the rainforests', go for something more subtle and write a piece that celebrates the positive aspects of nature. Try to create something unusual or different that will atttract people's attention. Look at the adverts in magazines – how do they attract your attention? Perhaps, like in 'Rainforest Song', you could finish your poem with a question.

SONG LYRICS

Find a song that you like and write new lyrics to the melody. Sing the original lyrics around in your head and then look around for something to sing about. It could be something funny and amusing or something more serious. Aim for a couple of verses and a chorus.

Brian Moses

Lost Magic

Today I found some lost magic –
a twisty-twirly horn
of a unicorn lying at my feet.
And when I stopped
to pick it up, to hold it
in my fist, I remembered
how once upon a time
you could always find unicorns,
but there are no unicorns now.

You would find them on the shoreline,
flitting in and out of caves in cliffs,
or climbing hills at twilight.
They would lead you through forests,
sometimes hiding behind trees,
and if you lost them or they lost you,

you could always find them again,
but there are no unicorns now.

And it didn't matter
if you followed them all day,
the edge of the world was miles away,
there was nothing to fear.
And none of the unicorns we knew ever
changed into dangerous strangers.

Once upon a time there <u>were</u> unicorns
but there are no unicorns now.

(from *Barking Back at Dogs!*: Macmillan)

'Lost Magic' is a **free verse poem**. Here, Brian Moses talks about the writing of the poem and discusses **assonance, chorus, imagery, internal rhyme, stanzas** and **titles**.

BRIAN MOSES: This poem stems from my childhood and the fact that childhood then was quite different to how it is now. When I was 10, my parents never worried about me. We lived in a seaside town and I was always out on my bike. I'd go round the harbour or down to the beach or the cliffs or the park. My parents didn't worry, just so long as I got home for mealtimes.

Us parents today, we're reluctant to let our children have that sort of freedom. Sadly, the world isn't as safe as it used to be, and we need to know where our children are and what they're doing at all times. In this poem there's the line 'The edge of the world was miles away' – as when I was young I was free to explore, but children aren't today.

The poem was written over a period of three to four months. I began with that phrase 'the edge of the world was miles away' and started adding things to it, ideas which I didn't use eventually. Then later I got the idea of finding some lost magic. I felt that so much of the magic of childhood had been lost, and I thought to myself, if I found some lost magic today, what form or shape would it come in? And I suddenly thought of this idea of a horn of a unicorn and that it would be a magical thing.

I'm very much attracted to mythic creatures like unicorns and dragons because the unexplained gives you great possibilities as a writer. Because nothing is definite about these creatures, there's so much that you can invent. I see the unicorn as a symbol of a more purer and more innocent time. I've always been fascinated by unicorns and whether they actually existed or not.

The first stanza – once I had the idea of the unicorn's horn at my feet – came very quickly. Once I got the line 'but there are no unicorns now', I knew that it would be a hook or a chorus around which the poem would be based. And the title is significant because the poem is all about a magical time that is now lost – even though it was only forty years ago – the late 1950s and early 1960s. I could have called the poem 'There Are No Unicorns Now' I guess, but I do like the word 'lost' and 'Lost Magic' sums up the poem more for me. Though I've used 'Lost' in another title – 'The Lost Angels' – so I'd better stop using the word!

I underlined the word 'were' in the final stanza because I wanted to emphasise the fact that unicorns are no longer with us. Also, at the end of the poem I could have linked the final two lines on to the previous stanza, but I wanted those last two lines to stand alone as I like the pause between the two stanzas.

With a free verse poem like this, I like to use assonance – such as 'a twisty-twirly *horn* of a *unicorn'* and '*changed* into *dange*rous *strangers'* – because that type of internal rhyming gives the poem a strength that it needs. There are a lot of 'i' sounds in there which strengthen the first verse – for example in the words 'unicorn', 'magic', 'it' and so on.

In the very first stanza I'm talking about myself. It's written in the first person because it's all about my own personal fantasy experience, though the next stanza is in the second person – and talks of 'you' – because I'm saying that unicorns were once available to everybody, that this was a universal experience.

I'm pleased to say that this poem has had some good reactions. One teacher at a private school in Eastbourne I visited recently complimented the poem. This teacher took a copy of the poem and used it as a focus for a creative writing activity with her class of 12 year olds – to look back at their own childhoods. And I actually made a couple of changes to the poem in response to her comments. One of her comments was regarding the line 'And none of the unicorns we knew ever changed into dangerous strangers.' Before, I had put '*to* dangerous strangers'. Also, there was an extra line in verse two, which wasn't very good. It was something like 'Climbing the hills at twilight, silhouetted against the sky' – which was just forcing the image, and laying it on too heavily.

I perform this poem now at most of my readings in schools. However, I'm not sure if children fully appreciate the poem, but they certainly seem to like the idea of the unicorn, and rate unicorns as a subject for a poem. Really, I think I read this piece as much for the teachers as I do for the children. And I usually preface the reading by talking about my own childhood and comparing it with childhood today.

I'm pleased with this poem as I feel I've achieved what I wanted to say with it. It's my favourite one from my new collection, *Barking Back at Dogs!*

Workshop activities: mythic creatures and distant memories

MYTHIC CREATURES

Make a list of all the mythic creatures you can think of – such as the Loch Ness Monster, Big Foot, dragons, trolls, elves, fairies – or, if you want, invent one. Which one interests you most of all? Why does it interest you? Write down your thoughts or feelings about the creature, again in a list. Now write down some words and phrases that describe what you think the creature looks like. Be imaginative and adventurous in your descriptions. Try to avoid any description you've heard or read before. Then think about what the creature might do if it appeared today, and how people would react to it – and then write down these thoughts and ideas too.

Now start thinking about a poem. Use each of your lists of ideas to make up a stanza each. So, the first stanza could be about your feelings towards the creature, the second stanza could be a description, the third could be about the creature appearing in a nearby street or local park. Write the poem in free verse – like Brian Moses' 'Lost Magic'. And even though you are not thinking about rhymes – think about the rhythm of the lines, how they flow, and also take time to think of the best way to describe the images you have. See if you can use some assonance, like 'dangerous strangers', or alliteration like 'twisty-twirly'. And perhaps, as with 'Lost Magic', you could find a line to repeat – say either at the beginning or the end of each stanza.

THERE ARE NO UNICORNS NOW

Take the line 'there are no unicorns now' and change it, to something like:

> There are no dinosaurs now

Or

> There are no dragons now

And use one of these as a first or last line for every stanza of a new poem.

DISTANT MEMORIES

Think for a while about when you were five. Write down a list of some of the things that you used to do at that age. Is there one object that was important to you, something personal to you that brings back memories of those times – a toy, a book, a teddy bear, a photograph or a present from someone? Use that object as the focus for a poem. Like 'Lost Magic', make it a free verse poem, but see if you can include some internal thymes occasionally. In your piece you might want to describe the object, how it looked then and perhaps how it looks now, if you still have it. Also think about why that object was important. What did you used to do with it?

Andrew Fusek Peters

Fire at Night

It's ready steady sticks for fiery fun,
The strike of the match is the starter's gun.
Up go the flames, long-jumping sky,
The smoke catches up, hurdling high.
The crowd stamp their frozen feet
Clap their hands for the winning heat.
Guy Fawkes sits on top of the pyre,
Easily beaten, eaten by fire.
Who is quickest in the scorching race?
Flames of gold grab first place.
Who beat the day? The crowd then roars
The moon made silver to the stars' applause.
Who has come third? No-one remembers,
As they all sprint home, leaving only bronze embers.
As clouds shuffle by with a marathon creep,
Children in bed clutch the prize of sleep.

'Fire at Night' is a poem written in **rhyming couplets**. Here, Andrew Fusek Peters talks about the writing of the poem and discusses **alliteration, assonance, conceit, couplets, draft, ending, image, metaphor, pun, structure, syllables** and **wordplay**.

ANDREW FUSEK PETERS: This poem began when I lit a fire outside the house. It was twilight and the village was just going quiet. It was a magical late summer evening. I'd been burning everything that we'd cut down in the garden, and the flames were leaping up into the sky. There's something about fire that I love. Suddenly a few lines came to me. I had my notebook on me and I started jotting the ideas down. These are the original notes I made sitting by the fire:

> Night fire
> Guy Fawkes
> The flames have won the high jump
> Balls of paper crumpled like loose faces
> Dried nettles
> Old fern into the heap ready to burn
> Wrinkled elder
>
> Now begins the fiery fun
> The strike of the match is the starter's gun
> We give you the silver, the moon
> The flames are gold in a scorching race
> Bronze are the embers, we came third and last

So by this point I was starting to think about rhymes and structure:

> No-one cheers, the fire goes past in this winning heat

By now I'd begun to think of the wordplay – the pun on the word 'heat', and turning the whole piece into a conceit. A conceit is an extended metaphor, or, put another way – it's a set of images that are all linked to one idea. Here, the conceit is athletics. What I was doing was moulding the two sets of images – the fire and athletics – together. Aristotle said that good metaphor implies an eye for good resemblance. And that's, for me, what poetry is all about – comparing one thing to another. This gives us a fresh way of seeing things. And that's exactly what I'm trying to do in this poem. I like writing a conceit because it's a challenge, it's difficult, and it's a crafted piece – you've made a jigsaw, and it's lyrical and beautiful.

The final draft is written in couplets – pairs of rhyming lines. Between the rough notes and this final draft I made further changes. In the third line I originally had 'hurdling sky', but that became 'long-jumping sky' as it scanned better. Lines 5 and 6 were 'The crowd cheers and roars with their feet / and clap their hands for the winning heat', which didn't work. As with 'Clap their hands for the winning heat', I'm always trying to see how many images I can fit into one line, how many layers of meaning I can achieve. Shakespeare was really good at weaving hundreds of layers of meaning into one line – and that fascinates me.

In this poem I'm using things like assonance – 'ready steady' and 'easily beaten' – and alliteration – 'hurdling high', 'frozen feet' and 'moon made'. I do like using these, but I don't look for them deliberately. They just happen. What I was aiming at was getting the images right, finding beautiful phrases. Because with a conceit it can become mechanical, just fitting images together. I was looking for the lyric, the feeling within the poem. Also, I wanted to fit in the images of the gold, silver and bronze athletics trophies. I thought, how can I fit these in? What is gold, silver and bronze? – and I discovered it was the flames, the moon and the embers.

I wasn't particularly counting syllables as I was writing the poem, I was more concentrating on sound and the sounds of words that work well together: 'Who beat the day? The crowd then roars / The moon made silver to the stars' applause.' You can hear that it just feels and sounds right.

The poem needed a strong ending. That's one problem I do have with my poems. But I think this one works: 'As clouds shuffle by with a marathon creep /Children in bed clutch the prize of sleep.' So, I've kept the conceit – that is, the athletics metaphor – going right to the very last image. I remember as a child having those fantastic evenings – outside with a fire, eating hot dogs, and it was cold, and I'd go to bed feeling really tired. So, what I've got in this poem is the form of the rhyming couplets as well as the conceit. Also, it's something real – the poem tells of real experiences.

I've never performed this poem, but I probably would on 5 November! If I did, it would be with Juniors, and I would perform it slowly because it's quite complex, and I would explain the imagery beforehand.

Workshop activity: fire

Think about the image of a fire. Brainstorm all the words, phrases and ideas you can think of. Use the senses: what does a fire look, smell and sound like? Make a list of all the times and places that you may see a fire. As with Andrew Fusek Peters, think of some metaphors to describe fire – images that the fire is like. So, compare fire to something else – perhaps a dancer, or a fountain. Using the dancer image you could write a conceit – an extended metaphor: 'Rising high to a crackling beat / Shimmering, shaking on its feet/The fire . . .'. Or, perhaps you may want to have a string of different metaphors, for example, 'A fire is a dancer /A raging rhythm / A fire is a fountain /An angry river . . .'. Or, you could take one of these two examples and develop it into a poem.

Poetry workshops

Abstractions

This activity has been adapted from one of Matthew Sweeney's popular poetry workshops, which he in turn borrowed from Carol Ann Duffy.

Think of some abstract nouns, some that you have experienced yourself – such as happiness, jealousy, excitement, confusion, greed, compassion, tiredness, surprise, love, worry, hate, contentment or hope. Make a list and decide which one interests you most. Think about your abstraction imaginatively and put it into real terms by answering the following questions, which have been answered for the abstraction 'boredom':

1 What does it look like? *Grey as an afternoon that never quite rains*
2 What does it sound like? *Musak in a shopping centre*
3 What does it taste like? *White bread – no butter or jam*
4 What does it feel like? *So itchy you want to scratch it all the time*
5 Where does it live? *In a cupboard and falls out every time you open it*
6 What does it smell like? *School dinners*
7 What would it say if it could speak? *Anything – but it would go on and on and on!*

Matthew Sweeney stresses that the responses to each question must remain concrete, and no further abstractions – apart from the theme itself – are allowed.

Bring your own responses together and develop them into a free verse poem. Each answer could be expanded into a whole stanza.

Alphabets

BRIAN MOSES: This exercise is good for whole class collaborations. This one is the start to a 'Dragon Food Alphabet':

> A is for antelope, juicy and sweet
> B is for brains, cooked and stewed

Close observations

Go outside and collect something from the natural world – perhaps an empty bird's egg, a feather or leaf or stone; or, you could choose a picture of an animal. Take a sheet of paper and draw a vertical line down the middle. Label one column 'subjective' and the other 'objective'. In the 'subjective' column write about your own personal feelings and responses to your find – any words or phrases that come to mind. In the 'objective' column write only comments that are factual and descriptive, such as the size, shape and colour of the object/animal. Use all the senses – sight, smell, feel and so on – and include any similes or metaphors that you wish. Be as original as you can. Now write a free verse poem in which you interweave both subjective and objective responses.

Colours

Write a poem – in any form or style – in which you include as many colours as you can. Pick a setting or subject that has a wide variety of colours – such as a market, a beach, a fairground or a firework display. This colour poem was written by 8-year-old Laurence Fitz-Desorgher:

Colour of Day and Colour of Night
Yellow day has gone,
Birds go to sleep,
All but one:
The brown owl still peeks.
The black is here,
The yellow's gone,
But still in the sky
There's a golden twinkle.
Black bats hunt
While peach people snooze,
Yellow is back again,
Red bus is on a cruise.
Green trees rustle
While rosy children play,
Which colours
Will we see
Next
In this day?

Class anthologies

When poets collect poems for new anthologies they will often write to other poets asking for contributions. In the information sheets they send out they will detail the topic of the anthology, and give suggestions as to what types of poems they would like to receive. Here are a few recent anthologies – why not do your own class versions?

Brian Moses (Macmillan)
Aliens Stole My Underpants! (poems about space)
Hysterical Historical Series (Romans, Middle Ages, Tudors, Victorians)
Secret Lives of Teachers
I'm Telling on You (poems about brothers and sisters)
Minibeasts
We Three Kings (Christmas poems)

John Foster (Oxford University Press)
Dragon Poems
Dinosaur Poems

Paul Cookson (Macmillan)
Let's Twist Again (tongue twisters)

Conversation poems

Teacher-led activity.

MAGGIE MOORHOUSE, ENGLISH TEACHER, STOKE PARK SCHOOL, COVENTRY: A good way to start a poem is to have a conversation in pairs, taking on two different characters, e.g.

Police-officer and suspect
Teacher and student
Dentist and patient
Boss and job applicant

The way that people speak and the kind of language people use can tell us a lot about a person. Think about the words you choose for them to use, any accent or dialect they may have and how formal or casual their speech is. When you have acted out a conversation, choose one of the two characters and write in their voice. You could write as both characters or you and your partner could write as one each and combine the two voices in a poem.

Dreams

BRIAN MOSES: What do everyday things dream about? Here are some examples to start you off:

A shoe dreams of being worn by a princess.
A snowman dreams that the sun will never shine.

Forms of poetry

This book does not feature all of the different forms of poetry, so you may wish to explore some of the forms listed below, which are covered by these texts: Sandy Brownjohn's *To Rhyme or not to Rhyme?* (Hodder and Stoughton), Pie Corbett and Brian Moses' *Catapults and Kingfishers* (Oxford University Press) and Peter Abbs and John Richardson's *The Forms of Poetry* (Cambridge University Press):

ACROSTIC
CINQUAIN
DIAMOND
FOUND POEM
KENNING
LIMERICK
LYRIC
RIDDLE
SONNET
TANKA/CINQUAIN
VILLANELLE

John Foster – 'Grandma'

Grandma is navy blue.
She is a comfy cushion.
Grandma is a soft whisper.
She is a path through a winter wood.
Grandma is a warm scarf.
She is a cup of tea by the fire.
Grandma is a sleeping cat.
She is autumn sunshine.

(from *You Little Monkey*: Oxford University Press)

JOHN FOSTER: When I use this poem in my workshops I ask children to choose a character of their own – be it their brother, sister, parent or teacher – and to follow the pattern that I have set up in 'Grandma'. So the character is a colour, then a piece of furniture, then a sound, then a landscape, a piece of clothing, a food or drink, an animal and finally a form of weather. It's a very useful exercise to encourage children to consider figurative imagery. I've used this with children from Year 4 across to Year 8.

Group poems

Teacher-led activity. Pick a title/first line from those given below and copy them on to the board. Ask the class to copy these on to the top of a sheet of blank paper. Invite the group to think of a few lines of their own in free verse. After ten minutes ask five volunteers to read out one favourite line that they have written. Write these lines on the board and then ask the class to copy these down and to use them as the basis for a free verse poem. The group can add, delete or re-order lines to create their own individual poems.

'Moon Gazing' – The moon looks very different tonight . . .
'Sleepwalker' – While the city sleeps . . .

Headlines

Here, Brian Moses answers the question 'What makes a good title?'

BRIAN MOSES: People have told me that 'Aliens Stole My Underpants' is a good title. With that poem I was thinking of the headlines that you get in some of the less reputable Sunday newspapers, such as 'Baby Nessies Found In Garden Pond'! I just imagined that 'Aliens Stole My Underpants' could easily be such a headline. With this poem I thought of the title first, and wrote the poem to the title.

Write your own poem with a humorous newspaper heading. Either make up your own heading, or use one of the following:

'Baby Nessies Found In Garden Pond'
'Aliens Live In My Attic!'
'Dinosaurs Didn't Exist – Says Top Scientist'
'The Millennium Dome was a UFO: It's Official!'

House haiku

A haiku is a three-line poem in which the first line is made up of five syllables (or beats), the second line has seven syllables, and the third line has five syllables. Before reading this haiku poem by Tony Mitton, work out how many beats or syllables there are in your name. Tony Mitton's name, for example, has four: To / ny / Mit / ton.

Tony Mitton – 'Bathroom'
Steam rises whitely.
My knees are strange bare islands.
The bathroom is mine.

TONY MITTON: Think of your house and think for a while about each individual room. What memories do you have for each room? What has happened in each room? What does each room mean to you? How would you describe each room? Is this room different at different times of the day?

Write a haiku for each room. This exercise can be done in a number of ways – either as strict haikus of 5–7–5 syllables for each stanza, or the first two lines are made up of images, and the third line is a thought, or, alternatively, two lines of images and the third is a feeling, or even three lines of all images.

Here are further themes for a haiku:

- A bird diving into a river to catch a fish
- Dusk or dawn in a garden or park
- A busy city street at night
- Looking out of a railway carriage/bus/coach window

- A cat crawling along a wall
- One animal chasing another.

Haiku: Utopia and Dystopia

What would your Utopia – your perfect world – be like? And what would your Dystopia – your worst possible world – be like? For some, a Utopia might be a beach in a warm country or an endless supply of chocolate or a world without suffering. For some, a Dystopia might be a world where there are no school holidays or a world without music. Brainstorm ideas separately for the two worlds. Write one haiku for your Utopia, and another for your Dystopia.

Iambics

Read through this first stanza of the 'The Walrus and the Carpenter' by Lewis Carroll out loud. Concentrate on the rhythm.

> The sun was shining on the sea,
> Shining with all his might:
> He did his very best to make
> The billows smooth and bright –
> And this was odd, because it was –
> The middle of the night.

Read it again. What do you notice about the rhythm?

You'll find that every other beat – that is, every second beat – is emphasised. This type of rhythm is known as an 'iambic'. Here Andrew Fusek Peters talks about his poem 'When I Come to the Dark Country' (from *The Weather's Getting Verse*: Sherbourne Press), which is a ballad. In this ballad Andrew tells the story of when he went for a walk and noticed how the Shropshire countryside had become polluted with litter. This is the first verse:

> As I walked out one evening soft
> High in the hills of brown
> I came across a wonded land
> A queen without a crown

ANDREW FUSEK PETERS: Ballads are our oldest form of poetry. Many were written as lyrics to be sung or spoken out loud and they often told a story with a gloomy ending about ghosts, highwaymen, sad love affairs or historical battles. When you read a ballad aloud, it seems to flow along quite easily. This is the trick when writing your own ballad. Another way of finding the right rhythm is the very scientific *dum-de-dum* method. This is where the 'dum' lands on the syllable or word you stress most when speaking aloud. Thus, if we translated the first verse, it would go like this:

> de-dum de-dum de-dum de-dum
> de-dum de-dum de-dum,
> de-dum de-dum de-dum de-dum,
> de-dum de-dum de-dum.

This way of translating your words can be very helpful to check the rhythm of your own balladeer attempts.

Write your own iambic piece. You could begin with 'As I get up' or 'As I go out' or 'As I went out' or 'The sun was shining on the sea' or 'As I walked out one evening soft'. You could write about a walk that you have been on and tell of your observations. It could even be your journey to school.

Imaginary snapshot

TONY MITTON: In your mind take an imaginary photograph of someone in your family doing something – some domestic activity – that they often do, perhaps every day – such as digging in the garden, washing up, reading or laying the table. Then use a free verse form to celebrate them doing that act. Observe them very carefully in your mind's eye. Make your word pictures as clear, concrete and detailed as possible. Paint or film the images in well chosen words.

Improvising free verse to music

Teacher-led activity. Pick two instrumental pieces of music that last about three or four minutes. Find two pieces that are wholly different in terms of style, mood, pace and instrumentation. Film scores are often useful for this kind of activity.

Before you play the pieces, instruct the pupils to listen to the music very carefully and to find what images the music paints in the mind's eye. As soon as they have that first image they are to improvise an unstructured piece of free verse. If possible, they should write non-stop for the duration of each piece, writing as many ideas and descriptions of that image – or series of images – as they can. Some students may even choose to doodle or draw the images. You might choose to play each piece of music twice. The unstructured pieces can then be developed further.

It would be beneficial to examine a few free verse poems beforehand to remind the pupils of this particular form.

Let's begin: poetry

See the worksheet 'Poetry beginnings' on p. 75 for a selection of introductory lines from a range of children's poets.

List poems

BRIAN MOSES: Pick one of the phrases below and use it as a starting point for a list poem. Start every line or every stanza with the same word or phrase.

I wish I was . . .
It's a secret but . . .
I dreamt I . . .
Don't . . .
I'd rather be . . .
I like . . .
If only . . .

The Magical Cat/Oath of Friendship

Brian Moses' workshops 'The Magical Cat' and 'Oath of Friendship' feature in the report of his visit to St John's School in the Author Visit Guide.

Metaphors in the outside world

COLIN MACFARLANE: Go outside with a pen and notepad and describe anything at all – a tree, the weather, the sky, but without any clichés. Personify whatever you are describing. If it's a tree, think: is it male or female? Old or young? What emotions does it feel? What would it say if it were human? What would it do? What would it enjoy or complain about? Write down anything you come up with and later work some of your ideas into a poem.

Metaphor and simile

Teacher-led activity.

JAN DEAN: I have a particular exercise on constructing an image using metaphor and simile, without using those actual words as such, but using the word 'comparison'. Look at your hand. What does it remind you of? With outstretched fingers you might say it looks like a leaf, or that the knuckles on your fist look like sand dunes, or that the side of your fist looks like a tornado. So, you could write:

> My spread hand is like a leaf

But to make this comparison stronger you remove the 'like'. You could develop this further and write:

> My spread hand is a leaf
> My curled hand spirals into a tornado
> My knuckles are a line of sand dunes
>
> There is a desert on the end of my arm

Then I might go outside and encourage the class to find things that remind them of other things. If someone brings me a pine cone that looks like a hedgehog, I'll ask them to find other things that look like other animals. Or, if a church steeple looked like a rocket, I'll ask them to find other things to do with space. Once they've done that, they can put together metaphors and similes that are linked by theme and they can build up a series of images in a poem.

Monster poem

Teacher-led activity.

JAN DEAN: Children often tell me that they have no imagination. So I say rubbish! Imagination is simply a reshuffling of the known. One workshop I do in schools to prove this is to get a class to invent a monster with me. I'll ask them all kinds of questions – such as what colour is the monster? *Blue.* What shape will its head be? *Like a conker case with spikes.* What will it sound like? *Blowing bubbles through a straw into a milkshake.* And so on – until I give them a description of the monster that they have invented from their own imaginations. I show them that we might not have invented the colour blue, the shape of a conker case and so on, but that being imaginative is all about putting everyday things into a new shape. Once we have done this, we then go on to write a poem about the monster.

The Natural World/The Outsider

Andrew Fusek Peters' workshops 'The Natural World' and 'The Outsider' feature in the report of his visit to Stoke Park School in the Author Visit Guide.

Rapping yarns

A rap poem workshop activity is given at the end of Tony Mitton's discussion of 'Little Red Rap' earlier in this chapter (p. 46).

Rhyming dictionary

TONY MITTON: As a fun activity, why not use a rhyming dictionary and make up a fun or nonsense poem using one rhyme sound if you can. Build your poem around just that *one* rhyme, using it, playfully, as often as you can.

Tony Mitton – 'Nits'
If you're scratching your head to bits
You could have nits.

And if you've got nits
You need to give your head a blitz.

You can get kits
To deal with nits.

But if it can help it,
A nit
     never quits
It just sits
       Tight
until night.
And then it might
         bite.

Yes, having nits
Can drive you out of your wits.
They're the pits.
You're better off
      with the squits!

(from the collection *Plum*: Scholastic)

If you do not have a rhyming dictionary, just pick everyday words such as tall, boy, sun, hat, man, sky – and brainstorm all the rhymes that you can.

Tell me no lies

Teacher-led activity.

> **JAN DEAN:** One workshop I do is to get a class to think about the room they are in and to tell me three details that might make the room sound grim and scary, three details from the room that make it sound beautiful and exciting and three details that make it sound dull. We'll then take one of those sets of details and use it as the basis for a poem.

The shape of things

Shape poems can come about in a number of ways. You can turn a poem that already exists – one that you or someone else has already written – into a shape poem. The tear-shaped poem was written as a short rhyming piece but was later transformed into a shape poem on a word processor.

A

poem

is just like

a tear: a drop

of emotion – a tiny

explosion – a silent

commotion – an

act of de-

votion

The river-shaped poem started out as a phrase and a doodle and soon became literally a river of words.

from

a

tiny

spring

the

river

came

and

wound

its

way

for

days

and

days

first

east

then

west

but

always

south

always

down

even

when

it

c

u

r

l

e

d

itself

a

r   o

u   n

d

a

b

e

n

d

but

then

one day

something changed

and a river it could no longer be

for the river grew and the river knew that now it was

THE SEA THE SEA THE SEA THE SEA THE SEA THE SEA THE
SEA THE SEA THE SEA THE SEA THE THE SEA THE SEA THE
SEA THE SEA THE SEA THE SEA THE SEA THE SEA THE SEA
THE SEA THE SEA THE SEA THE SEA THE SEA THE SEA THE

Activity 1

Take a feature of the outside world – such as a road, a footpath, a mountain, a lake, a cloud, a tree or a house – and draw it in words. Or, doodle with words and lines and pictures and enjoy experimenting with shapes.

Activity 2

The word onomatopoeia (on-o-mat-o-peer) describes the way that some words reflect the sound that they represent. Think of CRASH! BANG! SWISH! HISS!. Take a sheet of A4 paper and fill it up with as many of these words as you can think of. Then see if you can develop some of these words into a poem. Think of a subject that unites these sounds – such as a firework display, an orchestra or a rock group. Then form a poem around that subject using as many of your sounds as you can.

Activity 3

As with the piece shown here, you can use a word processor to help you create a shape poem. Use all the functions available to you – the letters, numbers, punctuation, centralising, italics, various fonts, sizes – and use bold, underline, shadowing. You could even develop this piece further by including further shapes and sizes and even sounds.

Activity 4

Think of a musical instrument. Write a poem about the sounds that it makes, its appearance, the way that it is played, the styles of music it can play and also why you like it. Once you have a poem that is working well, use a personal computer to adapt your poem into the shape of that instrument. The instrument poem on p. 71 was first written in regular stanzas and was later changed into a guitar shape on a word processor.

I like electric guitars:
played mellow or moody
frantic or fast – on CDs
or tapes, at home or in
cars – live, pre-recorded
busked or in bars.
I like
electric
guitars:
played
choppy
like
reggae
or angry
like
rock or
chirpy
like
jazz or
strummy
like
pop or
heavy
like
metal – it
bothers
me not.
I like electric guitars:
their strings and their straps
and their wild wammy bars – their
jangling and twanging and funky
wah-wahs – their fuzz boxes,
frets and multi-effects –
pick-ups, machine
heads, mahogany necks
– their plectrums, their wires,
and big amplifiers. I like electric
guitars: played loudly, politely – dully
or brightly – daily or nightly – badly
or nicely. I like electric guitars:
bass, lead and rhythm –
I basically dig 'em –
I like ele
　　　c
　　　　t
　　　　　r
　　　　　i
　　　　c
　　　　g
　　　　u
　　　　　i
　　　　　　t
　　　　a
　　　　r
　　s

Activity 5

Take a song lyric and change it into a shape. The words to a love song, for example, could form a heart. Take a theme or an image from the lyric as your guide.

Snap, crackle, pop

NORMAN SILVER: The following poem comes from my collection *The Walkmen Have Landed* but none of the words in it are my own! I took them all from the back of cereal packets. I had only one or two cereal packets to choose from, so I went to a supermarket armed with a pen and notebook and copied out words and phrases from their wider selection. My rule for the poem was: *only use words and phrases from the back of cereal packets.* Read these two verses from the poem and afterwards I'll suggest how you can write your own version.

Snap, Crackle, Pop

Wake up sunshine, morning treat,
don't leave home before you eat,
hearty breakfast, fortified,
free collect-a-card inside,

protein, energy, sodium, vitamin,
niacin, fibre, calcium, thiamin,
sugar, glucose, chocolate, malt,
yummy, honey, marshmallow, salt,

barley (ground),
bran (baked),
wheat (shredded),
corn (flaked),

family, first established, milling,
children growing, vital, filling,
energy, daily, wholesome, nutritious,
natural, low-fat, balanced, delicious

pecan, coconut, almond, sultana,
apple, hazelnut, date, banana,
papaya, apricot, maple, strawberry,
pineapple, sunflower, sesame, cherry,

oats (rolled),
rice (toasted),
raisins (splitzed),
nuts (roasted),

special offers, details on the back,
trademark, tokens, two per pack,

cut-out dinosaurs, space-glo stickers,
genuine Matchbox die-cast replicas,

aprons, calculators, magic stencils,
wicked witches, coloured pencils,
new-look package, recycled, green,
by appointment to the Queen,

nuggets, loops, pillows, hearts,
clusters, rings, puffs, tarts,
Malties, Crispies, Shreddies, Munchies,
Toasties, Frosties, Sweeties, Crunchies.

Okay. Now choose your own product, e.g. ice-cream, pasta, chocolates etc. Then raid your food cupboard or go into a supermarket armed with a pen and a notebook. Remember the rule for your poem: *only use words or phrases which you have found on the packaging.* When your poem is written, please email it to me at: poems@storybook.demon.co.uk Have fun writing!!

Song titles

Have a look at the titles to songs in the charts or on CDs or cassettes. Write out a list of titles that you like. Can you put some of these together to form a poem or a new song? You do not need to stick to titles, you could include lines from lyrics and also add some lines of your own.

Take a line

Here are some beginnings to popular poems. Pick one and develop it however you wish.

> Have you ever seen a sheet on a river bed?
> Or a single hair from a hammer's head?
> Has the foot of a mountain any toes?
> And is there a pair of garden hose?
>
> (from Anon. – 'Have You Ever Seen?')
>
> I always eat peas with honey
>
> (from Anon. – 'Peas')
>
> The sea is calm tonight
>
> (from Matthew Arnold – 'Dover Beach')
>
> Hurt no living thing
>
> (from Christina Rossetti – 'Hurt No Living Thing')
>
> Up on their brooms the witches stream
>
> (from Walter de la Mare – 'The Ride-by-Nights')

Poetry word wheel

For this teacher-led activity, see Figure 2.4: 'Poetry word wheel: adjectives, nouns and verbs'. Photocopy one for each member of the class. Pupils can cut out the three wheels and join them together with a paper fastener. They then choose a combination of three or two words as a starting point for a poem. (This was adapted from the 'Surrealist Dreaming Wheel' of the Tate Gallery Education Department.)

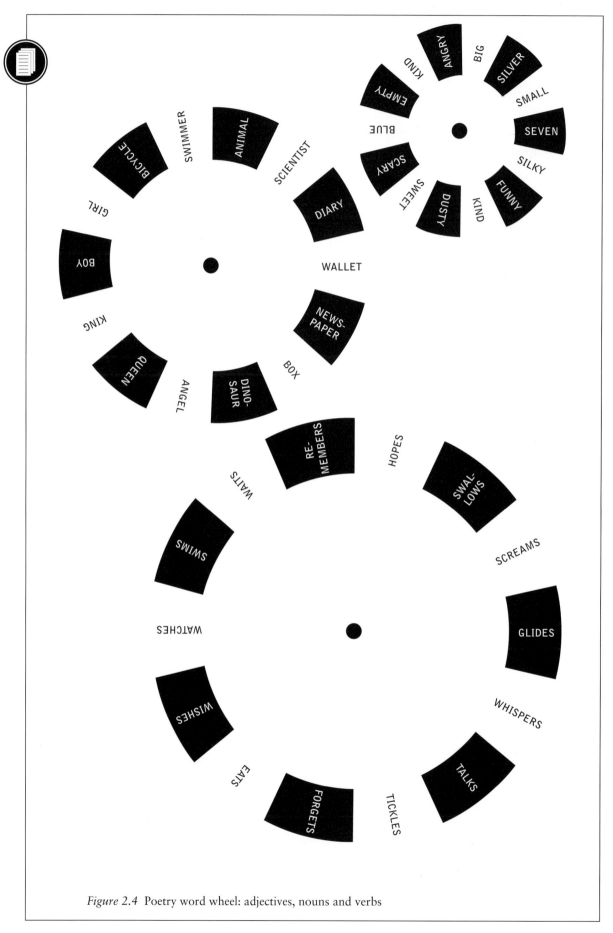

Figure 2.4 Poetry word wheel: adjectives, nouns and verbs

POETRY BEGINNINGS

Here are some beginnings to poems that have never been written. Find one that you like. Copy it on to the top of the other side of the page and then carry on with the poem. Before you begin, think – do you want to just start writing or do you want to brainstorm your ideas first? And what clues are there in the beginning you have chosen to help you find some way of growing it into a poem? Say the line out loud a few times to feel its rhythm.

VALERIE BLOOM
Underneath the bridge at midnight
Or
Last night I had soup for breakfast
Or
My monster is quite useless

JAN DEAN
Behind the dust, behind the cobweb
Behind the crack in the wall
Or
When they find out it was me

BERLIE DOHERTY
The earth is angry

JOHN FOSTER
'In the Cellar'
In the corner of the cellar

ROGER MCGOUGH
The afternoon is dropping to its knees
Or
Within reach of the shore I hesitate,
tread water

TONY MITTON
The door came crashing open
Or
Tell me your story, little box

BRIAN MOSES
I met a kid called Goliath

ANDREW FUSEK PETERS
She wove her anger into a box,
Closed her crying eyelid locks

NORMAN SILVER
When the last whale dies

MATTHEW SWEENEY
There are places in the forest
You must never visit
Or
The polar bear looked into the water,
Saw something he liked there

BENJAMIN ZEPHANIAH
Poems like this can cause

POETRY CHECKLIST

When you are reading through a draft there are many things to think about.

The questions below may help you to develop your poem.

Language

Do you repeat some words too often?

Is any of the phrasing awkward?

Are there too many adjectives or adverbs?

Are there too many overused adjectives (nice, beautiful, lovely etc.) ?

Are you using clichés (unoriginal phrases) that could be changed?

Are you using metaphors or similes? Are there too many?

Do your rhymes work well? Are you using words just for the sake of a rhyme?

Image

Are you painting a full picture for your reader?

Are your descriptions too vague or unclear?

Structure

Do you have a good beginning, middle and end?

Does the opening grab your attention and make you want to go on?

Have you got the best possible opening line or stanza?

Rhythm

Do the words, phrases and lines flow?

How well does it read out loud?

Is the rhythm working well overall?

Do you keep to the same rhythm throughout?

General

Are your lines the right length?

Should the poem be in a different form?

Is the poem too complicated?

Is the title right?

Is the poem original in any way?

Is there anything in the poem that you don't need?

Does the poem do what you want it to do?

Will the poem make sense to a reader?

How will a reader respond to this?

What are the strengths and weaknesses of the poem?

The next step

How could it be improved?

What needs to be done next?

If you have gone through the checklist and you are not sure what needs to be done next, leave your poem for a while and come back to it later.

POETRY GLOSSARY

alliteration and assonance Alliteration is where words begin with the same letters or sounds: 'table top', 'car keys', 'green grass'. Assonance is where words have the same sounds: 'green bean', 'new view'.

anthology A book of poems by different poets often on the same theme, for example Christmas or shape poems.

cliché An overused and unoriginal phrase or description: 'as black as night', 'as cold as ice'.

conceit A metaphor that is extended and explored throughout a poem: a poem about a bare tree in winter may compare the tree to an old man – stooped, with gnarled fingers and a threadbare coat.

drafting and editing Drafting is doing different versions to improve and develop a piece of writing. Editing is checking a piece for spelling, grammar and punctuation.

form The type of poem, for example rhyming, free verse or haiku.

free verse Poetry that does not rhyme or follow a set rhythm.

imagery Tony Mitton: 'The imagery is the kind of pictures in the head the poem makes'.

metaphor and simile Simile is when you say one thing is *like* something else: 'as cunning as a fox', 'she felt trapped like a bird in a cage'. Metaphor is when you say one thing actually *is* something else: 'it's raining nails', 'the city is a jungle tonight'.

narrative The story that a poem tells.

personification: A metaphor that compares something to a human being: 'the wind laughed', 'the moon stared'.

point of view Some poems either are told by a person or show the world as it is seen through one person's eyes; this is the 'point of view' of the poem.

rhyme When the sounds at the ends of lines agree with each other:
'Have you ever seen a sheet on a river *bed*?
Or a single hair from a hammer's *head*?'

rhythm The rhythm is the beat and the feel of a poem, and will depend on how long each line is, and how each word in each line is spoken.

shape poem A poem in which the words form a specific shape.

stanza The grouping of lines in a poem.

structure How the poem is laid out, with a beginning, middle and an end.

syllable A single beat. Po / em has two beats. Po / et / ry has three beats. How many beats are there in your name?

theme The main subject(s) of a poem.

3 Fiction

BERLIE DOHERTY: Fiction is the combination of *I remember* and *let's pretend*.

Facts behind fictions: initial discussion points on writing fiction

As Berlie Doherty says in the quote that opens this chapter, fiction is the coming together of 'I remember' and 'let's pretend'. In other words, it is the merging of fact and fantasy, our memories and our imagination. Morris Gleitzman explores this idea:

MORRIS GLEITZMAN: Where do ideas come from? This is what everyone wants to know, including me. The closest I've come to figuring it out is this. I reckon we all have a compost bin in our head. All our life's experiences – all the people we know, all the places we've been, all the books we've read, all the ants we've trained to juggle jelly babies, everything goes into the bin and mulches down into something rich and pongy and fertile. Our imagination grows seeds and ideas spring up in that compost between our ears. How do we get our imagination to sow the seeds? Lots of different ways. I sit in my writing room with the curtains drawn and I stare at the wall and I daydream. I spend a lot of my time daydreaming. It's one of the ways I get ideas and it's one of the reasons I like being a writer. As I daydream I try to forget who I am, where I am, what I'm doing, and most importantly, I try to forget the fact that I'm looking for ideas. When I do finally forget, that's when my imagination starts to take over and the characters' voices come into my head.

I also like being a writer because it's one of the few jobs you can do at home in your pyjamas. As a writer, you're indoors a lot, but it's never boring because you get out a lot in your imagination. I've spent days breaking into Buckingham Palace (*Two Weeks with the Queen*), giving a guinea pig a Viking funeral (*Water Wings*), shaving all my hair off (*The Other Facts of Life*), stealing a stuffed horse (*Second Childhood*) and carrying out a pirate raid on a school (*Bumface*) – all without leaving my chair. I can't wait to see where I go next.

A good starting point for writing any form of prose is to consider your own life, your own experiences. A method that many teachers and workshop leaders use is to encourage their students and pupils to tell each other stories from their own lives, perhaps significant experiences – events which are meaningful to them, or simply some amusing anecdotes. These oral stories can be shared with a partner or in small groups. Another way of doing this is for pupils to record their stories onto cassette tape, to transcibe them later and then rework the material into a piece of prose. (Please refer to the 'Non-fiction' chapter for workshop activities on writing autobiographical pieces as well as the 'Early memory' activity in the 'Narration' section of this chapter: pp. 171–2 and 127.)

So many published plays, short stories, poems and novels have begun as a result of actual events in their authors' lives. If you ever find as you are writing about your own experiences that the piece evolves into fiction, then that's fine – develop the idea and see where it takes you. Alan Durant addresses this very situation. He talks about when he took a real event and turned it into a short story entitled 'The Star' (published in his teenage collection *A Shory Stay in Purgatory*: Random House):

> **ALAN DURANT:** The original version of the story was quite wordy and caught up in real events – it wasn't fictional enough. Originally, I was the narrator, telling the experiences that happened to me. I was too close to it. And this is a problem when you write fiction based upon your own autobiography. You have to push aside the real events, and let the fiction in. The fiction should live and breathe and take over, so it's a story. The original version – which was called *Following the Star* – was more of a chronicle.

Because the various elements of fiction – such as plot, dialogue, character, setting and so on – are so interlinked it can be very difficult to talk about each one wholly separately. For, when you discuss your characters, invariably you will talk about what your characters do, and therefore you will be mentioning plot. When you talk about what your characters are saying, you will be discussing dialogue. So, to deal with these aspects of fiction in isolation is quite artificial, as they all exist and function together. Yet it is necessary for students to consider each of these elements individually in order that they can see how fiction works as a whole.

In the following quotes authors talk about stories and fiction writing. These could serve as useful discussion points in a workshop environment.

> **DAVID ALMOND:** I feel strongly that stories are the thing that holds us together. They're the way we pass on information, the way we educate children. Without stories, the world becomes just information – fragmented information. Narratives hold people together because you have to have a narrator and a listener or, put another way, a writer and a reader. This process attaches people to each other. There's also the idea that the world is a book, a book that has been written by someone or something else and we are acting that story out. So the whole notion of story seems to me such a hugely powerful metaphor for human life.

> **TERRY DEARY:** Writers learn how to write in the same way they learn how to speak. They imitate. And in the same way you develop your own way of speaking and conversing, you develop your own way of writing. But initially, if you want to be a writer, you imitate, like a parrot.

> **BERLIE DOHERTY:** Every book should have elements that make us laugh and cry.

> **MORRIS GLEITZMAN:** Sometimes I think dreams are stories trying to come out . . . I also think stories are a bit like X-rays. They show us what's happening inside people. Not to their blood and bones and spleens. To their hopes and fears and dreams and feelings.

> **RUSSELL HOBAN:** What happens next? . . . It's the essence of story.

> **PHILIP PULLMAN:** Writing a story is going on a journey without a map.
>   Advice to young fiction writers: Take an interest in the craft. Learn to punctuate. Buy several dictionaries and use them. If you're not sure about a point of grammar, look it up. Take a pride in the tools. Keep them sharp and bright and well oiled. No one else is going to look after the language if you don't.

Here are some further thoughts for discussion:

- What is fiction? Give examples.
- Why do we tell, read and write stories?
- Are stories important – and if so, why?
- Has the role of storytelling changed over the past 200 years?
- What are the similarities/differences between (a) oral stories, (b) stories in text form, (c) stories in picture books and (d) stories in the form of films and TV dramas?
- An adapted Picasso quote: '[Fiction] is a lie that tells the truth'.
- Stories help us to question, reflect upon and make sense of our lives and the world around us.
- Fiction gives shape and meaning to the chaos of our lives.
- Fiction helps us to see the world from other people's points of view.

Planning for fiction: ideas on brainstorming and planning for writing

Even if you do not want to do a full plan of the piece you are going to write – be it a story, drama or whatever – it is always useful if you can jot down a few initial ideas. As a result, you will have something to refer back to when you have begun writing. You can often have many ideas in your head at one time, so putting ideas down on to paper will prevent you from forgetting them. It is always a good idea to do some planning before you write a story, even if you don't stick to your plan. These two authors very much encourage pre-planning:

ALAN DURANT: I advise children to do some preparation. I do think this is useful – just spending a few minutes to think about where your story is going to go. So many children start and they'll be writing away and then get stuck. I don't encourage anything as formal as a detailed plan, but I'll get them to think how the story will start, roughly what will happen and how it will end. Endings are often where children get stuck. Too often you get, 'I woke up and it was a dream', because there hasn't been enough planning beforehand. I don't tell them to stick rigidly to their initial ideas – all I'll say is that they should know roughly where they're going with the story. You can know what the ending is going to be, but it can be left open as to how you will get there and how it will be presented.

MALORIE BLACKMAN: If it's a novel, I plan a chapter breakdown so that I know what will happen at each stage of the book. This gives me a framework for my story, therefore when I start a novel I know where it's going! That's not to say that I always stick to the chapter breakdowns. Sometimes, midway through the book, the characters may take me in another direction, but by then I trust them to know where they're going.

Morris Gleitzman will not begin writing a novel until his plan is ready:

MORRIS GLEITZMAN: I plan my books out on the computer and I write notes about each chapter of the novel. I do many drafts of that chapter plan. When I start writing the book, I'll have what might be draft 6 or 7 or 8 next to me printed out, but then as I'm working on the text I'll add to that plan as I go along.

(See Morris Gleitzman's chapter plan for *Bumface*, p. 93.)

Philip Pullman believes in not doing too much preparation:

PHILIP PULLMAN: I find that when I do plan a story it goes dead on me, so I have to keep some of it unknown. Otherwise I lose the curiosity that pulls me through.

David Almond's method of brainstorming ideas takes the form of story mapping (see Figure 3.1):

DAIVD ALMOND: If I'm working on a new book or a new story I'll do some story mapping. When I do a story map I might have just one idea to start off with. That idea might be that there is someone on a train going over a bridge. So I might write down 'train'. Then I'll give him a name. Frank. And I'll write 'Frank' down. And I'll ask myself questions about him, such as 'What's he wearing?' A T-shirt. A Nike T-shirt. I'll write that down. And Frank has got a bike with him. What kind of bike is it? A Raleigh. Where's he going? He's going to see his aunty – his Aunty Doreen. Where does she live? 17, Clacton Gardens. What's he got in his pocket? A letter.

Stories come from details like these. I find it very hard to look for plotlines. I explore these different details and these will give me my plot. You have to look hard and question everything you put down in your story map. And the more you look, the more you find. Every detail you find allows your story to grow in richness. So the story takes on a body organically. And rather than seek out a plot with a beginning, middle and end – you have a scenario from which you can work. You will eventually have a linear plot, but you achieve it in a very different way.

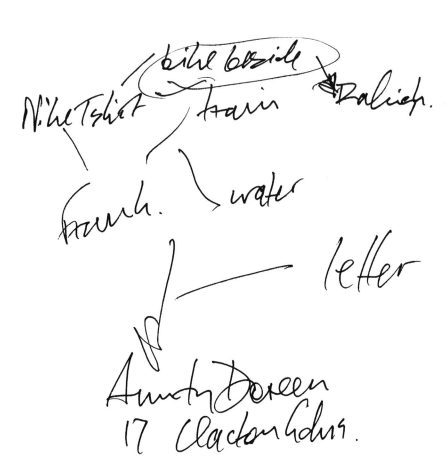

Figure 3.1 Story mapping notes made by David Almond

The 'Brainstorming' worksheet will help you to give shape and structure to your ideas. There is no reason why this sheet cannot be modified for non-fiction and poetry too. You could even change or adapt it to suit your own way of working. The other two worksheets – 'Story mapping 1' and 'Story mapping 2' – adopt David Almond's story mapping idea and can be used for finding an outline for a story.

When doing story mapping of your own, consider the questions Who? How? Where? Why? What? When? See if a story or scenario emerges. You might also want to write out aspects of your story in boxes, like a flow chart. Alternatively, you could try Philip Pullman's method, which is to write out various scenes for a story on to small yellow Post-it notes and to move them around on a big sheet of paper to find the best sequence for those scenes. But what is important is that you discover a system that works best for you.

BRAINSTORMING

It is always a good idea to do some planning before you start writing a story, even if it is only a rough outline – for example, the characters' names and how the story will start. This sheet will give you a chance to plan more fully if you choose to do so.

Write down your first ideas around this SPIDER DIAGRAM:

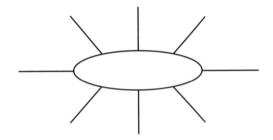

Now develop your ideas further:

Character(s): Name, age, likes, dislikes and details of personality and background.

Setting(s): Where will the story take place?

Now try to write out a structure for your story. You do not have to keep to your plan as you write.

Beginning:

Middle:

End:

STORY MAPPING 1

Use these questions as the basis for a story. If other ideas come to mind as you respond, write those ideas down too. Do not worry if you do not have answers for every question.

Someone is going somewhere . . .

Who is this person?

Where is this person?

What is she or he wearing?

What is she or he carrying?

What is she or he thinking about?

What has this person got in their pocket?

Is she or he worried about something?

How does this person feel about where they are going?

What does the person plan to do when they get there?

STORY MAPPING 2

Use these questions as the basis for a story. If other ideas come to mind as you respond, write those ideas down too. Do not worry if you do not have answers for every question.

Someone new has arrived somewhere . . .

Who is this person?

Where has the person arrived?

When did he or she arrive?

Why is he or she there?

Will he or she stay long?

What will other people think of this person?

Will things change because of this person? If so, how?

GROWING FICTION

In this section, two authors talk about the evolution and origins of one of their most popular titles: Malorie Blackman (Pig-heart Boy) and Morris Gleitzman (Bumface). Although these novels are very different in terms of style, plot and subject matter, both books – as the authors discuss here – have very striking and memorable opening sequences. These titles were both shortlisted for the prestigious Carnegie Medal.

Malorie Blackman – *Pig-heart Boy*

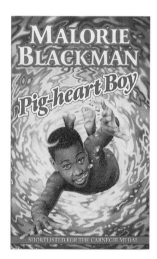

Figure 3.2 Cover of Malorie Blackman's novel *Pig-heart Boy* (Corgi Yearling)

One

Dying

I am drowning in this roaring silence.

I am drowning.

I'm going to die.

I look up through the grey-white shimmer of the swimming-pool water. High, high above I can see where the quality of the light changes. The surface. But it is metres above me. It might as well be kilometres. The chlorine stings my eyes. My lungs are on fire.

Just one breath. Just one.

I have to take a breath, even though I know that I'll be breathing in water. But my lungs are burning and my blood is roaring and my whole body is screaming out for air. If I don't take a breath, I'll burst. If I do take a breath, I'll drown. Some choice. No choice.

I close my eyes, praying hard. And kick, kick, kick. I open my eyes. The surface of the water seems even further away.

I'm going to drown.

A fact. A fact as clear, as real as the silence around me. Part of me – a tiny, tiny part of me – laughs. I am going to drown. After everything I've been through in the last few months, this is how I'm going to bow out. One thought rises up in my mind.

One thought . . .
Alex . . .
I stop kicking. I have no energy left.
I stop fighting. I'm so tired. I can feel my body begin to sink.
Now for the hard part.
Now for the easy part.
Now for the hard part.
Give in. Let go.
Just one breath . . .
Just one . . .
Just . . .

MALORIE BLACKMAN: A good introduction is absolutely vital – to grab and engage that reader. Being a very practical person, my view is that – and as I've been told – what sells a book is the picture on the cover, the blurb on the back and the first page. That's what people go to. If you get them with the cover, they might read the blurb, and if they like the blurb they'll invariably read the first page. So I aim to go straight into a story so that hopefully people will think, 'Oh, what's this about?' and it will grab them. You can bring in characterisation and everything else once you've grabbed the reader. But unless the reader knows your work and wants to read all your books and will trust you, if you start very slowly and build up you might lose a lot of people. My advice is if you want to grab your reader, get on with the plot on the very first page.

I always start by writing a synopsis of the book, an outline of the plot. My editors do like to have a rough idea of what they're getting. With *Pig-heart Boy* I gave them about a page, which outlined about three-quarters of the story. Usually, I'll plot the beginning, middle and end, so I have a framework to follow. I don't mind deviating from a framework, just so long as I know why I'm deviating and where the story is going to eventually. Though with *Pig-heart Boy* I deliberately didn't plan the ending because it was important to me that I didn't know how it was going to end until I was actually typing it.

I like doing a synopsis – it helps a lot – but putting too much detail into a story plan kills the whole thing dead. I just write three or four lines per chapter. My story plan for *Tell Me No Lies*, as with all my plans, wasn't that detailed, it was like 'Gemma does this, which leads to Mike doing that, which leads to this for Gemma' and so on. That way, I still have fun when I write each chapter as I'm still discovering things about my characters I didn't previously know. And I really like it when things happen that I hadn't planned, and I think, 'Oh gosh, where did that come from?!' That's the thrilling part of writing. That happened in *Pig-heart Boy* – I had no idea certain things would happen to Cameron's family at the end. It's funny because when I sit at the computer screen it sometimes feels as if I myself am not writing the story. It's almost as if the ideas are coming through me. I don't want to get too flowery or mystical about it, but ideas do seem to come out of nowhere sometimes! And I absolutely love that!

I mainly write in the third person at the moment, but I do use the first person too. It depends on the book as to which I use. What I like about the first person is that it allows you into a character's head and their feelings, and for something like *Pig-heart Boy* it was absolutely essential. When I first started writing *Pig-heart Boy* I wrote it in the third person and it didn't work – Cameron, the central character, was too distant, and the voice was all wrong. So I tried the first person instead, and it clicked, and I had the right voice. Although having said that, the way I write in the third person is often that of keeping very close to one character's point of view, but with *Pig-heart Boy* it was vital that I could actually hear Cameron's voice, and that he was narrating his own story.

When I was writing the book, I very much saw the plot as separated into three parts. This book is all about the choices we make, and they might be right choices or wrong choices, but we make them, and they have an effect, and they have consequences. It's like a chain reaction. I wanted to explore this idea. Cameron has to make various choices all the way through the book – and it's not that he does all the right things or makes all the right choices. So because of this I divided *Pig-heart Boy* into three separate parts, which are called 'Cause', 'Effect' and 'Consequences'.

I wanted to start in the middle of the story, with Cameron drowning in the swimming pool. This is taken from the 'Consequences' section, the final part of the book. At this point he's trying to touch the bottom of the swimming pool to prove that even though he now has a heart that was transplanted from a pig, he's still the same as anyone else, and that he can do what anyone else can do. It's his way of doing things in a normal way, and to restore some normality to his life. The reason I started the book off with this event from the 'Consequences' part of the book is because I wanted to show and highlight the outcome of Cameron's decisions.

I needed a beginning that would grab the reader. As I was writing it, I was aware of enticing my reader, and gaining their attention, but at the same time, I was probably more responding to the sort of introduction that the book required. It seemed the perfect place to start. This part of the story – where Cameron is drowning – is a pivotal point in the plot, and it just felt right to start with this. The book is all about Cameron having a heart condition and thinking he's going to die soon. And it's at this very point in the story that Cameron is convinced he's dying – and in a horrific manner. However, the reader won't know any of this unless they carry on reading the rest of the book, and will then appreciate this sequence in its true context in the story.

With this introduction I wanted to go straight into the action, and begin at the moment where Cameron realises he's not going to make it back up to the surface of the water:

> *I am drowning in this roaring silence.*
>   *I am drowning.*
>   *I'm going to die.*
>   *I look up through the grey-white shimmer of the swimming-pool water. High, high above I can see where the quality of the light changes. The surface. But it is metres above me. It might as well be kilometres. The chlorine stings my eyes. My lungs are on fire.*
>   *Just one breath. Just one.*

It's that moment when you're desperate for a breath and you know if you take a breath it's going to kill you. But you've got no choice. So, what's Cameron going to do? Drown or asphyxiate himself? Then it goes on:

> *I have to take a breath, even though I know that I'll be breathing in water. But my lungs are burning and my blood is roaring and my whole body is screaming out for air.*

Cameron is aware of every part of his body, and he needs oxygen, but he just can't get any. Here I wanted to convey this total desperation:

> *I stop kicking. I have no energy left.*
>   *I stop fighting. I'm so tired. I can feel my body begin to sink.*
>   *Now for the hard part.*
>   *Now for the easy part.*

Now for the hard part.
Give in. Let go.
Just one breath . . .
Just one . . .
Just . . .

Then he does have to take a breath and his lungs will fill up with water, and the reader will think 'What's going to happen next?' But instead of showing what happens next, the book then goes back to the very beginning of the story, to show how Cameron managed to get into this situation in the first place.

In this part I wanted a staccato effect – short, quick lines like musical notes, each one fading until finally there's nothing. It conveys his desperate struggle to stay alive, but finally, at the final line 'Just . . .' he has to take a breath. It's a bit like a poem here, with these separate lines. The layout of the lines was very important to me, because the lines as well as the words express Cameron's feelings and his situation, because as the lines get shorter he's gradually losing his struggle. My editor, Annie Eaton, was really enthusiastic about this idea of the separate, diminishing lines, and she left them exactly how I wrote them in my manuscript copy.

Throughout the first part of the book – the series of incidents that lead up to the event in the swimming pool – Cameron's time is running out, he's slowly getting, or so he thinks, closer to his death. And so too do the lines in this introduction get shorter and shorter, moving closer into nothing. Throughout this introduction, the sentences are mostly very short, which again highlights and reinforces his turmoil. Usually with prose, the shape, layout and structure aren't as important a consideration as in poetry. But for me, in addition to the words and what they're saying, the very shape of these lines here gives an extra meaning to the piece, and it's there for the reader to pick up on if they want to. I do like doing this kind of thing with my prose. I used a similar device in my short story collection 'Not So Stupid'. There was a line in which I took out all the spaces in between the words, and it went 'bloodbloodbloodblood'. In that passage I wanted to emphasise a continuous flow.

As Cameron is thinking all these thoughts, he's gasping within himself and his heart is beating wildly, and he's convinced he's going to die – hence the title for this short introduction is 'Dying'. And then there's the line:

After everything I've been through in the last few months, this is how I'm going to bow out.

Cameron has been through so much, and he never realised he'd be in this unusual situation. What I'm showing here is the unpredictability of life. You think things are going one way, and they go another way instead. As I said before, this for me was a book of cause, effect and consequences – with one decision leading on to something else, which in turn leads on to something else again. Cameron is aware that any decisions he makes will send his life off into all kinds of different directions. But nothing has turned out exactly how he thought it would – and he has to live and deal with that. For example, Cameron and his friend Julie like each other very much, but once Cameron has had his heart transplant, Julie is scared of Cameron as she's afraid of what she might catch. And some other people in his class feel exactly the same way too. This is just one of many consequences of Cameron's decision to go through with the heart transplant operation – a consequence that Cameron could never have anticipated.

I don't at any point in the story want to say that there is a right or wrong in this situation. I was adamant that I didn't appear to be on either side – that is, for or against the heart transplant from the pig. I wanted to highlight both sides of the argument as well as to show that you have to live with the consequences of your actions. I had to be very careful not to come down on one side or the other. As I was writing the book, I was forever thinking 'What would *I* do? – I'm not keen on the idea of having an animal's heart inside me, but I would want to live.' You really don't know until you're in that sort of situation. For me, that was the fascinating thing, and that's why I didn't want to know the ending of the book until I reached it. It was intriguing watching Cameron and watching him make those decisions and to see what the resulting consequences were. I wanted to explore the various issues surrounding animal heart transplants and all the different options available to those in Cameron's situation.

Once I got going, it was an easy book to write for me. This introduction took about three drafts. Originally, it was much longer and it was losing its impact, so I trimmed it right down and tried to make it more sparse and staccato. I can be very critical of my work, but I'm quite happy with this introduction. And here my language and prose style are perhaps a little more poetic than usual, with phrases like, 'I am drowning in this roaring silence', and 'the grey-white shimmer of the swimming-pool water' and 'my lungs are burning and my blood is roaring'.

As soon as this short introduction is over, it goes on to the 'Cause' part of the book. This part shows the events that lead up to Cameron making the decision to have the pig heart transplant. And then the 'Effect' part that follows shows the events that happen as a result of Cameron making that decision – how it affects not only his life, but his family's and friends' lives too.

This book originally came about when I read a newspaper article some four or five years ago in which a doctor was saying that because of the shortage of human donors by the year 2000 we'd have to start using animal organs for kidney and heart transplants. Before I began writing the book, I did a lot of research on the Internet. I was on the Internet every night for three months, to get as much up-to-date information as I possibly could. It was worth it, as I really wanted to get all my facts right with this book. I read recently that a man in Israel is going to have a pig heart transplant sometime this year. So it really is going to happen.

Workshop activities: *Pig-heart Boy*

IN THE NEWS

Write a short piece in which your character – like Cameron in the story of *Pig-heart Boy* – is regularly in the national newspapers for something that she or he has done or because of something that is happening in her or his life. You could, if you choose, begin with your character looking out of their bedroom window and seeing – for the first time – crowds of journalists and TV crews outside the house.

CRISIS POINT

Write an opening for a short story in which your character is going through a major incident or crisis in her or his life. As with *Pig-heart Boy*, start with the crisis point. Perhaps your character is running away from something, having a disagreement with someone or writing a letter to another person. You choose the right event to open with. Read through the introduction to *Pig-heart Boy* a few times and see how many of the sentences are short and clipped, to make them more dynamic and dramatic – and see if you can write some of your own sentences in this way.

CAUSE – EFFECT – CONSEQUENCES

As with Malorie Blackman's novel, write a story divided up into three parts: CAUSE – EFFECT – CONSEQUENCES. First of all, think of a character in a difficult situation. Once you have decided upon the situation, think about it in terms of the cause (what made it happen?), the effect (what effect will it have on her or him and other people?) and the consequences (what will happen as a result?). Also, think about how your character will deal with this situation. You could tell your story in the sequence in which the events happened, or as with *Pig-heart Boy*, you could start with the climax, the 'consequences' – and then go back and show how the chain of events began.

Morris Gleitzman – *Bumface*

> 'Angus Solomon,' sighed Ms Lowry. 'Is that a penis you've drawn in your exercise book?'
>
> Angus jumped, startled, and remembered where he was.
>
> Ms Lowry was standing next to his desk, staring down at the page. Other kids were sniggering.
>
> Angus felt his mouth go dry and his heart speed up. For a second he thought about lying. He decided not to.
>
> 'No, Miss,' he admitted, 'it's a submarine.'
>
> Ms Lowry nodded grimly. 'I thought as much,' she said. 'Now stop wasting time and draw a penis like I asked you to.' She pointed to the one she'd drawn on the blackboard.
>
> That's not fair, thought Angus. I wasn't wasting time.
>
> He took a deep breath.
>
> 'Excuse me, Miss,' he said, 'I wasn't wasting time. I was working on my pirate character for the school play. He lives in a submarine and –'
>
> 'Enough,' interrupted Ms Lowry. 'You know perfectly well play rehearsals aren't till tomorrow. Today we're doing human reproduction. I don't want to hear another word about pirates.'

MORRIS GLEITZMAN: With my introductions I ideally want a first line that is going to draw people immediately into the story, one that is going to let the reader know that this is a story that contains humour and contains the unexpected. We live in a world where there are so many things competing for our attention, and so many of them have honed that ability to grab the attention very quickly. You're not serving your story well if you're asking people to take a leisurely fifteen minutes to gradually work their way into five pages of description. I think it's a challenge that poets continually face, because twenty words can achieve a huge amount, as our great poets have shown us. Even though I don't attempt to write a whole novel with that degree of intensity, I think that it's really worth making your opening sentences and paragraphs earn their keep.

I spend a great deal of time working on my introductions and I always make a lot of changes to the first chapter of a book. The first chapter is where I'm really connecting with the voice of a character and the tone of the book – so I rewrite the first chapter over and over again. Rather than make those stylistic decisions in abstract, I just start writing as soon as I've got an inkling and I just go over and over it. Although I might only do a first draft and then a polish, I will have done maybe ten or twelve drafts of the first chapter.

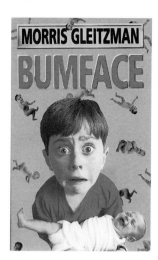

Figure 3.3 Cover of Morris Gleitzman's novel *Bumface* (Puffin)

When I plan a novel like *Bumface*, I do a breakdown of 100–150 words for each chapter (see Figure 3.4). I keep doing different drafts of that breakdown until I think the story, in a general sense, is working and ready to be written. I always do more drafts of the plan than I do of the book itself. With *Bumface*, I probably did half a dozen drafts of the plan. But I've done many more drafts with other books. With *Belly Flop* I did about nineteen. When I start writing a book I don't need to redraft much to change the tone of voice because I don't start writing until I know the character's tone well. For me, drafting is all about getting the structure right, and that's why I spend so much time working on the shape of the story during the planning stage. But with *Bumface* I did three complete drafts of the whole book, though I usually do just a draft version and a polish – because, as I said, I've done so much of my drafting, in a sense, in the planning. *Bumface*, as with most of my books, took about six months to write in total: two months of thinking, two months of planning and two months of actual writing. The quickest book to write was *Two Weeks with the Queen*. I wrote it in four weeks and it didn't need much reworking. I suspect that story had been building up inside me for years and years.

I got to know Angus, my main character in *Bumface*, by connecting with how he was feeling at certain times in the story. A simpler way of saying that is that – as I do with all of my characters – I just imagine myself in the situations Angus finds himself in. Angus is a part of me, so I don't have to do any exterior observation of children to help me build up a character profile. The truth of a character for me is how a character feels about the events and situations in his or her life. And that's something I just know, and if I didn't, I couldn't write the stories that I do.

My characters' names come from all over. I let names swirl around in my head. Sometimes I look in phone books, and I've got a book called *What to Name Your Baby*, and that has many first names in it. I chose the name 'Angus Solomon' because I wanted a name that denoted strength and reliability. I figured that subconsciously his parents would have had him earmarked to play a certain role, and would have chosen a name that represented the sort of figure they wanted in the family to compensate for some of their needs. In the biblical sense, 'Solomon' denotes parental authority and wisdom. The name felt right for a kid who is being asked to take on more authority than he wanted.

I now see that some of the ideas and themes of *Bumface* have, in a sense, grown out of some of my earlier books. The first seed of an idea for *Bumface* was just the notion of a boy feeling that he had to behave like an adult which left him very little time to be a kid – but at the same time he was being denied access to aspects of the adult world that he needed. This was just a

Dad hasn't got a clue about the realities of Angus's life. When Dad hears Mum arriving home, he scarpers, leaving a mess.

13/4/98.

Angus at the end of his tether. Tries to tell Mum, but she's upset with invasive story in tabloid mag about her relationship with the director. Too much unauthorized publicity could lose her her job. As a single Mum – disaster. Hopes this relationship will be 4th time lucky.

DENIAL

Won't accept Mum is neglecting them

As always, she thanks Angus profusely for being her top bloke, her good boy, her Mr Dependable. Leaves him folding her clothes. In bed, Angus wonders how much longer he can cope. Only one thing is keeping him going. The school play.

THREE FOUR [FIVE]

Next morning. Play rehearsal. Angus loves it. He's playing a pirate, Bumface, a scurrilous, energetic, self-serving rogue who roams the seven seas free of all parental responsibility, pillaging, plundering, flinging clothes to the floor and having heaps of fun.

By the end of rehearsal, life doesn't seem so bad. Until the teacher announces that from now on rehearsals will take place after school. Angus is horrified. He has to take care of Leo and Imogen after school. He tries to talk the teacher into keeping rehearsals in school time. Unsuccessfully.

Teacher – grow up.

Angus daren't tell the teacher the truth about his after-school commitment. He fears that if word gets out, Mum will lose her job. The papers will have a field day with the revelation that TV's best-loved mum is actually overworked and negligent in her real life. He must protect Mum's image at all costs or the family will have no money. But Angus is determined it won't be at the cost of Bumface.

Media would see it this way. Angus needs to believe she's got a reason

Supermarket. Sees mess. Condescending adult tries to help. Angus knows more than she does.

teacher – your mum. how does she do it?

FOUR FIVE [SIX]

Angus goes to see if his Dad can have Leo and Imogen after school for a few weeks. Dad has lots of excuses why not. He's broke and he has to get his book finished to earn some money. House full of kids running amok. Angus appalled. And jealous. Dad childminding for cash and observation. He tells Angus what a good boy he is, but a bit too serious.

Angus goes to see Leo's dad. Who has remarried since his divorce from Mum and has two young sons. With his new family and his part in a long-running stage musical, (Pirates Of Penzance?) he really doesn't have the time. Prima donna. Throws babyish tantrums. Despite his platitudes about being a good father to Leo, Angus sees that Leo is part of the old life that Leo's dad would rather leave behind. Shields Leo from this.

2

Figure 3.4 Manuscript page (chapter plan) for Morris Gleitzman's *Bumface*

very general idea I had. So it was a situation in which he was supposed to act like an adult, but only in ways that suited other people. In other words, he was given all the responsibilities of being an adult but he had none of the rights.

Interestingly, the title came very early and that doesn't usually happen with my books. Usually I'm well into writing a novel before I get the title. Even as I was considering these abstract ideas I've just mentioned to develop into a specific story, I knew I wanted a title that was defiant. I needed a title that was – and possibly even for adults – a confronting and subversive expression of this character's needs and ultimately, his determination to hang on to being a child.

I think my young stepson probably uttered 'bumface' around the time that these early ideas were developing. It just struck me as being the perfect title for this story, particularly as I'd then started to think about a fantasy pirate persona as being a vehicle through which this poor, beleaguered kid hoped he could express some of the child urges within him. A pirate is able to dispense with adult responsibility and constrained forms of behaviour, but does not lose that power that goes along with that conventional adult way of being. So in some ways, you could say, a pirate is like a kid with power.

Over a period of several months when I was working on other projects, I was having various thoughts and notions about the story that would become *Bumface*. Some of these ideas I jotted down, some I remembered, some I didn't. So when I came to sit down to start doing the outline for the book I had various ideas to work with. I remember that I woke up really early one morning – about 5.00 a.m. I hadn't been able to sleep. I went into my office and suddenly I felt I knew the shape of the story. I couldn't even wait for Windows '95 to load up on my PC and so I just scribbled the story out on a few pages by hand.

Before I reached that stage I got a few more specific ideas. I knew it was going to be a family story, as all my books are centred around the family unit. Then I very quickly had the idea that the main character's responsibility would be that of looking after younger siblings, and that if his mother had another baby it would be more than he could cope with. Therefore, the boy would have to try and stop her from having another baby.

I put a lot of thought into the first few paragraphs up to 'the one she'd drawn on the blackboard'. I not only wanted to – as I always do – grab the attention and establish the humour and the unexpected, but also to give the reader the idea that this is a story that goes places where kids' books don't often go. What this introduction also does is actually give a specific illustration of what the book as a whole is all about. For me, it's about the differences between the worlds of childhood and adulthood. It's about an 11-year-old boy who is a child but he is battling with the need to try and be adult. It's about a whole bunch of adults who have the power and privilege of adults but, in many ways, they're still children. So it's about all these reversals.

So I took one simple reversal, which is that we expect Angus – who's accused of drawing a penis in his exercise book – is being a naughty boy and that he's done something he shouldn't have done. That's our expectation as a reader. Then it's turned totally on its head. We find that in fact he's been drawing a submarine and the teacher is cross because he should have been drawing a penis. That reversal, I think, tells us that this is going to be a story about all sorts of reversals, a story in which our assumptions about who is responsible and who is irresponsible are going to be reversed, so, who is behaving in an 'adult' way and who is behaving in a 'childish' way is going to be reversed too. I did this very consciously. Though I don't expect any reader to read this opening scene and go 'Aah! – this is going to be a story about responsibilities and reversals' – but because they're laughing at the situation, I think it will resonate in an unconscious way, and in a way that will draw them into the story. So, what I've done is to encapsulate my major theme for the book in these few sentences at the beginning, up to 'the one she'd drawn on the blackboard'.

This opening scene is an exposition that sets up the context of Angus's world. At this stage I haven't established his specific problem, we ease into it much more gently than in my other stories where I set up the child's problem in the first sentence – like *Water Wings*, for example:

'What I need,' said Pearl, as she started to slide off the roof, 'is a grandmother.'

Generally, with my prose I would say that I look for concrete, active language. I prefer to use the sort of language, by and large, that my main character would use. So, even though I'm writing in the third person, it's my character's vocabulary and sentence structure rather than my own. I need to establish that in the first chapter for the tone of the book overall. Take for example, these lines from *Bumface*,

Angus's cheeks burned and his insides sank.
Not again.
Not more joking and sniggering behind his back. Not more rumours spreading round the playground quicker than head lice. Rumours that were completely, totally, one million per cent untrue.

The intention here is that these are Angus's thoughts. And this is where I'm – in a way – tiptoeing on the very edge between first person and third person. And these lines are his thoughts. One of the things I love about third person is that I don't have to quote his thoughts exactly. Note I wrote 'his back' and not 'my back' – so that alerts the reader unconsciously to the fact that there might be an element of paraphrasing or summary here.

Bumface was always in the third person. You see, I can get as much into Angus's head in third person as I can in first, and I've still got the freedom that comes with the third person. The way I write is such that it's third person – but it could almost be in the first person. The great pitfall with the third person is to have an adult authorial voice – a voice of power and authority. Necessarily, works of fiction manipulate their readers – that's the difference between a dictionary and a novel. What a novel can do is manipulate the reader through a series of ideas and feelings. Kids' lives are full of bossy adults and I don't want there to be any element of a bossy adult in my stories. In my books my main characters are all 11 years old, and thus far they're not particularly bossy towards other kids. So, my readers are being steered through the story – that is, told the story – by another kid.

My stories are about kids confronting the big problems in their lives. Those problems might be readily recognisable as big problems that we all face – or, for some of us, they might seem very small problems, but to that kid they might be very big problems. My characters don't shy away from the difficult feelings attached to those problems. They often discover in wrestling with these problems that they are things that don't have solutions or the possibility of a real solution. My stories are more about processes rather than end results. My characters always go through a change and it's always a positive change in terms of what they want for themselves. Rarely are their problems wholly and completely solved.

Workshop activities: *Bumface*

MORRIS GLEITZMAN'S ACTIVITY

Decide who your story is going to be about – it could be about you, somebody you know or somebody you've heard about or somebody you've imagined or even a combination of these. Find out what the biggest problem is in that character's life. Then, once you've thought about that, you can ask yourself what that character is going to do about it. Think about how that character feels about their problem, and how you would feel in that situation too. Before you start writing, consider if the character will actually solve their problem, or part of their problem. Most important of all, think about how they will feel about their problem at the end of the story. For me, feelings are the most important part of a story. You can turn to nearly any page of one of my books and know exactly how my main character is feeling.

BUMFACE *ACTIVITY*

Write a beginning to a story, in which, like *Bumface*, things are not what they seem to be. Perhaps you could begin with a conversation between a teacher and pupil, or parent and child. Go for a first sentence – or first paragraph – that will grab the reader's attention.

WATER WINGS *ACTIVITY*

Write a story in which, like Morris Gleitzman in *Water Wings*, you describe the main problem in your character's life in the very first sentence.

Short stories

Most of the text examples discussed in this 'Fiction' chapter are taken from novels. But you will only ever have time to produce short stories or pieces during the workshops. Yet the ingredients of fiction – such as plot, character, dialogue and place – are the same whether you are writing a short story or a novel.

David Almond's advice on writing shorter narratives

David Almond has the following useful advice for writing short stories:

- Scribble down lots of ideas first of all, but don't do too much planning.
- Have two or three main characters at the most.
- Keep to a short time scale. Keep the story within a few days, a week or a month at the very most.
- Think in cinematic terms. Write your story as a series of scenes.
- Try not to report or comment on action, *show* the action happening. If you had a sentence like, 'Sam was sitting by the river. He was wondering about what Donald had said last night.' That's just reporting something. Instead, you could say, 'What on earth was Donald on about last night?' You put it in the form of a question and it becomes more active, and involves the reader more. It doesn't refer inward to what Sam was thinking, but puts his wondering out loud directly on to the page. If you *show* things outwardly more in this way, it becomes more cinematic and more fast-moving. A short story needs to move fairly quickly and this helps you to keep it short. If you flounder about trying to explain everything then your story will become too long. The American author Raymond Carver had great advice for writing short stories: 'Get in, get out and move on!' So – show a scene, then move on. Show another scene, and move on again – and so on.
- Don't be frightened to leave a space on the page between your scenes. The best thing you can do in a short story is to leave a gap on the page so the reader just moves naturally on to the next scene.
- Try not to put in too much padding, anything that you don't need in your story. You don't

need to include details of how your characters are feeling the whole time. We should know how your character is feeling by what they are doing and what they are saying. *Show* your characters acting and speaking.

Further guidelines for writing shorter fiction

- Have an introduction that is brief – and get into the main part of the story as soon as you can.
- Use dialogue to help bring your story and your characters to life.
- Like David Almond, Celia Rees advises writers to keep the scale of the story small:

CELIA REES: Pick one small experience or event and explore that in a story rather than trying to achieve something more ambitious. Think small – perhaps just simply a description of someone walking into a house, just a small moment in time. You don't even need a real plot necessarily, but it does need some kind of structure – a beginning, middle and end.

Beginnings and endings

Ways of opening a story

What are the different ways of beginning a fictional story?

PHILIP PULLMAN: Stories must begin somewhere. Out of the welter of events and ideas and pictures and characters and voices that you experience in your head, you the storyteller must choose one moment, the best moment, and make that the start. You could begin anywhere in the chronology, of course; you could begin in the middle, *in media res*, or you could begin at the end of it if you wanted to.

JAN DEAN: I often like to start a story straight into dialogue, but it's not always the best beginning for every story. Sometimes you find that you just can't go straight into people speaking or into action, as you need to give some context, some background details on your characters or their situation. When you do go straight into dialogue or action, you can weave in the background details as you go along. But as a general rule, you need to have a big event, something important or exciting or intriguing, as soon as possible in your story, as you can't linger for too long.

Further to the examples given above, stories can also begin with a description of a character, atmosphere or location.

In previous sections, the authors Malorie Blackman and Morris Gleitzman have talked about the introduction to one of their novels. They stressed just how important a good opening is. Read through the introductions to their novels again. What do you think of them? Do they make you want to read on – and if so, why? How do you respond to them?

Celia Rees emphasises the need to make an early impact upon the reader:

CELIA REES: Most of all, you've got to suggest to the reader that something is about to happen or has happened and is disrupting your fictional world. And that event could be frightening, upsetting, all kinds of things – that will depend on the style of your story. Something significant has to occur early on. On top of that, you've also got to establish the place and the characters in your introduction so as to make the maximum impact upon your reader.

Now look at these three opening sequences and see how they aim to arrest and keep a reader's attention:

> *I found him in the garage on a Sunday afternoon. It was the day after we moved into Falconer Road. The winter was ending. Mum had said we'd be moving just in time for the spring. Nobody else was there. Just me. The others were inside the house with Doctor Death, worrying about the baby.*

> (David Almond – *Skellig*: Hodder)

This introduction makes you ask yourself – who is the 'I' that is telling the story? And who is the 'him' in the first sentence, and what was he doing in the garage? And who is 'Doctor Death', and what is the matter with the baby? David Almond gives the reader little snippets of information, but only so much – just enough to arouse our curiosity and to make us ask questions and want to find out more.

> *He came in the early morning, at about half past two. His feet padded along the balcony, slinking silently past the closed doors of the other flats. No one glimpsed his shadow flickering across the curtain or noticed the uneven rhythm of his steps.*

> (Gillian Cross – *Wolf*: Puffin)

This opening sequence may be very different in style from *Skellig*, but again it stirs our interest. We want to know: who is this character? What is he up to? Why is he sneaking about at this time? What it also does is to create an atmosphere. We are told that it takes place 'in the early morning', and the author uses sound to describe how the character is walking – 'his feet padded', 'slinking silently' and 'uneven rhythm', but she also gives us images – 'balcony', 'closed doors' and 'his shadow flickering across the curtain'. So not only does the author encourage us to ask questions, but also she allows us to know exactly how it feels to be there. Right from this first paragraph the reader is very much involved with the story.

With Helen Cresswell's bold and inviting introduction, who could resist reading on?

> *Listen, I have a story to tell. It's mad and sad in parts and beautiful as well. Most stories have a time and a place. They happen because a particular person was in a particular place at a particular time. Think about it. If Wendy Darling had not lived in a certain tall house in a certain street in London, we should never have known the story of Peter Pan.*

> (Helen Cresswell – *Snatchers*: Hodder)

Now imagine someone in a bookshop. They have just picked up a copy of your book. They open your book at the first page and begin at the first paragraph. What are you going to do to keep that person interested and entertained and to stop them from putting it down and picking up another book? This is certainly something worth thinking about when you are reading through drafts of your stories. The next time you are in a bookshop or a library select a few books and compare how they start. Also, consider what makes you decide if you're going to read a certain book or not. The cover? The title? The blurb on the back? For many people it's a combination of these, but in the main, it's the beginning – the first few paragraphs of the story.

When writing a novel, Norman Silver dedicates much time to the introduction:

NORMAN SILVER: More time is spent on the beginning of a story than anything else. I just keep working on those first couple of pages. Until I get the tone of my work, it doesn't move any further. So, the usual order of production is first to gestate the idea, then second, to go for those opening couple of pages to see what it's going to sound like. Then, once I've wrestled with it and got it nearly right – the train leaves the station! – and I'll begin the story proper. And now I'll work on it non-stop until I get to the end. This writing phase is pretty intense. Once I've finished, I might leave it for a bit, work on other things and then return to the polishing stage later.

Ways of concluding a story

As regards endings to stories, Morris Gleitzman and Celia Rees both stress the need to have credible conclusions:

MORRIS GLEITZMAN: I like to write books in which the characters' problems are not totally solved or wrapped up at the end of the book because so often in life problems aren't fully solved. I think it can be disappointing to read stories in which they are. It's unrealistic.

CELIA REES: Endings have to round off the story satisfactorily. Readers can feel cheated if a book doesn't end properly. An ending needs to have a sense of completion, but should also point forward to the future. Life is a continuum and carries on, and a book should reflect that. In a book you have to convince your reader that your characters are real, that they live in a real world and that real things are happening to them. In fiction, everything has to stop at the end of the story – so you need to put across the sense that 'This might be the end of this story, but another is just beginning'.

Jan Dean reflects upon the different forms of endings in fiction:

JAN DEAN: There are a number of different types of endings. There's the open ending in which certain events have come to an end but the reader is left to imagine what may happen next. There's also the twist ending in which either the unexpected happens or things are not quite as they seemed to be throughout the story. I don't like endings to be too neat, but it can be unsatisfying if there are lots of unanswered questions at the end of a story – such as what happened to so-and-so and what happened about such-and-such.

As Alan Durant has suggested earlier in this chapter, it is not essential that you know the ending of your story before you start, but it is good to have some idea as to how the story might finish or otherwise you might get stuck and have to go back and change aspects of your story. Above all, try not to think too hard about how your piece of fiction should begin or end as you write. You can make decisions about those details when you are doing a second draft. Also, an ending does not necessarily have to be happy and positive, but you will find that most readers will at least want the conclusion to the story to bring some sense of hope. And as a rule, it is good to have a fairly short, sharp sentence or phrase to finish off with.

(See the worksheet 'Story beginnings' as well as 'Genres: openings' in the workshop section at the end of this chapter.)

Workshop activity: endings

Write a story to one of these endings:

- And she/he/it was never seen again.
- And the three of them lived *fairly* happily ever after.
- She/he ran up the steps, and didn't look back once.

STORY BEGINNINGS

Below are the beginnings to stories that have never been written or published. Find one that you like. Copy it on to a piece of paper and then carry on with the story. But before you begin, think – do you want to just start writing or do you want to brainstorm your ideas first? Either way, try to think of how your story will finish. 'I woke up and it was all a dream' is cheating and it's not allowed!

DAVID ALMOND
Alan took the postcard out of his pocket again.

IAN BECK
He woke suddenly into darkness and the sound of wolves howling. His old nurse stood by the bed with a dark lantern. He could see the tears on her cheeks, and she was muttering a prayer.

'Quickly,' she said, and he scrambled into his clothes. From somewhere deep within the stone walls he heard a muffled explosion.

MALORIE BLACKMAN
I crept down the stairs, wincing each time the floorboards groaned under my feet. The house was night-time dark, but I knew the way by heart. Through the hall, through the kitchen, open the door and out into the garden. The moon was hiding behind a cloud. But at last the clouds drifted out of the way. The garden filled with moonlight, bathing me in its silver glow. And slowly, I turned into a . . .

MELVIN BURGESS
If I'd known you were my father I'd never have helped you in the first place.

GILLIAN CROSS
When Benjamin was eleven, his parents gave him an island off the coast of Scotland.

TERRY DEARY
She laughed all the way to the funeral.

ALAN DURANT
Wizzy had never seen a cow before and he found the sight – in particular the swollen hand thing that dangled from its belly – somewhat bemusing. What a bizzare place this planet was!

ANNE FINE
Robbie stood in the doorway. Seven beds. Seven quilts. And seven little bedside tables. A month ago, it would have been Robbie's mother reading 'Snow White'. Now, suddenly and horribly, it was a new home.

continued over

MORRIS GLEITZMAN

James was three when he first realised people were trying to kill him.

RUSSELL HOBAN

'Listen,' said Grandad, 'if it ain't working for you, it's working against you.'

ANTHONY MASTERS

José switched off the outboard engine and the rubber dinghy bounced on the wave crests. He exchanged glances with Adam, and could see the mounting terror in his friend's eyes.

The stink of the polluted Mexican shoreline was revolting – a kind of acrid rotting smell that neither of the boys had ever got used to, despite the fact that the Toxic had spread right round the coast over the last few years. That was why Adam's scientist mother was in Ensenada, studying the growth of the pollution.

PHILIP PULLMAN

At midnight, the crabs came back.

CELIA REES

She could never be sure whether she hated the house or it hated her.

JACQUELINE WILSON

I sat up with a start, absolutely terrified.

Characters: writing about fictional people

Writers and readers both agree that, in fiction, one area that is of great importance is good characterisation. But what is it, and how can it be achieved? Answer this question yourself when you have finished reading this section.

One way to describe fictional characters is 'round' and 'flat'. A 'round' character has been well crafted and, as a result, is believable and portrayed in detail. Take, for example, Jacqueline Wilson's *Double Act*. Over the course of the novel the reader gets to know the central characters, Garnet and Ruby – and also their immediate family – very well. The reader is informed as to what these characters are like, how they behave, what they think and how they feel about each other. However, the other, more incidental characters – such as the twins' teachers and friends – are not portrayed in such detail. These are 'flat' characters – characters that are more shadowy, ones that a reader does not get to know so well. And it can only be this way – for not every character in every book can be 'round' or otherwise every short story you started would turn out to be the size of a telephone directory! There simply isn't time or space to paint every character fully: it is the central characters that need most attention.

Celia Rees likes to get to know her central characters well, and she ensures that they are fully rounded:

CELIA REES: You've got to have believable characters that your readers can care about. You've got to care about them and you can only do that by developing credible characters within a strong plot. Sometimes your characters jump out at you fully fledged – they're there, they're that person, with that name and you'll know them well immediately. Other characters prove harder to get to know. I may begin by thinking this person is female, aged 16, has blonde hair and blue eyes, wears these clothes – but that character is still anodyne, not fully fledged. Usually I'll have to find one thing about that character that's different and then they'll become real. With my earlier novels I used to write pages of notes about all the characters. Now I do the notes in my head. I give a lot of thought to my characters, just waiting for that one quality or detail that will make them come alive. There's a science fiction film called *The Invasion of the Bodysnatchers* in which these zombie-type people grew out of pods. If you're not careful, your own characters will be like that, a pod character that's not whole or fully formed, and will just sleepwalk through the novel not doing very much.

Rarely do books these days – for children, teenagers or adults – contain lengthy descriptions of characters. Previously, writers would take up many paragraphs – if not whole pages of text – to provide detailed biographies of their characters. Nowadays, short character sketches are more fashionable, as these next two passages demonstrate.

> *He was tall and thin, and dressed in an immaculate black suit. From his shoulders, a long, black teacher's gown hung in heavy folds, like wings, giving him the appearance of a huge crow. Only his head was startlingly white. Fair hair, almost as colourless as snow, lay round a face with paper-white skin and pallid lips. His eyes were hidden behind dark glasses, like two black holes in the middle of all the whiteness.*

(Gillian Cross – *The Demon Headmaster*: Oxford University Press and Puffin)

> *The old woman's hair was grey and white in streaks, tied back in a bun. Her face was as thin and brown as cardboard, with deep lines round her nose and mouth. One leg was stretched stiffly in a bandage, her heel resting on a coil of rope. She*

was wearing a long brown skirt and a tweed jacket with leather patches on the elbows.

(Janni Howker – *Badger on the Barge*: Walker Books)

The descriptions in these two passages are most vivid. The prose is simple and direct and flows with a strong rhythm – and because of this, both pieces work well when read out loud. Note how both of these character portraits focus solely on *physical* description – for the characters' personalities come out elsewhere, in the events that occur in these novels.

> **ALAN DURANT:** Show rather than tell – that exact phrase is always in my head when I'm writing. And I always tell myself off if I think I'm telling rather than showing.

What Alan Durant means by 'show rather than tell' is that he aims to write fiction in which he shows his characters in action, doing things, talking, interacting – rather than simply *telling* his readers about those characters. Or, put another way, we as readers get to know his characters not so much by what he tells us directly about them, but what he shows his characters to be doing. But how does this work in practice? Well, rather than writing, for example, 'Joe was a gullible boy' – that is, directly *telling* the reader what Joe is like – you could show the character Joe in conversation, being tricked into believing something.

Plot and characterisation in a story are very much intertwined. Plot is the series of events that the characters initiate or are involved in. Clearly, you cannot have a plot without characters of some form – be they human, animal or whatever. Some stories and novels are not plot-driven, but character-centred, and are more concerned with either the personalities of the individuals in the story or the relationships between the characters. That is not to say that there is no plot at all in such books, but the writer is more interested in exploring the characters and their relationships rather than taking the reader through a series of events. Anne Fine is one writer who openly confesses that as she is writing she is more actively concerned with character than plot.

> **ANNE FINE:** To be honest, plots don't interest me nearly as much as people. When I stop to chew the pencil, it's rarely to wonder what the characters will do now, or where they'll go. Far more often it's what are they thinking? Or, how are they *feeling*?

But this does not mean to say that Anne Fine's books do not have plots at all, as they do, but when she writes she gives thought to creating interesting characters in interesting situations. Have a look at Anne Fine's book *Bill's New Frock* – in which the main character finds himself in a very unusual if not unique situation!

These two authors are very much aware of the relationship between plot and character:

> **NORMAN SILVER:** Generally speaking, plot and character work together for me – when an idea comes I have the feeling of a character in a situation or in a crisis. From there, my plotting starts with my main character's need to get out of his situation. And that will start to generate the plot. I then start to expand the character to make him go for one choice rather than another. I never think of a character in isolation – that wouldn't work for me. I'm always thinking of a character in a social or personal situation, or whatever, but in some kind of turmoil, usually. That scenario drives the plotting forward. But I'll also have various other plot ideas – I'll know that other events will happen down the line – so that will affect how my character

starts to be formed, and then the character takes a step forward, and I'll see that affecting the plot.

GILLIAN CROSS: I don't think of plot and character as separate. My characters express their personalities through the plot, the things that they do. I like to put them in extreme situations which highlight the moral choices they have to make. I think moral choices are important and I think children share that view.

But how do writers get to know their characters?

JACQUELINE WILSON: I do think about my characters quite hard before I write about them – particularly when I'm swimming in the mornings! I always know what my characters like best to eat, their favourite television programmes and things like that. I get to know them very well.

ANTHONY MASTERS: I know all my characters 'off stage' – outside of the story – very well. I keep a notebook in which I write down details about those characters. Often those details won't appear in the piece, but they'll help me to get to know the character. My characters can be quite stereotypical in my first few drafts of a novel, and by the later drafts they become much more flesh and blood.

MALORIE BLACKMAN: Once I've organised the plot framework for a book, I work really hard on my characters, getting to know them really well. I work out a full biography for the main characters, answering questions such as – What do they love and hate? What makes them happy or angry? What's their favourite food or colour? Do they have any annoying habits? What do their friends like or dislike about them? I might not ever use all of that material. Probably 70 per cent of it I won't actually need, but at least by doing the biography the characters have become real people inside my head. And I hope my characters act like real people in my books. Although some of my characters find themselves in bizarre situations, I try to make the way they behave in those situations realistic. I never base my characters on family and friends, and I do like writing both nice and nasty characters. I think it's true to say that most people are a mixture of both good and bad qualities. For me, playing about with the proportions of good and evil is the fun part when creating a character. I never start a story until I feel I know a character really well. The characters are all important.

As Malorie Blackman says, doing a character biography is a useful and practical way of getting to know a character, one that can help to make a character become fully rounded. (See the worksheet 'Invent your own character' for an example: p. 109.)

Celia Rees believes that pondering over characters is an essential part of the story writing process. Indeed, it is good to spend time thinking about your characters in action: talking, interacting, even doing everyday and mundane thing. You will also need to consider what makes them unique, what makes them different or special – do they wave their hands about as they talk? Do they have an unusual laugh? Do they dislike eye contact?

Many writers admit that their characters' personalities – often quite unintentionally – are made up of people who they have met or who they know well. A few writers will deliberately use friends or acquaintances as the basis for characters in their stories. They will start with someone they know but will change certain details around – their sex, their age, their appearance. However, the majority of fiction writers – such as Malorie Blackman above –

claim that although some minor aspects of their characters may be based upon people they know (including themselves), in the main, their characters are invented.

Morris Gleitzman talks about how he becomes acquainted with his characters, and reveals that he too does not base them on real people:

MORRIS GLEITZMAN: When I'm getting to know a character and I'm starting to think that I have a character whose story I want to tell, I always feel that I want to tell their whole story, I don't want to tell some peripheral aspect of their story. To do that, I have to know what the biggest problem is in their life at that moment. So I'm always building up stories around the character's problems. They don't have to be big global problems or issues, but they must be problems that are significantly important and preoccupy that character.

All of my main characters are a part of me, but exactly where my minor characters actually come from is a mystery to me because what I've never done is take people I know from my life and consciously put them into stories. My family are always telling me that they don't want to appear in my books! And that's fair enough, because it's my job to make things up, not to steal other people's lives. I suspect that what happens is that without even knowing it, I take very tiny pieces of people's lives, so tiny that they wouldn't even notice. These minor characters, I think, are combinations of lots of different people I've met.

Both Morris Gleitzman and Melvin Burgess believe in letting their readers know exactly how their main character is feeling and what they are doing at any moment in a story. Melvin Burgess adds that young writers should 'aim for vividness in both character and situation'.

It can be difficult to write about a character until you have the right name. One way of overcoming this situation is to call the characters 'A' or 'B' or 'C' until you find suitable names – but make sure that once you are writing your story, you have the names you need. Writers can source names for their characters from many places – such as 'Name Your Baby' books and telephone directories.

How do authors decide upon their characters' names?

JACQUELINE WILSON [on the toy rabbit 'Radish' in *The Suitcase Kid*]: I was looking for a name for the Sylvanian Family Rabbit. I got thinking about what rabbits like to eat, and 'Lettuce' cropped up. And I thought, no, it was too wet and limp! I was after something that was sturdy but little and then I came up with 'Radish' the rabbit. It sounded alliterative, and I went with it. I chose this particular toy as I had my own Sylvanian Family Rabbit as a mascot that had originally been my daughter's. And I have to say that Radish is definitely my most popular character to date.

ALAN DURANT [on Calico in *Publish or Die!*]: I have a notebook in which I write various bits and pieces – ideas for titles, jokes, interesting names, descriptions of interesting faces – all kinds of things. For example, I came across the name Calico – my main character in *Publish or Die!* – during one of my school visits, and I made a note of it in my notebook, and it resurfaced later.

HELEN CRESSWELL: My characters are never called anything like 'John' or 'Susan'. They'll be 'Arthy' or 'Jem' or 'Minty' or 'Else'. I used to have a notebook in which I'd collect names, and would sometimes look around graveyards for any good ones! In fact, the names 'Joshua' and 'Caleb' – from *The Night-Watchmen* – I've been told, come from a piece in the Old Testament. I must have read it when I was at school and I must have stored those names away in my mind.

One final word on characterisation: aim to create central characters that your readers can identify and sympathise with.

Workshop activities: characters

OUT OF THIN AIR

You are going to build your own character out of nothing – by simply answering a few questions and developing your character from there. Give yourself just a couple of seconds to answer each question.

- Is it a girl/boy/woman/man?
- How old is the person?
- Where does the person live?
- Who does the person live with?
- What does the person do?
- What is the person like?
- How would you describe the person's appearance?

Now you have built up some details to begin with, brainstorm some more of your own ideas in note form – or even use the 'Invent your own character' worksheet to learn more about your character. Do not worry about writing down everything, thinking about the person is just as important. Once you have as many details as you need, write a story based around this character in the first person. You could begin with 'My name is . . . and I want to tell you about . . .' or find your own opening.

EMPTY OUT YOUR POCKETS

Instead of writing about a character directly, write about the objects or possessions the character always has in their pockets, and say why these are important to her or him.

EAVESDROPPING

There are two people sitting on a park bench. They are having a row. Who are they? What are they rowing over? Go straight into writing the piece without any planning – and learn about the characters as you go.

THE HOT SEAT

(This activity has been adapted from one that Berlie Doherty and Gillian Cross have both done in their own workshops.) Volunteers in turn think of an imaginary character and (in character or not) answer questions about that person from the rest of the group. You can then write about one or a combination of these invented characters.

EVERY PICTURE TELLS A STORY

Teacher-led activity. Cut out pictures of people – but not famous or well known – from magazines or newspapers. There should be one picture per pupil. Ask the pupils to brainstorm various details about their character, such as age, background, family, the way they speak, their personality and so on. As they are writing these notes on their characters, sporadically ask the pupils a question such as:

• What important event happened to that character at the age of six?
• What birthday present have they always treasured – and why?
• Whose photograph do they keep in their pocket at all times?

Once the pupils have built up these notes, ask them to write about that character in a situation, perhaps one of the following:

• The character discovers that a friend/relation has been lying about something important for a while.
• The character finds a wallet on the street containing money and credit cards. What does she or he do?

WHAT'S IN A NAME?

Authors collect names for their characters from many different places – 'Name Your Baby' books, telephone directories, school registers and even gravestones! Celia Rees takes authors' names from the spines of books in the library and mixes them around – so William Shakespeare and Enid Blyton could become Enid Shakespeare and William Blyton. Collect a list of names – first name as well as surname – and then put personalities and characters to them. Write a short piece in which you describe your character doing something that they do every day. You may want to use the 'Invent your own character' worksheet to find out more about your character.

DOUBLE SEAT

Imagine this: You are sitting on a train. You have a long journey ahead of you. To your delight you have managed to find a double seat. Just as the train pulls away, somebody takes your spare seat. You are annoyed. But your annoyance soon fades when you discover a few minutes into the journey that the person sitting next to you seems most upset.

Think: Who is this person that is sitting next to you? Why is she/he upset? How would you describe her/him? Brainstorm as many things as you can about that person. Draw the person if you wish.

Then: Write a piece in the voice of this person about a secret that they have kept for a long time.

INVENT YOUR OWN CHARACTER

When you write a story, it is good to know your main characters well. One way of getting to know them is to do a character file. With this activity, you can invent the character *before* you write the story. This character – as with all your characters – must be made up, and must not be based on anyone that you know. Write down your ideas in the spaces below. If you think of other ideas, write them on the other side of this sheet. You may want to draw your character too. Answer as many of these questions as you can. Once you have finished, you could begin your story with your character doing one of the following:

(a)   saying to a friend 'Why didn't you tell me . . .?'

(b)   arriving home to a surprise

(c)   getting into trouble for something that she or he didn't do.

NAME:

AGE:

IS SHE/HE AT SCHOOL – IF SO, WHICH ONE?

DOES SHE/HE HAVE A JOB?

WHERE DOES SHE/HE LIVE?

WHO DOES SHE/HE LIVE WITH?

WHAT ARE HER/HIS HOBBIES?

FAVOURITE FOOD / POSSESSION / BOOK / COLOUR / NUMBER / ANIMAL:

WHAT DOES SHE/HE USUALLY HAVE IN HER/HIS POCKETS?

WHAT IS HER/HIS FAVOURITE PLACE? WHY?

WHAT IS SHE/HE REALLY GOOD AT ?

DOES SHE/HE HAVE ANY ANNOYING HABITS?

WHO ARE HER/HIS BEST FRIENDS?

HOW WOULD YOU DESCRIBE HER/HIS VOICE?

WHAT WORDS WOULD YOU USE TO DESCRIBE HER/HIM – HOW SHE/HE LOOKS
    AND HOW SHE/HE BEHAVES?

WHAT IS THE WORST LIE SHE/HE HAS EVER TOLD?

WHAT MAKES HER/HIM UNHAPPY/LAUGH?

WHAT ANIMAL DOES THIS PERSON RESEMBLE? WHY?

WHAT DOES SHE/HE WANT MORE THAN ANYTHING ELSE? WHY?

DOES SHE/HE HAVE A SECRET?

WOULD YOU TRUST THIS PERSON? WHY?

WHAT IS THE MAIN PROBLEM IN THIS PERSON'S LIFE?

Dialogue: the role of speech in stories

'Dialogue' is another word for talk or speech in fiction, and without it, stories would be very dull. Dialogue is vital in fiction and it serves as one of the major ways that a writer has to bring stories to life.

Dialogue has many roles to play within stories, including:

- to shape and form characters
- to give the reader an insight into what the characters think and feel
- to provide first-hand experience of how the characters behave
- to allow the characters to express themselves
- to develop the plot and to allow the story to progress
- to allow conflict to occur between characters.

For many people, dialogue is one of the easiest things to write. However, it is important to make sure that a story is not overtaken by dialogue, and that every line of dialogue serves a purpose.

In order that we can believe in the characters of a story, the words that they speak must be realistic and flow in the same way that real speech does. But just how 'real' should dialogue be? And should every 'umm' and 'err' that a character would say be included? In real life, people often say 'umm' and 'err', but it would be tedious to put all of these into a story. A good rule is to include utterances such as 'umm' or 'err' only when a character is hesitating or feeling anxious. And there is no reason whatsoever why your characters should not interrupt each other.

Berlie Doherty looks for specific things when reading her dialogue:

BERLIE DOHERTY: When I read through the drafts of a novel I pay close attention to dialogue – and whether something should or should not be in dialogue at all, whether a scene would actually move much faster if you take it away. And also, it must be that character talking. You should be able to recognise a character by the things they say and the way they say it. So, dialogue moves the narrative forward but also tells you something about the character. It's also got to sound like real people talking, though it hasn't got to have the monotony of real people talking.

Malorie Blackman has her own way of 'collecting' dialogue:

MALORIE BLACKMAN: I get a lot of dialogue from being incredibly nosy. I listen to other people's conversations whenever I get the chance. And I always have a notebook in my handbag so that I can jot down all the good expressions and phrases that I hear other people use.

These authors use the same method of testing out the dialogue in their books:

HELEN CRESSWELL: I always read my dialogue to see if it flows. And as I write it, I can hear the character's voice in my head.

ANTHONY MASTERS: When I'm writing the dialogue I'm in total immersion, and the process is so vivid for me that it's more like recording the voices rather than creating them. When I re-read the manuscript I speak all the dialogue aloud.

In the following extracts by Berlie Doherty, Malorie Blackman and Helen Cresswell, note how true to the rhythms of real speech the dialogue is.

> *'What's wrong?' I asked.*
>
> *'What d'you mean, what's wrong?' Ruthlyn's smile broadened. 'Why should anything be wrong?'*
>
> *'I can tell by your face. Where's Helen?'*
>
> *'Oh, Helen. She's gone home.'*
>
> *'She's supposed to be meeting me.'*
>
> *'She went a bit funny in afternoon registration and Miss Clancy sent her home.*
>
> *'What d'you mean, funny?'*

(Berlie Doherty – *Dear Nobody*: Hamish Hamilton)

> *'Mum?'*
>
> *'Yes.'*
>
> *'Can I ask you a question?'*
>
> *Mum smiled. 'Since when have you needed to ask if you could ask?!?'*
>
> *'Mum, I'm serious.'*
>
> *'Go on then.'*
>
> *'Why didn't you tell Dad that you were going to have a baby?'*

(Malorie Blackman – *Pig-heart Boy*: Transworld)

> *'Sit yourself down, Essie,' she fussed. 'Gravella'll fetch a spill and put in to the fire and it'll be cosy in no time. Oh! Getting quite dark outside, I see. Don't the evenings draw in? I'd best draw the curtains, or we'll have half the Dale peering in at us.'*
>
> *She went to the window, and drew the curtains with a grand sweep. They, too, were of brocade, and she secretly stroked her rough fingers down their softness before turning back to face Essie.*
>
> *'Ain't they new curtains, Jem?' she said sharply peering forwards.*
>
> *'What? Oh, them!' Jem shrugged. 'Newish.'*

(Helen Cresswell – *The Piemakers*: Oxford University Press)

In the passages by Berlie Doherty and Malorie Blackman above, each line of dialogue isn't always qualified with a phrase such as 'he said' or 'she said'. When writing a piece of fiction, you need to decide if you are going to explain who is talking every time a character speaks. Malorie Blackman talks about this issue as well as how she achieves realistic speech in her books:

MALORIE BLACKMAN: As I'm writing I hear the voices, the dialogue in my head. It's not me talking, it's my characters talking, and I'm just recording what they're saying. And because I imagine my characters to be real people in my head, it comes out as real people talking. Yet at times I've noticed that some of my dialogue has become quite flowery and poetic, and I've realised that *I've* taken over too much, and it doesn't sound like that character speaking, so I've had to change it.

With my dialogue I tend to use 'he said' or 'she said' more than anything else. In the main, a reader should be able to appreciate the way that something is spoken from the dialogue itself. Also, I feel that if you're using lots of adverbs to qualify how everything is spoken

– 'she replied softly', 'he answered quickly' – then the dialogue is not doing its job. Take for example,

> *'Come in for your dinner, John,' she shouted angrily.*

Here, the speech isn't enough, because it needs the adverb 'angrily' to explain. So, it needs to be something like,

> *'John! How many times do I have to call you? Come in NOW!' she said.*

There, you get it from the dialogue on its own. But that's not to say I don't use adverbs, there are exceptions where I do, such as when somebody is whispering something, and they're saying something normal and you want to tell the reader how it is being spoken – and then you'll have to put 'she whispered', or 'she replied softly'.

When you've got only two people talking, you don't need 'he said' and 'she said' for every time they speak, you can just let the dialogue do the work. It's actually been proved that when people read they skip over the 'he saids' and 'she saids' anyway, so you don't need to put them in every sentence! And anyway, reading a series of 'she saids' does slow the reading down.

Yet another effective way of showing how something is expressed is to focus on the character's facial expressions:

> *'I should send you to your room for the rest of the night without a bite to eat for that little stunt earlier,' Mum sniffed. 'You really had me going!'*
>
> *'Mum, that was the idea,' I smiled.*
>
> *Slowly she smiled back. 'Dominic, you had better watch that peculiar sense of humour you've got there. It could get you into trouble.'*
>
> *I just grinned at her. 'So what's for dinner then. Feed me. I'm a growing boy.'*
>
> *'How about we phone for a take-away pizza?' Jack suggested.*
>
> *'Yeah, OK!' I said, snatching his hand off.*

> (Malorie Blackman – *Dangerous Reality*: Corgi Doubleday)

Finally, one issue that one must not forget when writing dialogue – as Jan Dean rightly points out – is that it is wholly connected to characterisation:

JAN DEAN: Get to know your characters so well that you could take a line of dialogue out of the story and still know which character has spoken it, because it would be the type of thing that particular character would say – either because that character is the one that's always giving the orders, or always worrying, or whatever.

Workshop activities: dialogue

ACTIVITY 1
Write a conversation between two people. Do not worry about their names to begin with, simply call them 'A' and 'B'. Begin your piece with 'A' saying to 'B', 'Where are we?' See if you can write a whole page. Write it in this way –

A: Where are we?
B:

Give your characters names as soon as you want to. You could even use the 'Invent your own character' worksheet (p. 109) to discover more about your two characters.

ACITIVITY 2

Do the same as with Activity 1, but this time call your two characters 'C' and 'D', and begin with 'D' saying 'Where did you get that from?' or 'Why didn't you tell me that . . .'.

ACITIVITY 3

Take one of the pieces you have written in Activities 1 and 2 and turn it into a story in the third person. This time, try to use dialogue sparingly. Do not worry if the plot changes when you adapt the story – this is all part of the drafting process.

ACITIVITY 4

Often, what we say and what we think about things can be very different. Write a piece in dialogue in which you express this idea.

> PARENT: We've got apple custard for tea, John.
> JOHN: Oh, great!
> JOHN: *Not again – we've had apple custard every day for the last week!*

(For further dialogue-orientated workshops, see Workshop activities: drama, pp. 123–4).

Drama

Drama can take many forms, including

- a stage play
- a radio play
- an audio recording (on CD or audio cassette)
- a film
- a television programme.

What all these types of drama have in common is that they are all written to be performed.

Writing drama is not only about creating whole plays with three acts or full-length films. A good place to start is with a short dramatic sketch that lasts just a few minutes.

On the surface, drama may seem to have very little in common with the other forms of fiction, yet it has many of the same elements – such as dialogue, plots and characters, to name but a few. But if you look at a drama script it will seem very different from such forms as the novel or the short story because most of the text is in dialogue. Some drama scripts will include stage directions, which can be not only short background details of the characters and the set design, but also instructions to the actors as to how they should speak certain lines, how they should be standing or what physical actions they should be doing. Look at some play scripts for examples of stage directions.

When you are writing a piece of drama you can do a lot of work on developing your plots or your characters, or you can just write about situations – small events, such as two people arguing, one person in trouble, and so on. And as with a short story, you may find that you produce more dialogue than you actually need. So, when you are drafting your piece, remove any lines that do not really add anything to it. Here are the ideal characteristics of a short sketch:

- no more than three or four characters
- one setting
- a short period of time.

Once you have written your drama, why not perform it with others? If certain lines or aspects of the piece are not working, don't be afraid to rewrite them and then try the piece out again.

The drama workshop activities are at the end of this 'Drama' section after Terry Deary's discussion of his play *The Mad Millennium* and Jacqueline Wilson's discussion of her play *The Dare Game*; both discussions have related workshop activities.

Terry Deary – *The Mad Millennium*

ACT ONE
SCENE ONE

Pupils enter classroom talking over the top of one another about the exams and the last lesson. 'HISTORY' is chalked on the roller backboard with instructions disappearing under the board.

MARY:	I've lost my timetable! What lesson's next?
JAMES:	Actually, Mary, it's History.
HENRY:	(*mocking*) Actually that's jolly bad news, James, old chap.
CATHERINE:	Yeah! I hated it last year.
ELIZABETH:	Oh Catherine! It was only bad last year because Miss Fitt was a hopeless teacher.
WILL:	Yeah, fatty Fitt was a *mis*-fit all right.
JAMES:	We have a Mr Minde this year, it says on my timetable. Who's he?
MARY:	New teacher.
JAMES:	But we're in the Performing Arts Studio?
MARY:	Probably the only room free at this time.
WILL:	Hey! If Mr Minde's a schoolmaster we can call him Master Minde! Mastermind – geddit?
HENRY:	(*sourly*) History will still be horrible.
WILL:	Horrible History? That's a good name, Henry.

(He goes to the keyboard in the corner and picks out a simple sequence of notes, then begins to sing.)

Ho-rib-bull Hiss-tor-ree, Hor-rib-bull Hiss-tor-ree.

(The other children begin to pick up the tune.)

TERRY DEARY: My background is very much in theatre. I studied drama at college and I worked as an actor-teacher for a TIE [Theatre in Education] company in Wales. We used to tour around schools and community theatres and I wrote our TIE projects and plays. After that I became

Figure 3.5 Cover of Terry Deary's play *The Mad Millennium* (A 'Horrible Histories' play: Scholastic)

a theatre director. From there I went on to writing for children and I eventually rewrote some of my TIE plays as children's books.

The Mad Millennium was premiered at the Sherman Theatre, Cardiff. The director, Philip Clark, is a friend of mine. Philip and I used to work in the TIE company together, twenty-five years ago. And it was Philip who commissioned me to write this play for his theatre. He said, 'Your books are very successful. Can we turn them into a large-scale theatre production?' I was delighted to get back into writing plays again.

The play covers British history of the last thousand years. It could have been a bit of light entertainment, taking the funniest stories from history, but I didn't want to do that. I didn't want a pantomime or an end-of-the-pier piece of theatre. What I've done is to take the *Horrible Histories* concept and to write a play about a group of young people discovering themselves through history. And because it was a *Horrible Histories* play, in the writing of the play I didn't diverge too much from my *Horrible Histories* books. I used certain aspects of the books deliberately as I didn't want people to read the books and then see the play and find them too different or be disappointed. So I used funny poems to convey information, 'faction' stories and television-gameshow parodies. All are in both the books and the play.

The setting for the play is a classroom. Seven kids come into the classroom and they have tensions and relationships amongst themselves. There's one character you don't meet until the end called Master Minde, who's the history teacher. He leaves messages on the blackboard and on tape: 'This is the work you have to do before I get back and test you . . .'. He's very much the traditional teacher. Then in comes Miss Game, the drama teacher, who says, 'Don't worry, we'll look at history through drama'. And so they begin to re-enact scenes from history with her. It soon becomes clear that the characters of the people in the classroom are reflected in the historical characters they play. The bully in the classroom is called Henry, and he plays Henry VIII. The wimp in the classroom is called Edward, and he plays Edward II. And in turn, each of the seven children becomes a key historical figure.

The play is also a musical and it's interactive, in that the audience get involved as well. As the play develops, the more the relationships between the characters in the classroom develop, and they eventually become more tolerant of each other. At the very end, Master Minde turns up, and he's hideous. The children put him in an electric chair and fire questions at him. And because it's a *Horrible History*, the questions are about *interpretations* of history – they're *not* about facts. And so Master Minde gets them all wrong and he's zapped into unconsciousness.

When the kids take Master Minde's mask off, it's really Miss Game, because history is about what both of these teachers represent. History can be about facts but it's also about enjoyment and interpretation. Adults will come away from the play thinking, 'Wow, the layers of meaning in that!' It may sound boring and profound, but actually it's fun and very fast moving!

In the play I wanted to represent events that were spectacular, and I looked for the major turning points in history. I had to choose the best way to dramatise these events. But I also wanted the play to convey something about education, which can be as threatening and as horrible as history itself, because there is always the terror of the test. Kids live in fear that whenever they study something that they will be tested on it. That became a major theme of the play. So there are two themes throughout – one is about education today, as I've said, and the other is British history. The way I link the two together is to make the schoolchildren step from the school setting into various key scenes from history.

For me, each period in British history over the last thousand years has its own flavour, so it was important to treat each period in the play differently in performance. So there is a very different tone and feel for each era that the play goes through. For example, the Middle Ages is done as a dramatic scene from the Black Death. For the Georgian period we use some of Handel's choral music. The cast sing four-part harmonies whilst dressing Miss Game, the teacher, in Georgian dress – with a big wig and make-up! Whereas the Victorian era is done more like a television play, and on stage it appears far more intimate and small-scale. The scene from World War I, in which the English and Germans stop fighting on Christmas Day and play football, becomes quite large scale and is actually mimed.

For me, one of the most important parts of writing this piece was the rehearsal stage – working the play through and seeing it come to life. On the page certain scenes looked really good, but in rehearsal they dragged. So I made cuts. In fact, we made rather more cuts than I expected. And this really improved the pace of the play.

What I like about theatre is the danger and the unpredictability. Theatre relies far more on the audience than books do. You can write a book but then you're shielded from the audience's reaction. In live theatre the reaction from the audience can actually influence the actions of the actors. And you never know how an audience will react or which moments they will laugh at. That can sometimes change a play quite a lot. I have been known to rewrite my text according to how an audience reacts to various scenes.

Workshop activities: Terry Deary

TERRY DEARY'S DRAMA ACTIVITY

There's a big difference between drama and theatre. Drama is what you do in school when you do such things as explore issues through role play. Theatre is performance to a script on a stage for an audience. Drama doesn't need an audience, but theatre does. I like to write theatre wherever possible through drama and I use improvisation as a starting point. I let the actors improvise and contribute and build their characters around ideas. And that's what I'd advise children to do – to get together a small acting group and say 'Let's improvise this'. When you're happy with the improvisation, then you can write it down and script it. I've written quite a few plays this way. It's my preferred way of working.

So if you want to learn how to write a play, the easy and the best way is to use actors first of all. Put your pens and scripts away to begin with and get people improvising any ideas you may have. Then you'll start to see all kinds of things happen that you wouldn't have thought of if you'd just written the piece. This is my personal way of working. Many people in theatre work this way, and many don't. Shakespeare did. He knew his cast very well indeed and wrote parts for specific actors because he knew what they were capable of acting out. Some parts he would act himself. If Shakespeare did it, then I'm justified in encouraging this method of writing plays!

As Terry Deary suggests, rather than starting with pen and paper, begin with yourself and some friends. All of you can take part. Choose one of these scenarios or work on some of your own:

- Something happens when a group of friends miss the last bus home.
- A parent has kept an important secret from their child; the child finds out.
- Someone meets their hero/heroine and discovers they are not what they seem.
- Two people are travelling on a coach together; one is crying as she or he reads a letter.

You could even record your improvisations on to cassette and write them out from there.

MAD MILLENNIUM *ACTIVITY*

Choose a period in history. Research that time and pick a moment that would work well as a short drama. Find out as much information as you can. If you do not know all of the facts, invent some of the details. Here are some historical events just to give you a few ideas:

- Sir Walter Raleigh has just returned from America and is presenting the first potato and tobacco plant to Queen Elizabeth I.
- The morning before the three astronauts Neil Armstrong, Buzz Aldrin and Michael Collins took off on the first trip to the moon in Apollo 11. What conversation did the three of them have?
- William Shakespeare has travelled to London to sell his first play to a theatre. What conversation might he have had with a theatre owner?
- Imagine the ghosts of the six wives of Henry VIII – Catherine of Aragon, Anne Boleyn, Jane Seymour, Anne of Cleves, Catherine Howard and Catherine Parr – meeting up to discuss their murdering husband.

Jacqueline Wilson – *The Dare Game*

JACQUELINE WILSON: I originally wrote *The Dare Game* as a play for The Contact Theatre in Manchester, which, before it was burnt down, was going to be a wonderful theatre for children and young people. A while ago the artistic director for the theatre commissioned me to do an original play. He wanted a play with three or four child characters. I was thinking hard about this and decided that I wanted to write about a really fierce, sparky determined girl. I had this framework of a story about truancy and children who, for various reasons, bunk off school and meet up together. So I was thinking about how all this could be dramatised in some way and become a stage play.

I kept thinking about this girl – who started to seem suspiciously like my Tracy Beaker character, but a year or two on. Usually when I've written a book, the story will go out of my mind and I won't think much about it afterwards and the character will disappear out of my

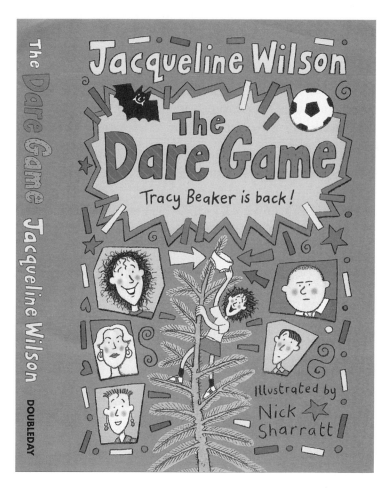

Figure 3.6 Cover of Jacqueline Wilson's novel *The Dare Game* (Doubleday–Transworld. Playscript unpublished)

head. Yet Tracy Beaker has remained with me ever since I wrote the original book. Also, I've had more letters asking what happened to Tracy – after the point in the story where the book finishes – than any other of my characters. So I thought I would write a play that would be a continuation of her story, but wouldn't require the audience to know the original book (see Figures 3.7 and 3.8).

I asked the director how he felt about me writing a new play about one of my old characters and he was happy about it. One advantage of using the Tracy Beaker character was that many people would know the character already and it would encourage them to come along. The book is read a great deal in schools, so I suggested that teachers might want to bring their classes along for school trips.

As the play was originally going to be performed in Manchester, a city that most people associate with football, I decided that one of my characters would be a football fan and that he would have 'Football' as a nickname. I thought it would be quite effective if he was forever dribbling a football around on stage. And if the ball bounced into the audience, then the children in the audience could bounce it back. The Contact Theatre is all about getting children who wouldn't usually see plays to visit the theatre. Because of this, I wanted to have this type of audience participation – not simply a crude 'Oh yes he is, oh no he isn't!' sort of thing, and to actually get the children involved. At times in the play I have the characters turn and ask the

```
THE DARE GAME          ACT ONE

SCENE ONE

A DERELECT TWO*STOREY HOUSE DOMINATES THE STAGE.
TRACY WALKS PAST, DRAGGING HER SCHOOLBAG.  SHE LOOKS
AT THE AUDIENCE AND GIVES THEM A CASUAL WAVE.  FOOTBALL
COMES RUNNING IN, DRIBBLING HIS FOOTBALL.  TRACY
INTERCEPTS, GIVES IT A HEFTY KICK IN THE WRONG DIRECTION,
AND RUNS OFF STAGE.  FOOTBALL GLARES AFTER HER AND
RUNS OFF STAGE TOO.  ALEXANDER IS IN THE HOUSE, PEERING
OUT OF THE TOP WINDOW.  HE BOBS OUT OF SIGHT AS THE
PLAY BEGINS.
A SCHOOL BELL RINGS OFF-STAGE.  THERE ARE SOUNDS OF
CHILDREN CHATTERING, GIGGLING, GENERALLY MESSING ABOUT.
```

TEACHER: (off-stage) Settle down, you lot! Qui - et!

Thank you. Now, I don't want to hear so much as a mouse

squeak while I take the register. Isla?

CHILD: (off-stage) Presnt.

TEACHER: (off-stage) Duncan?

CHILD: (off-stage) Present.

TEACHER: (off-stage, speeding up) Meethal?

CHILD: Present.

TEACHER: (off-stage, so speedily there isn't always

time for a response) Hannah, Hanif, Zara, Eleanor,

Richard, Marcus, Ashley, Dean ...

CHILDREN: (off-stage, very quickly) Present-present-

present-present-ppesent ...

TEACHER: (off-stage, loud and clear) Tracy? _Tracy?_

TRACY DASHES ON AND GOES TO THE FRONT OF THE STAGE,

LAUGHING. SHE POINTS TO HERSELF. ALEXANDER BOBS OUT

OF SIGHT.

TRACY: Absent!

SHE STANDS ARMS AKIMBO, TOSSING HER HAIR.

TRACY: I'm skiving off school. I can't _stick_ it.

Can you? Here, you guys - hands up who likes school.

Pause.

TRACY: Aha! So hands up who _doesn't_ like school!

Figure 3.7 Manuscript page for Jacqueline Wilson's play *The Dare Game*

THE DARE GAME

a sequel to THE STORY OF TRACY bEAKER

No Home

You know that old film they always show on the telly at Christmas, 'The Wizard of Oz'? I love it, especially the wicked witch of the West with her cackle and her green face and all her special flying monkeys. I'd give anything to have a wicked winged monkey as an evil little pet. It could whizz through the sky, flapping its wings and sniffing the air for that awful stale instant-coffee-and-talcumn-powder <u>teacher</u> smell and then it would s-w-o-o-p straight onto Mrs Vomit Bagley and carry her away screaming.

That'll show her. I've always been the absolute Tip Top at writing stories but since I've been at this stupid new school Mrs V.B. just puts 'Disgracefully untidy work, Tracy' and 'Check your spellings!'. Last week we had to write a story about Night-time XXXX and I thought ~~this~~ it an unusually cool subject so I wrote eight and a half pages about this girl out late at night and ~~how~~ she nearly gets raped and she runs away and then this crazy guy ~~nearly~~ almost murders her but she escapes by jumping in the river and then she swims right into this bloated corpse and <u>then</u> when she staggers onto the bank there's this strange flickering light coming from the nearby graveyard and it's ~~this~~ an evil occult sect wanting to sacrifice a virgin to the devil and she's <u>just</u> what they're looking for ...

It's a truly GREAT story, better than any that Cam could write. (I'll tell you about Cam in a minute). I'm sure it's practically good enough to get published. I typed it out on Cam's computer so it looked ever so neat and the Spellcheck took care of all the spellings so I was all prepared for Mrs V.B.

Handwritten margin notes:

Full page Picture at start of chapter of Tracy looking forlorn, wondering the streets, lots & lots & lots of houses — but none of them her home.

? Tracy as witch with winged monkey pet

? maybe comic-book scenes like violent American comic

Figure 3.8 Manuscript page for Jacqueline Wilson's novel *The Dare Game*

audience questions. I thought the footballing thing would be a good way in for boys who are football mad! During the writing of the play I panicked at one stage because I don't know anything about football, though I've come to realise that mostly – apart from two or three lines of dialogue, which any football fan would be able to help me out with – it's not really about football at all, but more about what's lacking in his life.

How would I sum up the story? Tracy is being fostered by a writer called Cam. Things aren't going well and Tracy is regularly playing truant from school. She hangs out in a derelict house where she meets up with two boys, fierce Football and timid Alexander. Tracy starts up a Dare Game which escalates dangerously, none of the children knowing how to back down. Tracy's real mum appears on the scene and Tracy thinks she's found her happy ending at last, but, by the end of the play Tracy finds out who *really* cares about her. And I'm going to have the same actress playing Cam – the woman who fosters Tracy – as well as Tracy's mum. Because of this, these two characters can only be on stage at different times. It's interesting to me that there's these two mother figures for Tracy – and they're very different types of women. To have the same actress playing both is quite a pleasing idea.

I really enjoyed writing this play because in my books the dialogue is usually the easiest bit to write. In fact, much of my books are dialogue, and I tell the stories through my characters' speech. So having only dialogue to write, as in a stage play, is quite a nice way of telling a story. Though one limiting factor is cast. In a book you can have a whole class for example, but in a play you may be limited to six people in total. Also, you can't generally have very young children in the cast. I had to bear these limitations in mind, and, as a result, they very much shaped the story. And because of the small cast, I had to arrange it so that certain actors would be able to double up certain parts. I had to give them time in the story to get off stage, to change costume and to then get back on stage again.

Overall, I wanted *The Dare Game* to be very lively and eventful, with lots of action. I also wanted it to be very modern and funny too. I wanted there to be a few rude bits as well, because children always respond to these! On top of all this, children's plays need to have an interval, and therefore I needed to have a really dramatic moment just prior to the interval, something powerful and exciting that would get them thinking 'What's going to happen next?' rather than 'Oh come on Miss, let's go, this is boring'. So, having to have that dramatic climax about halfway through affected the shape and structure of the play. And with the introduction I wanted to suck the audience straight into the drama and make them feel that Tracy is their friend.

In my book *The Story of Tracy Beaker*, there are a series of rude and silly dares. In *The Dare Game* there are more dares, but in a new context – that of bunking off school – and the dares get more and more scary. The play looks at issues such as courage and common sense and the way that groups of children can sometimes egg each other on to do dreadful things, whereas individually they wouldn't do these sorts of things.

It's more likely that you write a book and then later it might become a stage play or a television drama. So it was weird doing it the other way around, writing the play and then adapting that into a book. The book is in the form of a journal that Tracy has written. I didn't simply take all of the dialogue I used in the play, but I did use some of it. As I was writing the book I had the play beside me to refer to. Most of the time, I knew what was happening in the story and I let Tracy tell the story in her own way in her diary. The advantage of writing the book – as opposed to the stage play – was that I could put across exactly what Tracy is thinking at any given moment. You can't do that so easily in a play. In the book I also play around with the idea of the 'unreliable narrator' – the type of narrator that doesn't always tell the reader the truth. You see, Tracy writes things in her diary which are whopping great lies, and other times she's being very unkind about the people around her. By the end of the book the reader will hopefully realise what she's made up and which bits are true. Also, the plot structure of the novel was different – for a start, I didn't have to worry about the dramtic climax at the interval.

I hope that when *The Dare Game* is performed there will be music and songs composed for the play. The play of *The Lottie Project* is currently being performed at the Polka Theatre in Wimbledon, adapted and directed by Vicky Ireland. She's made a *brilliant* job of it and I'm absolutely thrilled. The music in *The Lottie Project* – by Andrew Dodge – is particularly effective.

I was a little bit nervous about writing a stage play because mostly my books are about the internal lives of my characters. To achieve this as well as having lots of action on stage is very difficult. It may sound arrogant, but with writing children's books I feel quite comfortable now and to an extent I feel that I know what I'm doing, but with the theatre I'm very much a novice. I have written for radio, but that's a very different medium again. I do think you have to have things on stage which are great to look at. I've been going to see lots of plays recently to see how other people do it – like Carol Ann Duffy's *Grimms' Tales* and also *Shock-Headed Peter*. Both productions were so visual and inventive and clever.

My advice for writing drama? Write about a situation that really interests you – with lots of dramatic possibilities. Don't be *too* wordy and try and have lots of different things happening.

Workshop activities: Jacqueline Wilson

THE DARE GAME *PLAY*

Read through Jacqueline Wilson's manuscript page of the introduction to the play. What will happen next? Even if you have read the book of *The Dare Game*, make up your own alternative version of the story. Write it as a series of short scenes to be performed on stage.

THE STORY OF TRACY BEAKER

Take one event from the book of *The Story of Tracy Beaker* and rewrite it as if it were to be performed on stage. For example, you might choose the time that Tracy and Cam go to McDonald's. But you will have to invent much of your own dialogue. Imagine what they might talk about – and remember that Tracy has a habit of exaggerating. And perhaps it is her exaggerating that makes their conversation interesting. If you can, use stage directions too.

CHARACTERS IN A SCENE

Take a character from any Jacqueline Wilson novel and write a short scene for them that could be performed on stage. You might choose Tim or Biscuits from *Cliffhanger* and *Buried Alive*, or Andy from *The Suitcase Kid* or the twins from *Double Act*. Or you might even want to mix and match characters – and have, for example, Charlie from *The Lottie Project* meet Dolphin from *The Illustrated Mum*. For this activity, you could even start off by improvising a few scenes with friends from your class.

A MONOLOGUE

As with the previous activity, pick a Jacqueline Wilson character and write a monologue for that person. In your monologue you could include details from the book that the character comes from. (See 'The monologue' activity on pp. 124–5.)

Workshop activities: drama

STARTING POINTS

Use one or some of the lines below as starting points for a short drama. Don't
worry who A and B are when you begin writing, just get them talking together first
of all. When you have written half a page or so, you might want to go back and
make some notes on the characters or their situation. Give your characters real
names as soon as you like.

> A says to B – 'Do you want the good news or the bad news first?'
> A says to B – 'It was supposed to be a secret. We promised. Remember?'
> A says to B – 'You haven't heard a word I've said. What's the matter?'
> A says to B – 'Hey – what's that over there?'

You can, if you choose to, include stage directions. Also, in a short introduction,
you can describe the set and give some background details to the characters.

WHY DID YOU LIE TO ME?

You have two characters on stage. One of them, a boy, is lying on his bed reading
a book. A girl enters and stares at the boy. The boy does not notice her. She moves
back as if to go away, but decides to stay. As she whispers 'Why did you lie to me?'
the boy is startled. Write down their conversation with stage directions from here.

RECORDING DRAMAS

These are to be done in pairs and do not have to be recorded, but if they are, you
could do a transcript of your recording and rework it into a short piece. Below are
some scenarios for you to act out. Or, you could use some of the opening lines
from 'Starting points' above. And why not do some of your own?

- Two people find themselves locked in a theatre overnight.
- On a very hot afternoon, a lift in a department store gets stuck between two floors. The
  two people in the lift have never met before but very quickly discover that they do not like
  each other.
- Two strangers are sitting next to each other on a plane. One suffers from vertigo.

SCENES FROM SOAPS

What is your favourite soap opera? Write some short scenes using characters from
the programme. You can use one of the following scenarios or write your own.

- One of the characters has been away for a few days. The person went off without telling
  anyone where they were going. In the scene you will write, two characters are talking to
  the one that has been away and are trying to find out where they have been. Think the scene
  through for a while before you write anything. Also think about the characters' personalities,
  the way that they speak and the type of language (words, phrases) that they use.
- Much of the drama in soap operas is based around the family. In your scene, imagine one
  character has done something to disgrace their family. First choose a character or family –
  then decide what they have done. In your scene write a confrontation between that character
  and other members of the family. You could start off with just two characters, and then
  perhaps you could bring in other family members.

BEGIN WITH A BOOK

Malorie Blackman talks here about adapting a novel into a television drama series. Malorie has adapted some of her own books into television series, including *Whizziwig* and *Pig-heart Boy*:

MALORIE BLACKMAN: How do you adapt a novel? You use the novel as a starting point. It's fatal to get too hung up on trying to use every single word and detail from a book. Television and books are totally different media, and that's the first thing you have to realise. With *Pig-heart Boy*, I put the novel to one side and started afresh thinking, 'Okay, I've got to write six episodes'. And with the television script of *Pig-heart Boy* I begin the story further back in Cameron's life.

With television drama you have to turn everything – all the events in a book – into something that can be either seen and/or heard. So much of what happens in the novel of *Pig-heart Boy* is going on in Cameron's head – his thoughts and feelings – so you have to think, how am I going to present that on the screen? How will I show that in a visual way? The convention I use for the TV drama is that Cameron talks directly into a camcorder, which, on the TV screen will look as if he's talking directly to the viewer. Whereas with the book, being in the first person, it's as if Cameron's talking directly to the reader. So I had to find a way of achieving the same thing – that intimacy – and the camcorder approach is absolutely perfect for that. Also, with children's TV, you have to keep the momentum going. Whereas in a book you can have two people talking for a whole chapter, you can't do that on TV – it would quickly get very boring.

My advice for writing drama? What I try to do is to imagine the story as a film or TV programme running in my head. I think to myself – what is the camera seeing? Where are the characters? What time of day is it? And as you watch this going on in your head you have to record what the characters are saying.

Choose a book that you like and know very well. Think about how you could turn it into either a television drama or a play for the stage. To start off, read the opening to the book. How could you adapt that? If it was to be a TV drama, what would the opening scene look like? What would the camera be showing the viewer? As Malorie Blackman says, books and television are very different media and you may need to make many changes. Would you go straight into an event or have a slow introduction, perhaps with the camera following or observing a character or even showing the setting for the drama? You could first organise the plot as a story board, a series of images like a comic strip.

If it is to be a stage play, what would the set look like? How many characters would you have on stage for your opening? Would it start at the same place as the book, or would you need to write a new scene to introduce your characters?

A VISITOR FROM ONE HUNDRED YEARS AGO

Imagine a character who has a dream in which she or he meets an ancestor who died exactly one hundred years before.

What would they want to ask each other? How different would they be? How would they react to each other? This is not a ghost or horror story – the ancestor will seem as real as your present-day character. And for once, this will be a piece in which your character will wake up and it will all have been a dream! Write your stage directions alongside the dialogue. What props – other than the bed in the bedroom – will you include on the stage?

THE MONOLOGUE

This is a performance or a text in which there is just one character, who will talk often about aspects of their life, their experiences, interests, observations or problems. One of the benefits of writing a monologue is that you don't have to worry about a plot. Nothing *has* to happen at all. You just have one character that talks. However, you have to know that character very well, you have to get to know their voice, their mannerisms, their way of speaking – and what they say has to have a purpose. Most monologues give an insight into the personality of the character. Also, like conversation, the monologue will no doubt drift from one subject to another, but there will usually be a central thread running through, one theme or subject that the character will keep returning to and discussing.

It does not matter whether you like your character or not, what is vital is that what they say is of interest to your audience. Here are a few starting points for writing a monologue:

- Your narrator has kept a secret for a few years, but now they are going to reveal all – but gradually as it is difficult to talk about.
- Your narrator is someone who loves complaining about everything.
- Pick a narrator talking about their job: a ticket inspector on a train, an ice-cream vendor, a vet, a police officer or a dentist.

Or begin with an opening line, and get to know your narrator as you write:

- 'It all started the day I met . . .'
- 'It was one of those times when I didn't know whether to laugh or cry. I just stood there and . . .'

(Also see monologue activity at the end of Jacqueline Wilson's discussion of her play *The Dare Game* on pp. 122–3.)

Narration and point of view: writing in the first and third person

In fiction there are two main forms of narration:

First person, in which one person tells the story, an 'I'. For example:

> *'It all began last year when I met . . .'*

> *'I'm going to tell you this story because I can't keep it a secret any longer . . .'*

Third person, when someone unknown is telling the story. Characters in the story are referred to as 'he' or 'she' or by their names. For example:

> *'She couldn't remember a single thing about the dream, but she knew that . . .'*

> *'Joe heard another scream out in the hallway. He ran to the door and . . .'*

Narration and the point of view of a story are very much linked together. Every story is told from one or a number of points of view. A first person story is told from the point of view of a single person, that is, the narrator of the story. Everything that comes into the story is communicated by that person, so as readers we are limited to that individual's viewpoint, knowledge and experience. Even if we are reading dialogue, it is there because the narrator has decided to tell us about it.

In the third person, a story can be told from one, two or even a whole number of viewpoints. The third person is the oldest, most traditional form of narration. Think of fairy tales – 'Once upon a time there was a . . .'. Find two books that are written in the third person and see which point(s) of view they are told from.

One of the most important decisions you can make about a story is whether to write in the first or third person. Your choice of narration will affect how the story is told and, as a result, the way the reader responds to the story. Sometimes a writer makes a decision – 'This story ought to be in the third person because –', and at other times, will just begin writing in whatever voice – first or third – comes to mind.

Some writers avoid the limitations of one point of view by having two different first person narrators; see how imaginatively this is done in Malorie Blackman's *Tell Me No Lies* or Jacqueline Wilson's *Double Act* and *The Lottie Project*. Another way is to include letters, postcards or diary extracts written by other characters, as in *P.S. Longer Letter Later: A Novel in Letters* and *Snailmail No More: A Novel by E-Mail* by Paula Danzinger and Ann M. Martin and also *Billy's Drift* by Charles Ashton. (See 'Epistolary' workshop on p. 145.)

Most writers believe that the third person gives you more freedom. Unlike the first person, you do not have to stick with one character telling the story, and you can tell your story from many points of view.

> **GILLIAN CROSS:** Most of my novels are in the third person – but close to a character's point of view. I always imagine that I'm a particular person looking at the scene. But I don't always keep to the same point of view throughout the book. For example, in most of the *Demon Headmaster* books, it's alternately Dinah and Lloyd.

In addition to this, third person allows you to write not only what your characters are saying, but also what they are thinking.

These authors enjoy the 'freedom' and 'flexibility' that the third person can offer:

> **ANTHONY MASTERS:** I prefer writing in the third person because I like 'playing god' as I'm such a control freak. The third person also gives me freedom with the language I want to use, and gives me access to the different experiences of the various characters. The first person is like tunnel vision and it's limiting because you are restricted to the language, knowledge and experience of your narrator.

> **PHILIP PULLMAN:** I like the third person voice because I like swooping in and drawing back, and giving a panoramic view – in the same way a film camera does. I like directing the story as one would direct a film.

> **MORRIS GLEITZMAN:** I didn't ever consciously choose to write in the third. When I started writing books I wrote in the third person because that's the one that most books tend to be written in. I then realised that I didn't want to ever write in the first person unless I had a really good reason to. When I wrote the *Blabber Mouth* trilogy I decided that the stories would involve Rowena Batts talking in her own head, in an interior monologue. First person seemed appropriate to these books. Now I've got to the stage where I think I could write any book either in the first or third person, and that it wouldn't hugely alter the story.
>
>   With the third person I can vary the degree to which we experience every moment, every thought, every feeling with the central character. Or, I can vary the degree to which I pull back slightly and do a bit of summarising. There's more flexibility in the third person. Sometimes you can show an event in real time, and there'd be five minutes of the character's life in such detail that it takes fifteen minutes to read. And then, in the next chapter or paragraph or sentence you can cover five days of their life. You can do that in the first person too, but there's

slightly more flexibility in the third. When I've used first person with *Belly Flop* and the *Blabber Mouth* trilogy those stories are both told as internal monologues, directed at the reader, and that's why I've used it.

Berlie Doherty and Alan Durant enjoy the first person because of the intimacy with the narrator:

BERLIE DOHERTY: With the first person narration, you get to know your characters better. And I prefer writing in the first person, I think. It helps me to get inside a character.

ALAN DURANT: When I write in the first person I get more involved, because I am that character, and in a way that keeps my interest going. Third person, I feel, is more difficult. If I was writing a novel in the third person I might lose interest a bit because I wasn't the character, I was just observing the character. First person is much more immediate for me, and it keeps me going. I find it easier to sustain than third person.

Workshop activities: narration and point of view

NARRATION: EARLY MEMORY

Think back to an early memory, one that you have not thought about for a long time. Spend a couple of minutes going over the details of that event. Now, write it down in your own voice and in your own language, just as the memory comes to you. All you need is a few paragraphs, but write more if you want to. Sometime later, go back to the piece and rewrite it in the third person. So, instead of 'I' you will write either your name or 'he' did this or 'she' did that. When you have completed the piece, ask yourself:

- Which was easier to write?
- Which felt more natural to write?
- Which do you prefer?
- Were there things you could do in the third person and not in the first and vice versa?

POINT OF VIEW: FAIRY TALES

All traditional fairy tales are written in the third person. Some modern versions have started to retell fairy tales in the first person and from the point of view of one of the characters in the story; one well-known example is Jon Sciezka's *The True Story of the Three Little Pigs by A. Wolf*. Try one of these or think of one of your own:

- *Jack and the Beanstalk* from the giant's point of view
- *Hansel and Gretel* from Gretel's point of view
- *Cinderella* from one of the two sisters' points of view
- *Beauty and the Beast* from the beast's point of view.

When you have finished, think:

- Does it affect the story? If so, how?
- Does it seem unusual? Why?
- Does it work?

Places and descriptive writing

Stories tend to have fewer and shorter descriptions of people or places nowadays – as authors concentrate more on storytelling and creating interesting characters and situations.

Looking at prose styles

When you are writing your own descriptive passages, try and be as original as you can without going over the top. Think of interesting similes and metaphors and adjectives that you could use. Look at these two sentences:

> *The sea was nice. The sky was beautiful.*

These sentences actually tell us very little. Why was the sea nice? What was beautiful about the sky? As a rule, adjectives like 'nice' and 'beautiful' are greatly overused and are best avoided! An unoriginal or overused phrase or description is known as a cliché. Here is an example of a cliché:

> *The beautiful blue sky was full of cotton wool clouds.*

Instead, you could try something like:

> *A platoon of clouds marched across the ice-blue sky.*

This phrase has an unusual but powerful metaphor – that of a 'platoon' of clouds marching. And the second part of the sentence gives the reader a vivid description of the sky with just two simple words – 'ice-blue'.

Aim to be creative but also specific with your descriptions. So rather than saying something like 'the man walked down the street' – you might want to consider how the man was walking. Think – is there a better way to describe his action? You could use an adverb – 'the man walked *swiftly* down the street' – or better still, you could use a more expressive and descriptive verb – 'the man *hurried* down the street'.

The following passage is from the classic early twentieth-century novel *The Wind in the Willows* by Kenneth Grahame, and demonstrates a very poetic style of description. At this point in the novel, Ratty and Mole are walking through a snow-covered village. As you read this extract, look out for the metaphors, alliteration and assonance.

> *The rapid nightfall of mid-December had quite beset the little village as they approached it on soft feet over a first thin fall of powdery snow. Little was visible but squares of a dusky orange-red on either side of the street, where the firelight or lamplight of each cottage overflowed through the casements into the dark world without. Most of the low latticed windows were innocent of blinds, and to the lookers-in from outside, the inmates, gathered round the tea-table, absorbed in handiwork, or talking with laughter and gesture, had each that happy grace which is the last thing the skilled actor shall capture – the natural grace which goes with perfect unconsciousness of observation. Moving at will from one theatre to another, the two spectators, so far from home themselves, had something of wistfulness in their eyes as they watched a cat being stroked, a sleepy child picked up and huddled off to bed, or a tired man stretch and knock out his pipe on the end of a smouldering log.*

Some authors, for example Helen Cresswell, write their prose as if it were poetry:

HELEN CRESSWELL: Although I don't do drafts as such, I will spend a long time on certain passages, polishing them as if they were a poem. I did that with *The Bongleweed* in the section where the plant takes over the graveyard. I think of my major fantasies – like *The Piemakers*, *The Night-Watchmen*, *The Bongleweed* – as almost being poetry. Those books were written in the same kind of process. It was as if my poetry skills were still there, even though I hadn't written poetry for a while. In fact, I would say that some of my best descriptive passages are in *The Bongleweed*. This is one of them:

> *The flowers were brimful with sunlight, suffused with it so that each individual blossom seemed itself to be a source of faint, glowing light. The heads were alive, they sniffed the wind like pale, fluorescent foxes.*

> (Helen Cresswell – *The Bongleweed*: Oxford University Press)

Here, two authors reflect upon their prose styles:

MALORIE BLACKMAN: I've tried writing metaphoric and descriptive prose, but it doesn't ring true for me. Though I do love reading lyrical poetry and evocative prose myself. I guess I write in a straightforward, down-to-earth way because that's the kind of person I am. If I've got something to say, I'll just say it, and get on with it. I have tried changing my style and being more lyrical, but when I read it back I get a bit bored with it! And I always think that if I'm bored reading it, my readers are going to be bored too. However, I hope I don't write every book in the same style. But I have found what works best for me – which is getting to the point and getting on with the story.

GILLIAN CROSS: The main quality I aim to achieve in my prose is that it's invisible – I want it not to interfere with the story. I don't want the reader to be conscious of my language – though I think that this approach can make me too conservative and not as daring as I ought to be. I don't want people to read something I've written and think, 'What beautiful prose this is!' I just want them to be thinking about the story.

As Philip Pullman says, prose can be more of a challenge to write than dialogue:

PHILIP PULLMAN: When you're writing a story, the dialogue is easy to write. It's just a question of writing down what the characters in your head are saying. Narrative prose is much harder. You have to choose just the right words to tell the story with.

Melvin Burgess comments that you should 'write in a clear, lucid way so it is easily understood. This is the essence of good writing.' The opening to his novel *The Cry of the Wolf* demonstrates how direct and simple yet very striking Melvin Burgess's own prose style is. Notice in the introduction below that he does not use any long words or complicated phrases, but concentrates on painting a picture using everyday words:

> *Ben Tilley lay on the banks of the River Mole keeping very quiet. It was a still, hot day. The river moved silently below him and around him in the grass there were tiny rustlings and scratchings from insects about their business. A robin was singing nearby and the sun beat down, baking into his back, pressing him into the dry mud. Ben could quite easily have fallen asleep if he had not been so excited.*

> (Melvin Burgess – *The Cry of the Wolf*: Puffin)

Melvin Burgess further believes in being economical with words:

MELVIN BURGESS: You should never use two words where you can use one. And never use a long word where a short word will do.

Morris Gleitzman advises that you should 'stick mostly to the words you use when you talk to your friends. The trick is to bung them together in new and exciting ways.'

Two further important issues to consider with your prose style are:

- using sentences of varying lengths
- not repeating the same words or phrases too often. If you find yourself doing this, a dictionary or thesaurus may help.

CELIA REES: Sentences can stretch and shorten depending on the mood and subject and events of a story. Short, sharp sentences – and even sentences of just one or two words – can be good for anger or for sudden events, for slowing a story right down or building up suspense. Long sentences are generally more suitable for detailed descriptions. Very long sentences can be hard to follow and are best avoided.

(For a further example of descriptive writing, see the workshop activity 'Painting animals with words' on p. 185.)

Writing about places

Writers spend far less time now describing the various settings in fiction than they used to and will only fully portray a place – be it a room, hallway or park or wherever – if it is relevant to the story in some way. And generally speaking, a story in the first person – that is, a story told by one narrator – will have fewer descriptions than a story in the third person. Exceptions to this rule are when a place is either significant to the narrator or to the story they are telling, or it says something about that narrator – that they are the type of person for whom detail and descriptions are important. In the main, writing in the third person can lend itself to more detailed and descriptive passages. (See extracts from *The Wind in the Willows* above and *Blood Sinister* below.) Also, fiction in the first person does not tend to use as many poetic devices as in the third person because the prose will be mainly in the everyday language of the narrator. However, there are many exceptions, which would include Berlie Doherty's *Daughter of the Sea* and David Almond's *Kit's Wilderness*.

When writing about a place, try not to think only in terms of the visual aspects of the setting – call upon the other senses too. Take a room, for example. What does the room smell of – and are there a variety of smells? What sounds are in the room – a clock ticking, a creaking floorboard – or is it totally silent? Are there noises outside – a road drill or a train rushing past? Is the room warm or cold – and is it warmer by the window where the sun comes in? What are the textures of various items in the room – the carpet, the chair, the cushions, and so on. As Morris Gleitzman suggests, 'Let your readers see, hear, smell, taste and touch your story'. And as Anthony Masters encourages, when you are writing a descriptive passage, close your eyes occasionally and imagine the setting in your mind's eye as vividly as you can.

Next, three authors discuss the issue of place in their work. After each discussion follows a short passage from one of their titles:

MALORIE BLACKMAN: Unless it's got direct relevance to the plot, I don't tend to describe places – I let the reader use their imagination. One exception would be *Thief!* Because the book is set in the future I needed to put details into the story to make that world seem futuristic. And it was great, because I could make it all up, such as with the tunnels and the mood wallpaper. Usually, I'll give just enough detail so that the reader will know the setting and where the events are taking place. However, if I feel that a room or a place reflects the personality or the mood of a character in some way, I will describe it. Otherwise, people have to fill in the details themselves when they're reading my books. Generally, I'm not one of those people that likes spending fifteen pages on describing a sunset, I like to get on with the story!

Lydia put out her hand to steady herself. Out of the corner of her eyes Lydia saw the wallpaper around her slowly begin to change colour. She turned around and stared at it. The wallpaper had been a pale pink colour but now it was turning into a deep, sun-yellow.

(Malorie Blackman – *Thief!*: Transworld)

ANTHONY MASTERS: Sense of place is probably *the* most important aspect of my work. To an extent, I don't care what the story is, just so long as it is powerful and atmospheric and introspective. As a reader myself, I want to be in another world – I want to step outside the boundaries of my own life and I want total immersion. For me, a sense of place is often the ultimate driving force of a book.

Miserably, Terry gazed around the room. It was a kitchen containing a few badly burnt bits of furniture – a table, some chairs, a couple of wall cupboards, a partly broken mirror and a singed calendar with a picture of a large house, its smooth lawns running down to a lake.

The walls were black and peeling and the ceiling was bubbled and scarred. The calendar was headed:

English Country Homes and Gardens
1965

All the scorched surfaces in the room were covered with a thick coating of dust, which clearly had not been disturbed for a long time.

(Anthony Masters – *Ghost Blades*: Mammoth–Egmont)

CELIA REES: Place is fundamental to my work. For me, it's one of the most important elements. I need to have a strong sense of place in my books – it's one of the areas that lends novels realism. When, like me, you're working within genres that are inherently unreal, say horror or the supernatural or even a thriller, you need to tack it into a reality. A strong sense of place will give it just that, and makes it possible, believable, which is vital. I always have an actual place in mind when I'm writing – even down to small locations like bus stops or shops. Everywhere is a real place. But it will get changed as I fictionalise it. I hope I give my reader a sense of a real place but also something they can relate to. With each new place that my characters go to, I put a brief description in, but I choose places common to anywhere, so they can fill in the rest of the details themselves. I put in a few pointers, and they'll know what a McDonald's or a school hall is like. I think long descriptions put young readers off, so I keep them short.

> *Whatever its original purpose, the room had been transformed from the last time I'd seen it . . . Oil lamps and candles compensate for the lack of natural light and cast a suffused glow over everything. Richly patterned carpets adorn the floors and walls, a heavy brocaded curtain, encrusted with gold and silver thread, cordons off the sleeping quarters. The more public area contains comfortable chairs and sofas. A beautifully carved table holds an exquisite chess set.*
>
> (Celia Rees – *Blood Sinister*: Scholastic)

Celia Rees adds that researching a place is important:

CELIA REES: Every story has to have a setting, a place where things happen. Make sure you know that place well. Make it real in your head by mapping it and collecting pictures, photographs and postcards of the actual place or places like it. The more real the setting, the more believable the story.

In contrast to the authors above, Morris Gleitzman believes that by not describing the settings in his books in great detail, he is empowering his readers:

MORRIS GLEITZMAN: My books have very little description at all – which leaves a lot of space for readers to fill in.

Workshop activities: places and descriptive writing

NO ADJECTIVES
Write a short descriptive piece about a place you know very well without using any adjectives. If you get really stuck, you are allowed to use two – but in different sentences.

NO LOOKING
Describe a place – a room, a house, a building, anywhere – that you know well. Describe it in terms of senses other than sight. Imagine you are walking around that place with your eyes closed. Concentrate on smell and feel and sound. What are the different smells you come across? What are the different textures you can feel? What sounds are there? If it was a kitchen there could be a kettle boiling, cars driving past outside the window or a radio playing in the background. For this activity you might choose to use a combination of your own, everyday language as well as some interesting metaphors and similes. You could even write this piece in the first person and in the present continuous tense – for example, 'It is the middle of the night and I am walking around . . .' or 'It is Friday afternoon and I am walking around the market in . . .'

INVISIBLE SOUNDSCAPES

(Adapted from a poetry workshop by Colin Macfarlane.) Go outside. Close your eyes. What can you hear? The more you listen, the more your ears will begin to pick up the smallest of sounds. Keep a notebook with you and make a list of the sounds every now and then. You could even compare what can be heard at different times of the day. Think of imaginative ways of describing what you can hear. You could use metaphors ('The wind is breathless, gasping in my ear'), similes ('The train beats past like a stuttering drum') or alliteration ('branches bristle in the breeze') and assonance ('more cars roar by'). If your piece of writing wants to become a poem, then let it – and you could even do a verse for each sound. You might even end up with a piece that is a cross between prose and a poem.

OPPOSITE SNAPSHOTS

Think of a place in your mind's eye and take a snapshot of it. What would the opposite of that scene be? If you picked a busy beach on a hot summer's day, one opposite might be the same beach deserted and bleak on Christmas Day. Another scene might be that of a bridge in a city that crosses a river. One snapshot of it might be at 9 a.m. in the morning with pedestrians, cars and buses rushing off to various destinations. An opposite for this might be the same bridge but at night, and it is snowing, with only the occasional car or person crossing. Find two opposites for your place and write about them. Get your ideas down first. Do not worry about your words and phrasing. In a second draft go back and particularly look at how you can improve your phrasing and give the reader the best image possible. Use imaginative similes and metaphors as well as alliteration and assonance.

SETTING FOR A GHOST STORY

Teacher-led activity. Here Berlie Doherty talks about a workshop that she has done in schools. Read the passage and then write your own ghost story. Begin the piece with an atmospheric description of the place where the story is set.

BERLIE DOHERTY: In a workshop we might start off with a kind of brainstorm where we talk about the place we're going to set a story in. This would be with 9 or 10 year olds. And perhaps we'd be going to write a ghost story. I like to tell the children that I like to know the landscape that I'm writing about. Then I ask them if they can think of anywhere they know which might be suitable – and they'll all know somewhere, it might be a disused railway station or a shop that's all boarded up or a big house. And then we'd describe the place, talk about it. And I then give them ten minutes to write about it with all the sounds and smells and all the things they can feel, using all their senses. We're not going into a story yet, we're just writing about the place.

PLACES: SNAPSHOTS

Spend time looking at the three photographs (Figures 3.9, 3.10 and 3.11). Make notes on them. Choose the one that interests you the most. Write a piece or a story that begins and finishes with a description of that place. Or, find a story that will link two or three of these settings together.

Figure 3.9 Photograph of beach by Rob Vincent

Figure 3.11 Photograph of cottage by Rob Vincent

Figure 3.10 Photograph of city at night by Rob Vincent

Plot: a sequence of events

Otherwise known as the storyline, plot is the sequence or series of events that happen in a fictional story – be it in a film, television soap opera, cartoon, play, novel, short story, comic strip or picture book. Put another way, the plot is the bare bones of a story, a story pared down to its most basic parts. Consider how the plot to the fairy tale Hansel and Gretel might begin:

> *Hansel and Gretel's parents can't afford to keep their children any longer so they try to lose them in the wood. The children come back and once again the parents . . .*

This is not the story as such. The story, with all the incidental details and dialogue included – the details that make the tale exciting and engaging and much longer – might begin:

> *Once upon a time there were a man and woman who lived in a cottage on the edge of a wood. They had two children – a boy called Hansel and a girl called Gretel. Times were hard and the man had no work. One night, after Hansel and Gretel had gone to bed, the man and the woman sat by the fire talking.*
> *'We have no food left,' said the woman. 'The children will have to go.'*

Writers have their own individual ways of finding plots.

MALORIE BLACKMAN: I tend to get the storyline or plot first, then I think about the people in the story. And I play 'what if' games. For example,

'What if a girl goes into the future and meets herself as a grown up?' (*Thief!*)
'What if a boy and his sister have to prove their dad didn't steal one million pounds from the bank where he works?' (*Hacker*)
'What if a boy and his friend get involved in a dare game which goes horribly wrong and one of them goes missing?' (*Deadly Dare*)

So, I'm always wondering 'What if, what if . . .' and then I find a plot. With all of my books I try to build up my novels to a climax where each incident is the direct result of something which happened previously and inevitably leads to something else – usually worse!

Some writers seem to be more motivated by writing about their characters' feelings and situations rather than actually working out a plot for their characters – see 'Characters' section. Yet Celia Rees is interested in both:

CELIA REES: I'm as concerned with plot as I am with character. When you write for young people, you have to have a strong plot. Equally, you've got to have believable characters that your readers can care about – particularly if you're writing in the genres that I do. Otherwise, you wouldn't care if the characters were killed or whatever. You've got to care about them and you can only do that by developing credible characters within a strong plot. And plot, for me, has got to work and have an internal logic. There can't be any boggy areas where nothing much is happening, or any loose ends that don't make sense. There's got to be a coherent sequence of events that work by cause and effect – a knock on from one to the other. You have to be able to see that *this* happened because of *that*. You have to be able to look forwards and backwards at any point.

A story cannot simply contain non-stop action or the reader would lose interest eventually. Quieter moments are necessary as you do not want a book equivalent of a car chase going on all the way through your story! Some dynamics – a balance of busy and quieter moments – are important.

Most novels will have a series of plots – perhaps a main plot and a minor subplot, or a number of subplots. But in a short story, as David Almond commented in the 'Short story' section earlier in this chapter, there is no room really for much more than a single main plot.

However, it is only too easy to worry about the plot, and to lose sight of what you are trying to achieve. A storyline, as Philip Pullman advises, does not need to be a complex chain of events and should ideally be kept as simple and as straightforward as possible. If you are worried about writing a plot or storyline – as Celia Rees suggested earlier – why not begin by writing some short pieces that focus on one single event or character, and you may find that a plot develops out of one of these. Philip Pullman has his own unique way of describing the process of choosing the events for a story:

PHILIP PULLMAN: With a story, you have a path and a wood. The wood is the world of the story – everything that could possibly happen to all the characters. The path is the story itself that goes through the wood – and some things happen and some things don't. But with every turn in the path something else could have happened. Cinderella could have thought, 'Stuff it, I don't want to go to the ball at all'. Or, the ugly sisters could have said, 'All right, Cinderella, come to the ball'. All sorts of things could have happened. You need to know many more details about the fictional world you have created than you will actually tell in your story. So it is the role of the storyteller to decide which path to take – that is, which details to include and which to discard.

Russell Hoban says that 'what happens next' is 'the essence of story'. The 'what happens next' – that is, whatever the chain of events in the story will be – is for the writer to work out and the reader to wonder and to enjoy. As a writer, you want your reader to be interested in your story and to anticipate what the next event will be. Now imagine you have a character, and that character is called Tom, and your story begins 'Tom awoke one morning to find . . .'. Well – what will happen next? You are in control of your story and it is up to you what you do with Tom. Is Tom going to find out that it's only 4 a.m. – so he goes back to sleep? Or, is he going to find two pairs of eyes peering at him? Or, is he going to find himself in a strange place that he doesn't recognise? It is your decision – you have invented your characters, and you must decide what you want to do with them, and how you will entertain your reader. One way is to inject suspense in your story, which is dealt with later in this chapter.

Here, Philip Pullman explains how he works out the plot for a novel:

PHILIP PULLMAN: I use those Post-it notes – the smallest yellow ones. I use them for planning the shape of a story. I'll write a brief sentence summarising a scene on one of them, and then I'll get a very big piece of paper and fill it up with sixty or more different scenes, and move them around to get them in the best order . . . I have pictures in my mind like daydreams. Like dreams, they can stay with me. If they're good, they will keep coming back. Such ideas can come unexpectedly and stay with me for a long time. For the *Northern Lights* trilogy, I had a whole series of images. My task was to discover how I could connect each of these images together and to find the narrative thread that joins all the images together – a story to connect the pictures. The only way I can do this is by sitting down and working the whole thing out.

Jan Dean has some useful advice on checking if the plot of a story is working well. Like Philip Pullman, she describes plot as a 'path':

JAN DEAN: Once you've written a story it is often a good idea to look at the plot by dividing your story up into its key scenes. A plot is like a path. You don't want it to meander too much. You want it to be reasonably straight, though you might want a few surprises along the way – something that jumps out at you. Do a storyboard, a series of simple pictures, and break the story up into its scenes. If you've got lost with your story, this can help you to see where you have gone wrong. If you want to, you can even do a storyboard as a plan for your story before you write it out. Whenever I write a book, I think: which are the bits that people will really want to read? So I look at my key scenes and work out how I can tell the story so that I can get as quickly and as neatly as possible from one scene to another. Try and imagine your plot as a series of beads on a string.

Most stories – whether deliberately or not – follow a set pattern. This pattern or formula can be divided into four parts (adapted from Peter Abbs and John Richardson's *The Forms of Narrative*):

OPENING – COMPLICATION – CLIMAX – CONCLUSION

Every fairy tale follows this pattern. Consider 'Cinderella':

OPENING: Cinderella lives with her two bullying sisters.

COMPLICATION: All three sisters receive an invitation to the ball. The two sisters insist that Cinderella cannot attend as she does not have a suitable ball gown.

CLIMAX: Cinderella goes to the ball thanks to her fairy godmother, but forgets that the magic wears off by midnight. As the clock strikes twelve she flees the ball, dropping her glass slipper on the steps outside.

CONCLUSION: The prince that Cinderella had been dancing with finds Cinderella's slipper. After scouring the region many times, the prince finds that Cinderella is the true owner of the slipper and they consequently marry.

Think of books or short stories that you have read recently. Do they follow this pattern? Write out the basic plot of some of the stories in terms of Opening – Complication – Climax – Conclusion. Then invent a few of your own plots with this model – using the worksheet 'Plot overviews'.

PLOT OVERVIEWS

Write out a few plots that follow this structure. Start with an everyday situation in which everything in your fictional world is fine – a man is reading a newspaper on a park bench, a family are eating their tea, a teacher is talking to a class, and then go from there. When you have a plot structure that you like, write out the story in full.

O P E N I N G:

C O M P L I C A T I O N:

C L I M A X:

C O N C L U S I O N:

Workshop activities: plot

SCENARIOS

Read through the following scenarios and decide which one you would like to develop into a full story. Think to yourself – how should I start? Should this scenario open the story or appear later on?

- *Empty Pocket* – A person has something – an object – in their pocket at all times, day and night. It is extremely important to them. That object goes missing.
- *Window Gazing* – A person is gazing through a window at something that they need or want. Who is that person? Why do they want it? Will they get it? Where is the window?
- *The Waiting Room* – A person is waiting to meet someone that they have not seen for a long time. Who are these two people? Why have they not seen each other for so long?
- *Escape* – Someone is getting on a train/bus/coach/plane/boat. They are escaping from someone or something.
- *Lost and Found* – Someone is lost somewhere. They do not know where they are or how they got there. Who is this person? Where are they? Why do they not know? How will they return home?

WHAT IF

Write stories for one of these scenarios:

- What if . . . someone is travelling on a train and overhears two people in the seat behind plotting a terrible crime?
- What if . . . someone walks through the car park of a railway station – and as they enter the ticket office they walk into the past?
- What if . . . someone was granted three wishes?

DREAM WORLDS

Here is Malorie Blackman talking about adapting her dreams into stories :

> **MALORIE BLACKMAN:** With my first short story collection, *Not So Stupid!*, I used my dreams as starting points. One or two of the dreams were full stories, and all I had to do was to remember them and write them down. With others, like 'Such are the Times', I had a dream about rain being so acidic it would dissolve the flesh off your body. I used that as a starting point. I thought, 'Okay, what would the rain do to people?' As ever, I was playing a 'What if . . .?' game. I was thinking about what would happen to the character if *this* happened, and if *that* went wrong, *then* what would she do? And so on. I'm always trying to escalate events in a story. But with short stories, it's a tighter framework, and there's not so much room to expand your story.

For a week, write down your dreams as you wake up. Choose one event from a dream and use it as the basis for a short story.

OUT OF ORDER

With a partner write a few scenes for a short story. Do this in note form first of all. Then either write a brief summary on strips of paper or yellow Post-it notes or draw them in the form of a storyboard. If you choose the storyboard approach, cut out your individual scenes. Now, move either the strips of paper/Post-it notes/

storyboard pictures around, changing the order of the scenes. Find the sequence that works best for a story. Do not worry if some scenes have to be removed.

STORY MAPPING

See the worksheets 'Story mapping 1' and 'Story mapping 2' on pp. 84–5 for further ways of discovering plots.

PICTURE THIS

On the worksheet 'Picture this', the artwork has been generously donated by the illustrators Jilly Wilkinson (Figure 3.12), Peter Bailey (Figure 3.13) and Ian Beck (Figure 3.14). Ian Beck's illustration © Ian Beck 1993. Taken from *Tom and the Island of Dinosaurs* by Ian Beck, published by Doubleday, a division of Transworld Publishers. All rights reserved.

PICTURE THIS

Look closely at the pictures by Jilly Wilkinson, Peter Bailey and Ian Beck.
Grow a story around one of these. Where will this event in the picture occur in
your story? Spend time thinking about your plot before you write. Or, find a
story that will link two or three of these images together.

Figure 3.12 Illustration by Jilly
Wilkinson

Figure 3.13 Illustration by Peter Bailey

Figure 3.14 Illustration by Ian Beck

Suspense and atmosphere: engaging the reader

Here Philip Pullman talks about the role of suspense in fiction:

PHILIP PULLMAN: It really does help to know that surprise is the precise opposite of suspense. Surprise is when something happens that you don't expect: suspense is when something doesn't happen that you do expect. Surprise is when you open a cupboard and a body falls out. Suspense is when you know there's a body in the cupboard – but not which cupboard. So you open the first door and . . . no, not that one. And up goes the suspense a notch.

Suspense can occur in any form of story – be it a novel, film, play or TV drama – when the tension is being built up. As Philip Pullman says, suspense is when the reader/viewer knows that something is going to happen. It is the build-up to a climax, a moment in which something horrifying, alarming, unusual, frightening, whatever, is going to take place. At these times the events or the action in the story will slow down and the reader/viewer will read/watch the event taking place in something close to real time. As a writer, suspense is one of the most effective tools that you have to engage, grip and excite your reader. Just occasionally, you might choose to have an anti-climax: you will build the tension up only to reveal that there was nothing to worry about – the strange noise outside was actually a cat or the banging against the window was simply a branch.

Celia Rees concentrates on how her reader will respond:

CELIA REES: Most fiction relies on suspense to make the reader actually carry on reading. As a reader myself, I read to find out what is going to happen. As a writer I do exactly the same, I impel the reader to find out what will happen in the story. For me, suspense is all about setting up a series of problems and then slowly answering them. My advice would be not to give away too much too soon – to pace the story slowly and subtly. Think of how you would feel if you were the reader of your story. What would scare or interest or intrigue you?

Atmosphere – often connected with suspense – is all about letting the reader know how it feels to be in a certain place at a certain time. For this you will need to picture your setting clearly in your mind's eye and then choose your words and phrases very carefully. Consider all the senses that you might call upon – sight, sound, feel and smell. Describe the weather too – the wind, fog, snow or rain – as well as the heat or the cold and also the quality of the light – is it bright, dim or totally dark? (For ideas on writing about settings, please refer to the 'Places and descriptive writing' section.)

Celia Rees says that atmosphere stems from clear and vivid descriptions:

CELIA REES: With atmosphere, you need to learn how to describe well, and to use every sense. And it's a case of 'showing' and not 'telling'. You can't just 'tell' the reader directly 'It was very scary in the house'. You have to do much more than that, and 'show' by describing the place in detail – how it looks, feels, sounds and so on. You have to discipline yourself into writing detailed descriptions of places. Usually, you'll write too much, so you'll have to select what you want to keep and edit out what you don't need. Think of what kind of mood you are trying to create, and foreground those details that will achieve that.

Anthony Masters reveals that aspects of his dreams are a source of ideas for writing atmospheric and evocative prose:

ANTHONY MASTERS: Some ideas come from my dreams. I dream an awful lot and I keep a dream diary. I'll wake up after a particularly emotive dream and try to write down as much as I can. It will all go otherwise. I dream in the same way that I write. The dreams are very impressionistic and are to do with landscape sense of place and are generally the beginnings of narratives. Aspects of my books come from dreams. The surreal sequence at the beginning of *The Dark Side of the Brain* from the Weird World series comes from one of my dreams:

> *Tim jumped as high as he could, punched the ball out of the goal and hit his head hard on the post.*
>
> *A dark tunnel raced towards him. Inside were a few brightly coloured stars, but they soon faded away and he felt himself plunging down a sharp incline into a pit where a black sea foamed. Silvery waves crashed on a deserted shore, burnt out in sharp relief like a photographic negative. A high-pitched whine filled his ears and a creature, half dog, half lion, loped across the charcoal beach. Familiar and unfamiliar voices called out and strange birds flew over Tim's head with trowel-like beaks and scraping transparent wings.*
>
> (Anthony Masters – *The Dark Side of the Brain*: Weird World series, Bloomsbury, p. 5)

In fact, all of the Weird World, Ghost Hunter and Dark Diaries series are partly based on dreams I've had. But what originated as a dream won't just become a dream within the book, but part of the story itself.

Here are two more passages of atmospheric writing – both very different in style, subject and overall effect. What techniques can you notice each author using? Are there any devices that you would wish to use yourself? In this first extract, from David Almond's *Skellig*, there is both atmosphere and suspense. At this stage in the novel, the reader knows that the character will meet someone in this tumbledown garage, but not who it is or what they are doing there.

> *I switched the torch on, took a deep breath, and tiptoed straight inside.*
>
> *Something little and black scuttled across the floor. The door creaked and cracked for a moment before it was still. Dust poured through the torch beam. Something scratched and scratched in a corner. I tiptoed further in and felt spider webs breaking on my brow. Everything was packed in tight – ancient furniture, kitchen units, rolled-up carpets, pipes and crates and planks. I kept ducking down under the hosepipes and ropes and kitbags that hung from the roof. More cobwebs snapped on my clothes and skin. The floor was broken and crumbly. I opened a cupboard an inch, shone the torch in and saw a million woodlice scattering away. I peered down into a great stone jar and saw the bones of some little animal that had died in there. Dead bluebottles were everywhere. There were ancient newspapers and magazines. I shone the torch on to one and saw that it came from nearly fifty years ago. I moved so carefully. I was scared every moment that the whole thing was going to collapse. There was dust clogging my throat and nose. I knew they'd be yelling for me soon and I knew I'd better get out. I leaned across a heap of tea chests and shone the torch into the space behind and that's when I saw him.*
>
> (David Almond – *Skellig*: Hodder)

> *A faint crack of light did in fact splinter the otherwise inky eastern sky, and as Henry watched, a nearby bird let out the first jubilant call of the day. By the time*

he was dressed and had carefully let himself out by the back door the dawn chorus was in full, amazing song. He stole down the dark, deserted streets and from every garden came such ear-splitting whistles and deafening song that he expected at any minute to see windows thrown open and heads peering out to see what the din was.

'I sleep through this every day,' he thought with wonder.

He had never heard birdsong so echoing and clear. It was as if the darkness had its own edges, as if it were a tunnel with its own echoes. As the light strengthened, so the birdsong blurred and softened. Below he could make out the shape of the Town Hall dome and rows of rooftops like cardboard cut-outs. He stole by a complicated zig-zag route to by-pass the market-square and approach the canal bridge from the far side, as he had the night before. And all the while the gaps in the sky were widening until when he finally turned on to the canal road it was to find the sun itself before him, spilling fire into the smooth, dark water.

(Helen Cresswell – *The Night-Watchmen*: Hodder)

Workshop activities: suspense and atmosphere

SUSPENSE

Inject some suspense into one of these scenarios below. Portray the event moment by moment, in real time. You could even tell the story in the present tense. Aim to let your reader experience your story as if they were there:

- Someone has broken down in their car by a wood at night.
- You are all alone in the house. You are brushing your teeth before going to bed when you hear a noise.
- Someone is cycling past a moonlit canal. They feel that they are being watched.

ATMOSPHERE

Write about these places in the most original way that you can and conjure up an atmosphere:

- a disused bus station/hotel/swimming pool/factory
- a cellar or attic
- an underground tunnel
- a clifftop during a storm.

One way of extending this is to work in pairs and to take two atmospheric pieces – perhaps one of a bus station and another of a cellar. The partners write one descriptive piece each and then devise a story that will link these two pieces together.

(Also see Celia Rees' and Anthony Masters' writing workshops in the Author Visit Guide.)

Fiction workshops

Animal → human

Teacher-led activity.

> **JAN DEAN:** Think of an animal and turn it into a person. Take a bear, for example. If that bear became a person, what would they look like? They'd be big and shambling. They'd have big hands and big feet, and they might bump into furniture. They'd be quite strong. They might have a sweet tooth – and eat a lot of fish! So, you can get a character simply from an animal's physical characteristics. Now write a paragraph or so about that character coming into a room. Give clues as to what your original animal was, but without mentioning the animal's name.

Collages

Collect all kinds of pictures from magazines, newspapers, brochures or leaflets. Cut them out and make a collage. Spend time looking at your collage and see if you can find a story by connecting two or three of the images that you have brought together.

Comic strip

Instead of telling a story in words, tell one in pictures as a comic strip. Have a look at some *Tintin* and *Asterix* books to see how the strips are laid out. If you are writing your own story, work out your plot outline first. Alternatively, you could adapt a scene from a favourite book – such as a *Harry Potter* or *Point Horror* title or a Jacqueline Wilson novel, or even a scene from a live action or cartoon film as a comic strip. (See 'Picture books for a younger audience', pp. 148–9.)

Epistolary

Begin a piece of writing in the 'epistolary' form, that is a story told in the form of letters, postcards, faxes or e-mails between two people. These two people may or may not be related, may have never met before, and may even live in different parts of the world. First brainstorm details about these two characters – such as their backgrounds, and how they got to know each other. Write a letter from one character to the other and then respond. What you will need to do – apart from including all the many different things these two may write about (such as updating each other with their news) – is to find an interesting plot or storyline to weave in and out of the letters. You will probably discover one as you are writing. Before you start you might want to look at some examples of epistolary novels and books – such as *Cliffhanger* by Jacqueline Wilson (which includes postcards), *P.S. Longer Letter Later: A Novel in Letters* and *Snailmail No More: A Novel by E-Mail* by Paula Danzinger and Ann M. Martin, *Dear Nobody* by Berlie Doherty, *Charlie's Drift* by Charles Ashton or even the picture book *Dear Greenpeace* by Simon James.

Another way would be to select a book that you know very well. Write a series of letters between two of the characters. If a whole new story emerges from these letters, then develop it as far as you can.

Fairy tales

Think of all the fairy tales you've ever seen, heard, read or watched. What do they have in common? What elements occur over and over again? Here's a few:

- 'Once upon a time . . . they all lived happily ever after'
- set 'a long time ago' in 'a faraway place'
- set in woods and forests
- good and bad characters
- wishes
- magic
- a moral
- a rhyme
- good behaviour is rewarded / bad behaviour is punished
- talking animals
- shapeshifting.

What others can you think of? Make a list. Now write your own fairy tale using at least four of these elements.

Teacher-led activity: an oral, whole class activity. The teacher or workshop leader begins, 'Once upon a time . . .' and, in turn, each pupil contributes a phrase or sentence of their own. So, one example may go something like:

TEACHER: Once upon a time –
PUPIL 1:   there lived a lonely prince –
PUPIL 2:   in a huge empty castle.
PUPIL 3:   One day the prince set out on a journey.
PUPIL 4:   Passing through a wood the prince met a –

The teacher may need to intervene occasionally and encourage responses and contributions. If the tale dries up or finishes, then start again. This oral story can later be written out and developed.

You can also mix and match existing fairy tales. For example, what if Goldilocks went to the home of the seven dwarfs instead of the three bears? Or, what if Hansel and Gretel came across a giant beanstalk in the forest?

Fairy tales: points of view

Yet another way to write a fairy tale is in small groups and to consider point of view. If there are five in your group you might choose 'Cinderella'. Each of the five adopts a different character – Cinderella, the fairy godmother, the two sisters and the prince – and can write (or even tell) the story from that character's point of view.

Fairy tales: modern

Read 'Fairy tales' above. Instead of writing a traditional fairy tale, set 'a long time ago' in a 'faraway place', write a fairy tale set in the present, in a town or city – using four or so of the fairy tale elements. There can still be the fantasy ingredients such as magic or talking animals.

Genres

Here are some of the many genres of fiction:

- fantasy
- horror
- thriller
- crime
- teenage romance
- hospital / school / family / police / football drama
- science fiction
- time travel
- mystery stories
- ghost and supernatural stories
- adventure stories
- fairy tales
- myths and legends
- comic strips
- and not to forget, pony stories!

Which of these do you like most of all? Pick just one. Think:

- What types of events happen in these stories?
- What types of characters are there?
- What types of places are these stories set in?
- Do these stories usually begin and end in the same way?
- Are these stories usually told in a particular way using certain words and language?

Once you have made a list of these, write your own version of a story in that genre.

Genres: mix and match

This activity can be done in pairs or small groups. One partner begins a story in one genre, say science fiction. The other partner continues the piece in another genre, say a horror story. Together the partners swap over until the piece is written.

Or, pick two of the genres and write a piece in which you mix them together, such as a sci-fi crime story or a time travel school story.

(For a workshop on writing horror and ghost stories, refer to Celia Rees' Author Case Study.)

Genres: openings

To get you started on writing in various genres, here are some openings. Read through them all first and identify which genre each is from:

- It was a dark and stormy night.
- 'All right, 5b,' barked the teacher. 'Have it your way. But no one goes home until I have found out who did it.'
- By the fifth millennium most planets had been colonised by Earth – all except XX8, of course. So why had Mission Control sent her there?
- The crowd roared with disbelief at the referee's decision: a penalty.

Historical fiction

See 'Non-fiction' workshops (pp. 181–2).

Notebooks

Many authors keep notebooks to write their ideas in. Keep a notebook of your own. Have a different theme for each week, so one week you might want to write down your dreams when you wake up, another week you want to make notes of interesting people that you have seen around, another week you could make a list of places in which to set stories. Once you have collected a week's worth of ideas, pick just one and develop it into a piece of fiction. You could even decorate your notebook with pictures and drawings. In your notebook you do not need to worry about neat handwriting, spelling or punctuation; it is your private place for writing and even drawing and doodling.

Mini-sagas

A mini-saga is a story in exactly fifty words. This one has a 'twist' ending:

Dying?
Thrown in with a crowd,
the door slams shut.
I hear water.
I feel redness oozing from me
colouring the water.
Gasping for air,
blood runs to my toes.
Knocked out by arms and legs,
I come round
hanging on the washing line –
a red sock
among pale pink laundry.

(Lucy Ogbourne – from Wells – age 11)

Write your own mini-saga in as close to fifty words as you can. You can include a title with up to five words. Write your story first – perhaps about a very small event – and then prune it down to fifty or so words. Use only those words that you need.

Picture books for a younger audience

IAN BECK: Try and remember what it was like to be really young. What scared you? What sort of things made you laugh? Try and build a story around one of those things. Keep it simple, but shape it so it has an ending, which seems right. Remember that really young readers like to look at pictures as well. Select the important bits of the story to make pictures of. These might be the funniest bits or they might be the scariest bits. Some of the pictures might be small and some might fill a page to make the story more dramatic.

Try and write the picture story with as few words as possible, perhaps only one or two lines on a page for instance. Look at some picture books for younger children and count how many words are used to tell the story, and see how the pictures are used. Remember that the pictures do some of the work of telling the story as well as the words.

Write a story that you are interested in, making it exciting for yourself to write and picture, and it will be exciting for the younger children. Try out the story on some of the younger nursery children in the school, or on your younger brothers and sisters, and gauge their reaction to it. You might amend the story slightly depending on how you think they reacted to it. It might be worth trying out the pictures for your story on rough paper first, that way you can correct any mistakes before making your finished pictures. Above all, enjoy making the story and the pictures – if you enjoy making it then the younger children will enjoy reading and looking at it.

As Ian Beck encourages, write a story to be read aloud to a small group of pupils younger than you – lower Juniors or Infants. Before you read your story, prepare your performance first – practise it with friends or siblings or read it into a tape recorder. Make sure your illustrations are large enough for your audience to see from a distance. And why not read some picture books to give you some ideas?

Sequels

Find a book or story that you have enjoyed and write a sequel. Spend time thinking about the character(s) and think about what they may do next. Perhaps you could read the last few pages of the book again and make notes on possible ideas.

Short exercises

Philip Pullman suggests:

- Write the story of Cinderella in exactly 100 words.
- Write the story of Little Red Riding Hood without using any adverbs or adjectives – not even Red or Riding.
- Write a paragraph without using the letter a.
- Write a paragraph in which every word begins with the last letter of the previous word.
- Describe a room, and without using any abstract words, suggest an atmosphere of foreboding or evil.

Song titles and lyrics activity

Here, Celia Rees talks about titles in fiction:

CELIA REES: A title gives a story an identity. A title should say something about the story and should grab a reader's attention in some way. Finding the right title can be very difficult. I've used and adapted lyrics and titles from pop songs for three of my novels: *Every Step You Take*, *Colour Her Dead* and *Midnight Hour*.

Have a look at some song lyrics and song titles on various CDs. See if they suggest a story to you. Or perhaps you could create a story in which a certain song is played or sung by the main character. The theme of the song could be reflected in the theme of your story.

Themes

Every story has at least one theme, that is a subject that it addresses. Write a fictional piece in which you explore one of these themes, or choose a theme of your own: loneliness, mistaken identity, friendship, sibling rivalry, greed, favouritism, destiny, good versus evil, discrimination, history repeats itself.

Titles

The title is one of the most important aspects of a piece of fiction. It's the first thing that you come across when you hear about a book for the first time. The title will help you to decide whether you are going to read that book or not. Many authors do not give a new piece of fiction a title until they have thought of something that they are happy with, which can often be when the piece is finished. However, David Almond has a different way of working:

> **DAVID ALMOND:** Originally, my novel *Skellig* was going to be called *Mister Wilson*. I knew it was wrong, but I just needed a title. Unless a story has a title at the top of the page, it doesn't exist. It has to have a name from the start – so I just put something at the top, even if it's just *Mister Wilson*! The year before I wrote *Skellig* I had been to Ireland and there's a bunch of islands called Skellig Islands off the south-west coast in the Atlantic Ocean. Halfway through the book I looked up from my computer and saw the book about the Skellig Islands and I thought, that's the name. It's a beautiful word, so I pinched it really.

Write a piece based upon one of the titles below. Do a brainstorm first. You could even change the title once you have written your piece if you find something more suitable:

'Black and White'	'Home from Home'
'Dear Diary'	'Perfect Strangers'
'Deep Water'	'The Newcomer'

True fictions

Teacher-led activity.

> **CELIA REES:** One writing exercise I do is to take a local newspaper and cut out loads of stories and news items. In groups, I'll get the children to discuss the other possible details behind these stories. I'll tell them that the newspaper clipping only gives brief details, but behind it is a whole human story of what has actually happened. So, working from the short piece they'll make their own story around that event. Children like the fact that these events really happened, and they enjoy creating background stories to them – wondering why this or that happened, inventing names for other people involved and thinking of the various events that led up to this particular story.

Fiction word wheel

For this teacher-led activity, see Figure 3.15: 'Fiction word wheel: people, places and situations'. Photocopy one for each member of the class. Pupils can cut out the three wheels and join them together using a paper fastener. They then choose a combination of two or three words and write a piece that combines these features. (This was adapted from the 'Surrealist Dreaming Wheel' of the Tate Gallery Education Department.)

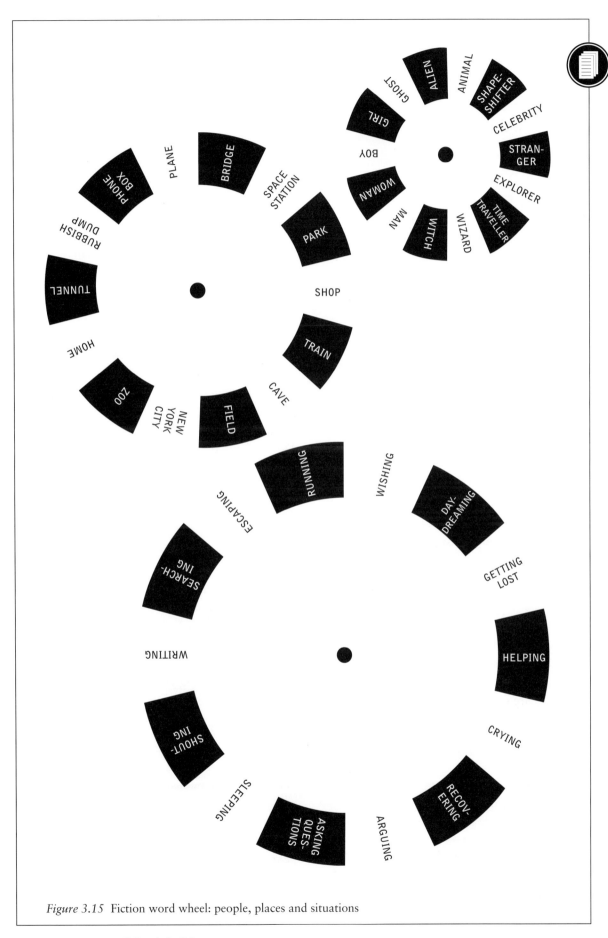

Figure 3.15 Fiction word wheel: people, places and situations

FICTION CHECKLIST

The questions below will help you to remember everything you have to think about when reading through a draft of a story.

BEGINNINGS AND ENDINGS
Does the opening grab your attention and encourage the reader to go on?
Do you get into the story as quickly as you can?
Have you got the best possible opening sentence or paragraph?
Have you chosen the right place in the story to start?
Do you have the right ending? Is it realistic?
At the end do you want to give your reader an idea of what might happen next?

PROSE AND LANGUAGE
Does your prose flow? How well does it read out loud?
Do you repeat some words or phrases too often?
Are there too many overused adjectives (nice, beautiful, lovely etc.)?
Is any of your phrasing awkward?
Are there too many descriptions?
Are there too many adjectives or adverbs?
Are you using metaphors or similes?
Are your sentences or paragraphs too long?

DIALOGUE
Does the dialogue sound real?
Can you recognise the characters by what they are saying?
Is there enough or too much dialogue?
Do you need to spend more time on thinking about how your characters speak?

PLOT
Does the story make sense?
Does the story build in tension or excitement?
Is too much information given away too soon?

Is your story too complicated?
Does too much / too little happen?
Is there anything in the story that you don't need?
Does it have a good structure: a beginning, a middle and an end?
Does the story drag at any point?
Do you move quickly from scene to scene?

CHARACTER
How does the reader get to know your characters?
Are you telling or showing?
Do you need to get to know your characters better?
Do you have too many characters?

GENERAL
What are the strengths and weaknesses of the story?
Is the title right?
Were you right to choose first person / third person for this story?
Is the story original in any way?
Does anything sound corny or clichéd?
Does the story do what you want it to do?
Is place important to your story – if so, do you portray the settings well?
Are you entertaining your reader / how will a reader respond to this?

THE NEXT STEP
How could it be improved?
What needs to be done next?
Is it ready to be published?

If you have gone through the checklist and you are not sure what needs to be done next, leave your story for a while and come back to it later.

FICTION GLOSSARY

alliteration Where words begin with the same letters or sounds: 'table top', 'car keys', 'green grass'.

assonance Where words have the same sounds: 'green bean', 'new view'.

atmosphere How it feels to be at a certain place at a certain time in a story.

characters The people in a story.

cliché An overused and unoriginal phrase or description: 'as black as night', 'as cold as ice'.

dialogue The speech in stories as spoken by the characters.

drafting and editing Drafting is doing different versions to improve and develop a piece of writing. Editing is checking a piece for spelling, grammar and punctuation.

drama A piece that is written to be performed.

fiction An invented story.

form The type of fiction, for example novel, short story, play, monologue or mini-saga.

genre The type of story, for example, fantasy, horror, science fiction and fairy tale.

'in media res' When a story goes straight into an event at the beginning.

metaphor and simile Simile is when you say one thing is *like* something else: 'as cunning as a fox', 'she felt trapped like a bird in a cage'. Metaphor is when you say one thing actually *is* something else: 'it's raining nails', 'the city is a jungle tonight'.

mini-saga A story told in fifty words.

monologue A performance in which one character talks about aspects of her/his life or makes observations about the world around her/him.

narrative The story in a piece of fiction.

narrator A person who tells a story.

plot The sequence of events that take place in a story.

prose Written language that is not poetry or dialogue.

setting The place(s) in which a story is set.

structure How the story is set out, with a beginning, middle and an end.

suspense The feeling that something is about to happen in a story.

4 Non-fiction

NEIL ARDLEY: Writing non-fiction is all about entertaining as well as educating your reader.

Creative with the truth: ways into writing non-fiction

Similarities between fiction and non-fiction

It may seem as if fiction and non-fiction are very different forms of writing. Fiction is the world of invention and make-believe whereas non-fiction, to an extent, is rooted in everyday realities, and is concerned with facts and real events. Yet, as the Fiction chapter has illustrated, much fiction can be inspired by actual events and happenings.

Like fiction, non-fiction can also tell stories. Take a look at any of Terry Deary's *Horrible Histories*. In every book you will find tales of human experience, endeavours and achievements. Think of the *Horrible Science* series: these books also recount stories of how individuals have made incredible discoveries about the world we live in. So fiction and non-fiction actually have a great deal in common and the boundaries between the two are often blurred.

When writing both forms – fiction and non-fiction – you will need to:

- entertain your reader
- maintain your reader's interest
- consider how to express what you want to write in the most interesting and appropriate way that you can
- ensure that your writing style is clear and easily understood
- use the best possible words – and be imaginative with your language, and use devices such as metaphors and similes
- use a good structure with a coherent opening, middle and conclusion.

In the specific case of non-fiction you also need to:

- enlighten your reader about a particular subject matter
- inform your reader what information you are going to cover, as well as guide your reader through the piece of writing; a contents page and bold headings are ideal for non-fiction projects
- if you are using technical terms or jargon explain what they mean
- use humour (if relevant!).

Text and graphics

Until quite recently, information books contained very informative but often dull and dry text. Nowadays, non-fiction writers are expected to come up with fresh and exciting ways of presenting facts and information to entertain their readers. Later in this chapter, both Terry Deary and Nick Arnold discuss this issue. In addition, they reveal how they write, plan and research their non-fiction titles. Presenting information – as Nick Arnold explains – is all about using visuals such as pictures, photographs, diagrams and maps as well as words:

> **NICK ARNOLD:** As I'm writing I'm always thinking in visual terms . . . I am always thinking to myself – how can I visualise this information? What cartoon could I include? Would this work well as a diagram? Considering all these visual details in this way is a very important part of the process of writing non-fiction.

Genres of non-fiction

Fiction has many forms – known as 'genres' – such as horror, romance and fantasy. Non-fiction too has a variety of genres but also covers many topics. This short list details just a few of the forms and subjects of non-fiction:

- reference books such as dictionaries, thesauruses and encyclopedias
- school textbooks
- biographies and autobiographies
- domestic texts – cooking, gardening, do-it-yourself
- religious texts such as the Koran, the Torah and the Bible
- books on science, geography, history and philosophy
- texts on the natural world – animals, plants, the environment
- car manuals
- books of song lyrics and sheet music
- travel writing.

This is not to forget that non-fiction includes magazines and newspapers, leaflets, catalogues, pamphlets, information posters and more recently, CD-ROMs and websites.

Choosing a topic

Nick Arnold and Terry Deary agree that the first stage in writing a piece of non-fiction is taking time to find the right topic:

> **NICK ARNOLD:** First, choose a subject you really want to write about. It has to be something that you find interesting. And you may discover that the more you find out about a subject the more interesting it will become. If that is the case, then that's brilliant, and you're on the right lines.

> **TERRY DEARY:** Choose something that really interests you. It's got to be something that makes you think: 'I'd like to share this information with somebody else'. When you do that, when you've got that enthusiasm, that's going to so much improve your own writing.

Researching

Nick Arnold encourages young writers to do much research and to produce a good plan from the start:

NICK ARNOLD: Be very thorough in your research. What you need to do is to get hold of and read as many books on your subject as possible. Use your school library as well as your local library. And don't just use books – watch TV programmes or videos on the subject. Use the Internet if you can. If you know anyone who is either interested in your subject or works in the field that you're writing about, then you might want to talk to them. Be so thorough that you think: 'I've got lots of material, but where can I get that extra exciting fact that will make my book *really* interesting?'

You will need to have a rough plan of what you're going to write – like a contents page to one of my *Horrible Science* books – before you start doing your research. You will almost certainly find that you'll have to change your plan according to the facts and information that you find.

As Nick Arnold says, planning in non-fiction is vital – and is as important as in any other form of writing. (See 'Planning and organising information', p. 157.)

When reading a non-fiction book as part of your research you may wish to consider the following points.

- Use the contents page at the front of the book and the index at the back to see which topics are covered and where specific information that you require appears in the text.
- Check if there is a 'glossary' in which special or technical terms are explained; you could even produce a glossary for your own project.
- Make notes in a notebook: if there is a lot of information you could devise your own shorthand (with abbreviated words) or even photocopy pages from the book if this is allowed.
- When using reference books you must not reproduce the original text word for word in your own project; you must rewrite and adapt the material into your own language; copying directly is theft.
- As you are reading through reference books, make sure you read the information carefully and that you fully understand the text.
- It is important to make a note of the books (as well as other media) that you have sourced information from and to put these titles in a bibliography at the back of your project; write down the title and author of each book, and the name of the publisher if you wish.
- Consider using other media for your research other than books, such as CD-ROMs, newspapers and magazines, TV programmes, videos and websites.

When you research your subject, you will come across much more information than you actually need. Selecting what is most necessary to the book or project you are working on is one of the key aspects of the non-fiction writing process. This book itself would have been something like 250,000 words – instead of just over 100,000 words – if some 150,000 words of research material had not been edited out.

When using a library to source information, ensure that you cover every possible source of information. Use the subject search on the PCs as well as the subject index cards. And you may wish to ask the librarians the following:

- the classification number of your subject – so that you can check the bookshelves for all the books on that topic
- if they know of any books/videos/other media that might be useful
- if there are further resources available at other libraries.

Depending on the nature of your topic, museums may be a further source of research information. But wherever your research takes you, make sure that you have a notebook with you at all times.

Researching on the Internet

Neil Ardley – co-author of *The New Way Things Work* (Dorling Kindersley) – gives advice on researching on the Internet, an increasingly popular place to conduct research:

> **NEIL ARDLEY:** The Internet is a great way of answering questions and finding information of all kinds. But, out of the millions of websites on the Internet, how can you find the one with just the information you want? A search engine does this job for you. It knows about most websites that are out there, and can take you wherever you want to go.
>
> A search engine is a super seeker – a special website that contains a huge list of websites. It presents you with a search box in which you key in the subject or name you are seeking. The engine then finds all the websites containing the words you have used, and lists them with a short description of each one. Click on any website in the list and you jump directly to it. Alternatively, you may also be able to key in a question and the search engine will try to find a website with the answer.
>
> However, this can be a bit hit and miss. You often get a long list of websites all containing the words you have keyed into the search box. Many of them will be no use to you at all, and it can be hard to find just the website you need. A good way to avoid this problem is to use the search engine called Yahooligans!, which is at the Internet address www.yahooligans.com. This is designed for children and it contains selections of good websites that have been specially chosen because they are interesting and useful. Just key in the subject you want, or choose from a list of subjects, and you'll get a list of good websites right away. Click on one and you should be there.

Planning and organising information

As with books, non-fiction projects need to have a structure and a logical sequence in which the information is presented. As Nick Arnold commented earlier, drafting a contents page can be a useful way of starting a project as it can help you to select what information you are going to cover, and organise a structure for your material. Here is a standard format for a non-fiction project that can be used and adapted:

COVER
CONTENTS PAGE
INTRODUCTION
CHAPTERS / SECTIONS
CONCLUSION
GLOSSARY
BIBLIOGRAPHY
APPENDIX

When drafting your project, it is wise to avoid long paragraphs as information is best presented in small chunks. In this way it is more accessible to the reader.

Interviews and questionnaires

Interviews and questionnaires are two very different but productive methods of getting information from people. An interview is ideal for acquiring material from an expert or if you want someone to explain a subject to you. Just two examples would be interviewing the manager of a local football team about the history of the club, or interviewing an older person about life in your local area during the Second World War.

Before an interview, do as much preparation as can. Spend time working on a list of questions to take with you. Try to avoid too many 'closed' questions which encourage a 'yes' or 'no' answer, such as 'Did you like doing that?' or 'Were you scared when . . .?'. Instead, ask more 'open' questions that give the interviewee a chance to talk and explain, such as 'How did you feel when . . .?' or 'What do you think about . . .?'.

Take a tape recorder and a blank cassette with you to tape your interview. Either use a tape recorder that has a mains lead or make sure you have some new batteries. Do not be afraid to ask the interviewee to explain something that you do not understand. And do ask any extra questions that come to mind during the interview. When you return, listen back carefully to the interview cassette. Then play it again, but this time write out all the important material that you want to use. This is called an interview transcript. (You may decide to remove all the 'ums' and 'errs' that people say – your interviewee will not mind at all!)

From there, select which quotes you want to use and decide where you are going to use them in your text. You could, if you choose, share the responsibility and conduct an interview with a friend. (See 'Interviews' activity in the workshop section of this chapter.)

A questionnaire is useful if you need to gather information or opinions from a number of people, perhaps friends in your class or people who live near you. Information from a questionnaire can be represented in the form of graphs and can help you to evaluate people's opinions and lifestyles. One example of a questionnaire might be on the topic of the environment; it might ask if people recycle paper, bottles and cans and if they use unleaded petrol. Another questionnaire could be on transport and would ask people how they travel to school and what transport they use at the weekends. Decide if you will fill out the forms as people answer your questions or if you wish people to write their answers themselves. You can include the questionnaires in the appendix of your non-fiction project.

The reader in the text

In addition to Neil Ardley, whose quote – 'Writing non-fiction is all about entertaining as well as educating your reader' – opens this chapter, Nick Arnold and Terry Deary stress the need to consider the reader at all times in non-fiction.

NICK ARNOLD: When you are writing non-fiction always think about how interesting and entertaining it will be for your reader. Just because you as a writer find that information interesting doesn't necessarily mean to say that your reader will be as interested and as impressed with the facts as you are.

You need to think very carefully about how you are going to present your information to your reader. This means you need to consider the tone of voice that you adopt in your writing. Imagine yourself talking to the reader – are you going to be constantly nudging them in the ribs and making jokes or are you going to be telling them in a very straightforward and serious way? Information and entertainment go together like a chicken and an egg. You couldn't have one without the other. Clearly, if your books aren't entertaining people won't want to read them, so you won't inform anybody of anything. On the other hand, if you are not informative, you've simply written a book of comedy – with jokes and puzzles. Most of all in your writing you need to be enthusiastic.

TERRY DEARY: Be aware of the fact that you are writing for a reader. You're not writing for yourself, you're not gathering information just to stick into a book or a word processor, you are writing to have an impact upon a reader. So always have your reader in mind.

Talking points

Here are some issues regarding non-fiction that you may wish to discuss in a workshop context:

- Is non-fiction more important than fiction or poetry because (a) it is based on facts and (b) it can have a more practical value?
- What is a fact – and is there such a thing? Give examples.
- Is the process of reading non-fiction any different from reading other forms of writing such as poetry or novels?
- Why do we use non-fiction books in different ways to other texts?
- What are the qualities of a good non-fiction book? Give examples.

Nick Arnold – *Bulging Brains* and the *Horrible Science* series

Figure 4.1 Cover of Nick Arnold's book *Bulging Brains* (Scholastic)

NICK ARNOLD: There a number of stages in the writing of each *Horrible Science*. At the start of every new book I have to find out what information is available on the subject I'm going to be writing about. So I'll go to my local public library to see what books are available that cover that subject. Then I'll do a rough plan – which is like a contents page for the book – to see what my chapter headings might be. Then it's a question of doing the research, reading about each area and collecting information for each chapter. For *Bulging Brains* I didn't need to use the Internet or go to medical libraries as my research was all from books from my local public library.

Take the 'Nasty Nightmares' chapter in my book *Bulging Brains,* for example. It's all about sleep. It was something I knew I was going to include right from the start as sleep is an important function of the brain. It would be impossible to sleep and to dream if your brain wasn't there to help you. I knew I would come across a lot of material about sleep. So 'Nasty Nightmares' was one of the headings I wrote down in a list that I knew I was going to research.

One thing I cannot do and that is to research only the areas I know that I will cover in the chapters of the book. That's a terribly bad idea. Although you can cut the amount of research work you do by a half that way, you may well miss out on some really fascinating and useful material. I would rather spend time looking at everything that is available on that topic – be it vegetables, insects, light, the brain, whatever – and then sample that and take the best information. If I spent less time doing research I could still end up with a reasonable book, but I would probably miss out an enormous amount of exciting information.

When I have finished my research I plan the book in greater detail and I work out exactly what is going to go in each chapter. I then begin writing quite intensively. My first draft is simply a matter of translating the research into my own words. If I'm writing well, this will come very easily and very fast indeed. I can easily produce a thousand words in an hour and sometimes even more.

I don't write to a set time schedule. I could research and write a book in a month quite easily but, on average, I write four *Horrible Science* books a year. *Bulging Brains* took longer than other books to research and write and that's to do with the fact that there was so much information available – loads of books have been written about the brain. The entire project took me from February to August 1998.

I never write my books by hand. Because I only ever work on a computer, it's difficult to talk of different drafts and versions of a book, but every section of each book will go through changes and each piece of text will get revised a number of times. I'll never send anything to a publisher until I'm really happy with it.

Of all the books in the *Horrible Science* series, *Blood, Bones and Body Bits* has been the most popular, so the publisher is keen for me to do more books on the human body. Whilst I was writing *Blood, Bones and Body Bits* I was aware of the fact that I had an enormous supply of information – far more than I would ever need in that one book. The body is a world in itself. With the chapters on the brain and digestion I knew that I could only use a small amount of the information that I had.

When I was talking to the publisher about the success of *Blood, Bones and Body Bits* they asked if there was anything else I could write about the body. I mentioned the brain and digestion. And these subjects have now become books in their own right – *Bulging Brains* and *Disgusting Digestion.* The chapter in *Blood, Bones and Body Bits* on the brain is called 'The Baffling Brain', and that's what I was originally going to call this book. As you can see on the manuscript page here, I drew up a whole list of possible titles (Figure 4.2). And to date, I have always come up with the initial idea for each of my *Horrible Science* books.

How do I decide how to present the information in my books – be it a quiz, joke or comic strip? For a start, it depends on the amount of material I have on a certain topic. And sometimes it can be obvious to me that I should present one piece of material as a story. If this material is not so much a scientific fact – but it is more about people, people struggling in their lives or

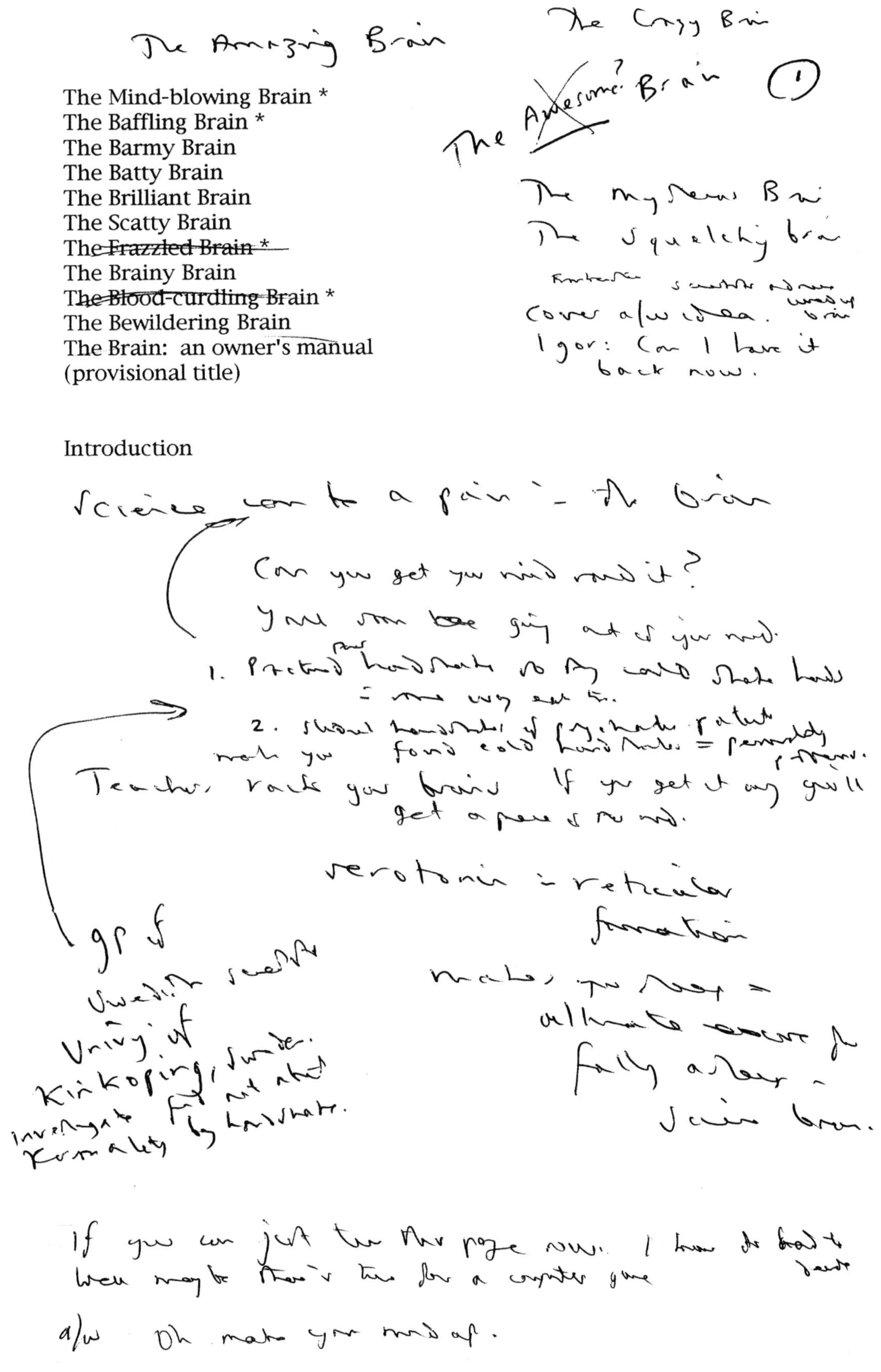

The Amazing Brain

The Crazy Brain

The Awesome? Brain ①

The Mind-blowing Brain *
The Baffling Brain *
The Barmy Brain
The Batty Brain
The Brilliant Brain
The Scatty Brain
The ~~Frazzled Brain~~ *
The Brainy Brain
The ~~Blood-curdling~~ Brain *
The Bewildering Brain
The Brain: an owner's manual
(provisional title)

The mysterious Brain

The Squelchy brain

cover a/w idea.

Igor: Can I have it back now.

Introduction

√ Science can be a pain - the brain

Can you get your mind round it?

You will soon be going out of your mind.

1. Pretend handshake so dry cold shake hands = one way out to.

2. Sweaty handshake of psychotic patient make you found cold handshake = personality.

Teacher, rack your brain. If you get it any you'll get a piece of my mind.

serotonin = reticular formation

makes you sleep = ultimate occur of fully asleep - Science brain.

gp of Swedish scientist

Univ. of Kinkoping, Sweden.

investigate Formality by handshake.

If you can just turn this page now. I know its bad to Well maybe there's time for a computer game

a/w   Oh make your mind up.

Figure 4.2 Manuscript page of rough notes for Nick Arnold's *Bulging Brains*

people discovering exciting things – then, the chances are that I will feature this information in the form of a story. In a way, that information is already a story, so it makes sense to tell it in that form.

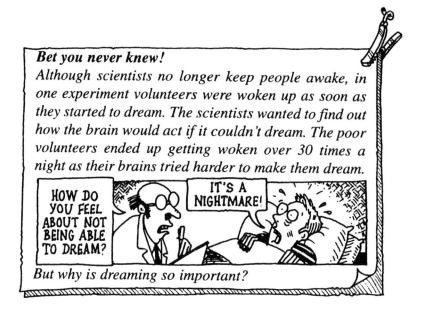

Figure 4.3 'Bet you never knew!', from Nick Arnold's *Bulging Brains*

When I've finished my research for a book I look at my notes and think: what am I looking at here? Could it be a story? Is it a little nugget of fact? If it is a scientific fact, I might decide to have it as a 'Bet you never knew!' (see Figure 4.3). If it's a piece of information that's quite unusual or unexpected, I might keep that as a quiz question. My rule with the quizzes is to include one question that is funny, one that is possible, and one that is correct. If the information I've got is just an exciting fact I might decide to put it into a sequence with lots of other facts. You've got to look long and hard at your material to discover the best or most effective way of presenting it. Doing this is like looking at something through a curtain – trying to make out what it is or what it might be.

I deliberately change the range of presentation forms from one *Horrible Science* to another. I think it would be very boring for children to read the same book with a different cover over and over again. But, to a degree, the content, my subject, will suggest the way in which I present the information.

Tony de Saulles' illustrations are vital to *Horrible Science* books. It's impossible to measure his contribution to the books, but it's very great. He is a really gifted artist – and also his jokes are much better than mine! In a series like *Horrible Science*, illustrations are so important. As I'm writing I'm always thinking in visual terms and making notes as to how a certain diagram should look or a page should be laid out. And I am always thinking to myself – how can I visualise this information? What cartoon could I include? Would this work well as a diagram? All this tends to come naturally. My mind just tends to work like this – I've always thought of information in terms of both words and pictures. Considering all these visual details in this way is a very important part of the process of writing non-fiction. I'm not an artist or illustrator, but occasionally I send Tony a rough diagram. Most of the time I will put a note in the manuscript asking him to do a certain diagram – say a cross-section of the brain – and then Tony will look that information up.

The editors always play a key role with each *Horrible Science*. I'll use *Bulging Brains* as an example. On the editors' advice, one story that was in the original manuscript was dropped as it was too sad and downbeat. Also, the editors were very keen that I explained things in more detail than I'd done with previous books because so much of the science of the brain is unknown to children. So as I was writing the book I was forever trying to anticipate what my reader might want to know. The editors also came up with the title *Bulging Brains*. They felt that with my own title – *The Baffling Brain* – some readers might not know the word 'baffling', but everyone knows what a *Bulging Brain* is! It's important that children can grasp a title – if they see a title they don't understand, they might not want to read that book.

In addition to Tony de Saulles and myself, the writer, the *Horrible Science* team includes the main editor, the copy-editor (who will check for such things as spelling and grammar), the book designer and two science consultants – specialists in the topic of the book. The stages that a *Horrible Science* goes through once I've finished a new manuscript are as follows:

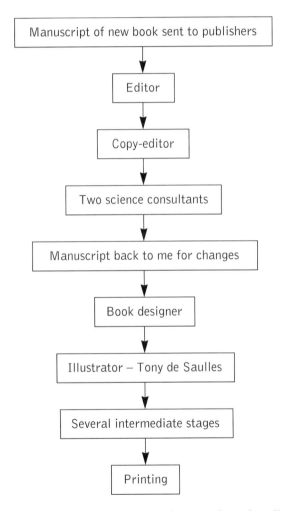

What struck me as I wrote *Bulging Brains* was how much yet how little we know about the brain and how much we're still discovering every month. Because it's such a developing area it's a very exciting topic to write about. Ten years ago we knew hardly anything compared with now, which is something that I talk about in the epilogue of the book. And this is something that I try to put across generally in all the *Horrible Science* books – the idea that science is something that is happening now and developing and ever-evolving. So I'm going to have to revise and update these books every few years to keep them up to date.

I'll talk through the introduction to *Bulging Brains*. There's a tradition in children's non-fiction that there has to be an introduction. It's there to lead the reader into the book – however, the different parts of the *Horrible Sciences* can be read out of sequence. In my introductions I always make fun of the boring side of science and I like to inform the readers that (a) this book is that little bit different, (b) they are going to be entertained and (c) they too can be experts in science. I think that this last point is an important thing to express because I've always felt that it's wrong to say that science is only about boffins in white lab coats. To an extent, we're all scientists. Anyone who seeks after truth – and that's what science is, it's what the word 'science' means – and anyone who wants to find out the truth of how things work or why things happen, is a scientist.

As I begin to write a new book I do the introduction first, and then I often come back to it during the writing of the rest of the book, adding and changing material. The introduction is so important to me. In the first sentence of the introduction to *Bulging Brains* I say:

> *To hear some scientists talk you'd think they knew everything about science . . .*

This is a common view of scientists – that they know *everything*. But the point is that scientists *don't* know everything about the brain. In addition, what I also try to achieve in an introduction is to introduce what the subject is, say what our understanding of the subject is, and in a humorous way I try to welcome the reader into the book. In the opening to *Bulging Brains* I tell of a recent discovery – the one about the girl who giggled when she was given an electric shock to the brain. The last line is an introduction to the reader to read on:

> *Now ask your brain to send a message down thousands of nerves to tell your finger muscles to gently lift the next page.*

That was a clever idea suggested by the publisher. And hopefully, once the reader has read this introduction and turned over the page, they're interested in the subject and hooked on the book! As for me, the whole point of an introduction is to encourage my readers to read the book.

Introduction

To hear some scientists talk you'd think they know everything about science . . .

But don't be fooled – scientists don't know everything. After all, if they did there would be no need for any new experiments. Scientists could sit around all day with their feet up. But, in fact, there are lots of mysteries left to solve. Lots of things we don't know or understand.

For example, there's one object that's so mysterious it makes the brainiest scientists scratch their heads. It's wet and squishy and looks revolting – and oddly enough, it's found between their ears. What is it? No, it's not their disgusting, snotty nose. It's the bit inside their heads – their bulging brain. Scientists aren't even sure how it works . . .

But if scientists are puzzled by their own little grey cells what chance do the rest of us have? No wonder learning about your brain can make your head ache.

Well, if science scrambles your brains, help is at hand. This book is bulging with brain facts. For example, bet you never knew that in 1998 US scientists found the part of the brain that makes you laugh. They gave an electric shock to this area of a girl's brain and she started giggling uncontrollably. And that's not all. Did you know that in one brain experiment children were forced to sniff their little brother's stinky old T-shirts? (Page 52 will give you all the smelly details.) Now that really is cruelty!

So by the time you've finished reading this book your knowledge will be so vast you could easily be the brains of your class. And who knows? Your teacher might even mistake you for a mega-genius. But to enjoy the full benefits you've got to ask your brain to help you read this book.

Your eyeballs scan the letters, your brain makes sense of the words, and your memory reminds you what they mean. But hold on – looks like you've already started . . . oh well, don't let me stop you. Now ask your brain to send a message down thousands of nerves to tell your finger muscles to gently lift the next page.

(Introduction to *Bulging Brains: Horrible Sciences* series, Scholastic)

My author's voice in these books is me talking, it's my voice but in written form instead of speech. All that enthusiasm that comes across is mine. Though at times – like when I'm telling a story in the voice of a fictional character or scientist – I'll adopt a different style or tone of voice, according to the person talking. This is the skill of a fiction writer.

I often write in the second person in my *Horrible Science* books – using such words as 'you' and 'your' in my text. See how often I have used these words in my introduction to *Bulging Brains*. The 'you' I talk about so often in my text is my reader, the person I'm talking to in my books. I am always aware of the fact that my reader may not be that interested in science, but they will be interested in themselves. Absolutely everyone's interested in themselves. If I'm writing a book about the human body, the reader will be interested in how the body works. If the book is about light, the reader will be interested in how they can see light and why the sky above them is blue. In fact, I'd say that the reader is a character in the *Horrible Science* books, in the same way that I'm a character – as the narrator – in these books. *Horrible Science* is a world which we all inhabit – a world in which we live and read about at the same time. The reader in a *Horrible Science* is as important as me the author. And above all, what I'm trying to do is to get the reader to go out and look at and interact with the world in a scientific way.

Workshop activities: Nick Arnold's *Horrible Sciences*

GRUESOME GAMES

NICK ARNOLD: In one library recently I did a writing workshop aimed at pupils creating their own *Horrible Science* books. We chose the title *Gruesome Games*. At the start I did a talk based on the science involved with playing various games to provide some raw material for the children's books. I talked about the science of throwing a ball, playing tennis, all sorts of things. The children worked in groups to produce their own quizzes, cartoons, book covers and stories based on the topic of *Gruesome Games*. They assembled these and made them into their own books.

Now create your own *Gruesome Games* – with cartoons, quizzes, fact files, diagrams and other *Horrible Sciences* elements. Pick a sport that you enjoy and consider what science is involved:

- Why does a ball spin?

- What does the brain have to do when someone (a) kicks a ball or, (b) hits a ball with a bat or racket?
- How do people swim – and what keeps them afloat?
- What muscles do we use when we jump or run?
- Why is exercise good for us – and what body parts does it help?

BODY PARTS

Pick a part of your body that interests you – it could be the eye, the brain, the foot, the lungs or the heart. Research that body part. What does that body part do when you are awake or asleep? What is its job? Does it help you to eat or digest food or what exactly? Do some diagrams in which you show what your body part does during different activities – such as eating, drinking, reading, walking or watching TV.

THE LATEST DISCOVERY

> **NICK ARNOLD:** Science is constantly in the news. It's happening now. It's changing the way our whole world operates. There are new discoveries being made in science every month.

Find out about a new discovery in science. It could be a cure for a disease, a robot, a new craft for space travel or a new machine for playing music. Write your own *Horrible Science* pamphlet – with text, diagrams and a quiz – explaining this new discovery to younger readers. Consider how you should present this information so that it will be entertaining and educational and also understood by a younger audience.

Terry Deary – *The Woeful Second World War* and the *Horrible Histories* series

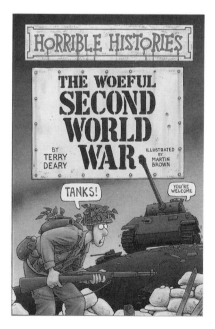

Figure 4.4 Cover of Terry Deary's book *The Woeful Second World War* (Scholastic)

TERRY DEARY: The fifth book in the *Horrible Histories* series was *The Blitzed Brits*. It came out in 1995, and quite accidentally, it coincided with the fiftieth anniversary of VE Day. As a result, *Blitzed Brits* went immediately to No.1 in the best-sellers list. Then, a couple of years after writing *The Blitzed Brits* I became aware that the book only really gave the British viewpoint of the Second World War. I realised that this was a very narrow way to write about history. Because of this I felt that I owed it to my readers to write *The Woeful Second World War* in which I show the war from a European viewpoint.

When I began writing *The Woeful Second World War* it was good to know that I didn't have to write that much about the British Home Front, as I'd covered that in *The Blitzed Brits*. Anyway, publishers don't like you covering the same information in two different books. So this enabled me to write more about France, Poland, Germany and Russia. And this time, *The Woeful Second World War* was published in September 1999 – to coincide with the sixtieth anniversary of the outbreak of the Second World War.

I have various research methods. For example, with all the *Horrible Histories* I have used researchers. For *The Woeful Second World War* I had a military historian. As a rule I always read the most up-to-date books on the period I'm writing about. And I find that I'm using the Internet more and more for research as well. As I do my research I completely absorb myself in that period so I'll know the whole historical context as well as all the events of that time. Within that framework my researchers will provide me with all kinds of information and facts. They'll say 'Did you know this . . .?' or 'Did you you know that . . .?'. As with most *Horrible Histories*, with *The Woeful Second World War* I ended up with far more information than I needed. There were a lot of boring facts that I didn't use, such as details about invasion plans and dates, dates and more dates! You see, dates don't matter. Human experience matters.

The vital thing for me when I'm writing a *Horrible History* is not to come over as, 'I'm an adult, I know this and I'm going to tell you. Are you listening?' What I am is an ignorant person saying, 'You'll never believe what I found out when I read this book. I'm going to share it with you.' That is my author's voice for *Horrible Histories*, anyway. It's this wonder of discovering about human nature: 'You'll never believe how people used to behave. Could you behave like that?'

I am a genuine enthusiast, and that comes across in my books. I am never an academic, I'm never a teacher and I'm not even an adult. I'm a big kid who wants to share this with other kids, big and small. I believe that a non-fiction writer has to *entertain* first and *inform* second. I haven't time for authors who write for their own entertainment or who stuff their books so full of dreary facts their readers fall asleep. Readers are more important than writers and their needs have to come first. If you don't engage your readers, then they'll read what you've written but they won't really take it in. But if they've enjoyed it, then they'll remember it.

I'm very aware of my author's voice. I ensure that my language and my prose style are always accessible. I'm very aware of speech cadences. Sometimes I'll go over what I've just written and adjust it so that it's more natural to speak. I don't sit at my computer screen and read it out loud, I'll do it in my head. I just love words and in my *Horrible Histories* I'll go over the top with alliteration or assonance. Poetry is often seen as a higher form of prose, but for me it's just another weapon in the writer's armoury. Poetry should be used in a far more relaxed way. Writers should feel free to slip into poetry whenever they want to. I do, even in my non-fiction books, and I feel very comfortable with it.

I deliberately use the second person in my books:

> *Any old boring history book will tell you about the battles and the dates and the*
> *facts and the figures. But what you want to know is what it was really like to live*

through those days. How did people really behave in the Second World War? And how would you have behaved?

(Introduction to *The Woeful Second World War*)

So many school textbooks use language that is very impersonal. It's alienating. I feel that by writing in the second person I bring the reader into the book. It's just part of my natural prose style. I want to talk directly to my reader, and when I'm talking to someone I don't use the third person, I use the second person. It's a very underused style of writing. You rarely get it in either fiction or non-fiction. If other writers don't want to use it, then that's fine by me!

I want to look at two sections from *The Woeful Second World War*. They're both mock newspaper articles. The first is an unusual story about an animal from the war. It's mysterious and it's quite lighthearted, in that nobody died in this particular story. The story reminded me of the type of article you come across in the *Sun* newspaper. So I imitated that newspaper's style. Hence I came up with that *Sun*-style awful pun in the title: 'Miaow did she do that?' I also adopted the newspaper's style of having an opening paragraph that states the subject of the article and a final paragraph that has a quote from a famous person (Figure 4.5).

Miaow did she do that?

The miracle mouser of London's St Augustine's Church has amazed her owner, Rector Ross. Yesterday he climbed from the rubble of his church to tell of the white cat's purr-fect prediction.

'Faith has been with us for three years,' he told our reporter. 'She kept her kittens on the top floor of the church house. But three days ago she carried them all down to the basement and tucked them into a corner. Every time I carried them back up she took them down again. Then, last night we had a direct hit. The top floor was demolished. But I found Faith and the kittens safe in the basement corner.'

The People's Dispensary For Sick Animals plans to give heroine Faith their silver medal. Even the Bishop of London admitted, 'It certainly makes us paws for thought!'

9 September 1940

Figure 4.5 'Miaow did she do that?', from Terry Deary's *The Woeful Second World War*

The other time I used a newspaper format in this book was in a very different context. For this piece I imitated a different style of newspaper – a broadsheet newspaper – because of the very serious subject matter. Perhaps if I had given this information in a different form it might have put my reader off. But by representing it in a newspaper format, my reader would approach it as they would approach reading a newspaper, in a more relaxed frame of mind than they would a school text. And this format will visually engage the reader. The broadsheet newspaper format also justifies my use of fairly short, punchy sentences. There is no humour here and no puns as it is a very serious subject matter.

Writers like myself can use a register such as a mock-newspaper article like this for different effects. Whether the readers are aware of it or not, they are getting the message that they too

Czechoslovakia Today

1 June 1942

Massacre at Lidice

Hitler's henchman, Reinhard Heydrich, was killed by a freedom fighter's bomb in the Czech capital Prague two weeks ago.

Heydrich – killed

Yesterday the German SS exacted their revenge on the small Czech town of Lidice.

They rounded up most of the 450 townspeople and shot 172 men. Seven women were shot as they were trying to escape and the rest were transported to a concentration camp at Ravensbruck. The 90 children were given new names and sent to Germany to be raised as Germans.

Today the SS will dynamite the town and the rubble will be levelled so that not a trace remains.

Figure 4.6 'Czechoslovakia today', from Terry Deary's *The Woeful Second World War*

could use different registers like this in their own writing – and that they too can use different media to create different effects. So, educationally, there is a message in *Horrible Histories* books about the way we use language and forms of writing.

The different media I use in the *Horrible Histories* – such as the diaries, the letters, newspaper extracts and so on – are simply a way of allowing a story to be told from the point of view of individual people. In *Even More Terrible Tudors*, there's a story about a young executioner who'd never executed anybody in his life. His first job was to behead Countess Pole. He missed her the first time he took a swipe at her and had to keep chopping. Now the interest for me wasn't from an onlooker's perspective, it was the executioner's, so I told the story from his point of view: 'Dear Mum, I'm here in the Tower of London and you'll never believe what happened to me . . .'. I'm trying to get away from the objective, and to get my readers to experience history subjectively, so that they become that executioner.

Compared with the other *Horrible Histories* books, what was unique about writing *The Woeful Second World War* was the sensitivity involved. The Second World War is an event that is still in living memory. Many people who will read this book may well know people who experienced the war or even died in that war. On top of this, a lot of people seem reluctant to discuss the Holocaust with children – but I think it's vital that children read about it. With a book like *Even More Terrible Tudors* you can talk about someone having their head chopped off after ten hacks and it's almost comical because you're so removed from it. But there's very little humour to be had from the Second World War. And people come to *Horrible Histories* expecting them to be funny. They're not so much funny as ironic. Even the story of the cat that I mentioned earlier has a menacing undertone.

A number of the children who read my books are reluctant readers. I get both parents and children writing to me saying, 'I like your books because I can pick one up, read a small section and then put it down again'. In a *Horrible Histories* book the reader is never faced with the long chapters that you have in fiction. In this way non-fiction can be a good alternative to fiction for the more reluctant readers. Also, you don't have to start at the beginning, you can dip in and out as you choose. And all the different media I use – such as the comic strips, quizzes – are yet another way of avoiding long chapters or sections of text.

With *Horrible Histories* I want children to think about how people in certain moments of history felt and also for them to consider what these people were experiencing. All the time I want the reader to look at the people, the individuals that make up history. History is never boring when you look at it on the individual level. In these *Horrible Histories* I'm asking, 'Why do people behave the way they do?' And, ultimately, 'Why do I behave the way I do?'

Workshop activities: Terry Deary's *Horrible Histories*

AN EVENT FROM HISTORY

Anton Campbell (aged 9) from Berkshire is interested in the aeroplanes of the Second World War. He enjoyed Terry Deary's *The Blitzed Brits* so much that he wrote his own *Horrible Histories* project – and included his own jokes, illustrations and quizzes. He called the project *The Potty Planes of the Battle of Britain*. What makes Anton's title so good is that some planes at that time actually were made out of recycled pots and pans!

What special time/event in history fascinates you? Do your own *Horrible Histories* project on that time/event. If you are unsure what to choose, read some *Horrible Histories* books for ideas. Once you have done your research, include some of these *Horrible Histories* elements:

- alliterating and amusing titles for each section
- timelines – pick just a few of the most important dates
- quizzes
- jokes
- fact files
- captions
- cartoons and comic strips
- diagrams, illustrations and photographs.

NEWSPAPER ARTICLE

Take an event from history and tell it in the form of a newspaper article – such as the Great Fire of London, the arrival of Pocahontas in England, the Battle of Hastings, the invention of the steam engine, the Romans invading Britain or the birth of Jesus. Like Terry Deary in *The Woeful Second World War*, you could imitate the style of the *Sun* newspaper – or another paper if you wish. If you choose the *Sun*, find a good title with a pun, like Terry Deary's 'Miaow did she do that?'. Also, begin the article stating what the subject is and finish off with a quote from someone who had been at or involved with the event.

SECOND WORLD WAR HISTORY

What was it like to live through the Second World War in the city/town/village where you live? Is there anyone in your area who can remember the war? Research that time. Go to your library and look out for books on your local area. Interview people. Visit your local museum. Use the Internet.

LOCAL HISTORY

Do you know anything about the history of the area in which you live? You could research the whole area, or pick a more specific aspect – such as families who have lived in the area for a long time, or a building, monument, park, railway station, a local company, industry or organisation, or even a farm – the list is endless!

Non-fiction workshops

Author profiles

Which authors do you enjoy reading? Why not create your own author profile or even a series of profiles? Publicity departments of children's book publishers will be happy to send you information on their current authors. Libraries can also be a good source of author information, and some fiction texts – novels and short stories – have short author biographies on the first page.

Your profile could be in the form of an illustrated leaflet or even an information poster. Or, each member of your class could pick an author and everyone could produce an author 'Fact File' with a standard format. Whatever format you choose, think about all the different types of information you could research:

- current books in print by the author
- a five-star rating for these books
- biographical details – such as where the author was born and now lives, what the author has done other than writing
- which awards the author may have won
- different forms of books written by the author (novels, poetry, picture books, information books); different genres of books – fantasy, horror, school drama etc.
- does the author have any favoured themes that he or she writes about?
- are there characters that appear in more than one book by that author?
- if the author is an illustrator too, how would you describe his or her illustration style?
- what are the author's favourite books by other writers?
- a few quotes from the author – often included in publicity blurb – such as 'I like writing because . . .'
- comments from your friends on the author: 'I like ——'s books because . . .'

Can you think of anything to add to this list?

(A list of publishers can be found in the *Writers' and Artists' Yearbook* (Black) and *The Writers' Handbook* (Macmillan). Young Book Trust (London) – 020-8516-2977 and Young Book Trust Scotland – 0131-229-3663 also provide author biographies and bibliographies.)

Auto/biography

Here are a few ideas for different forms of auto/biographical writing:

- What is your very earliest memory? How much of it do you remember? Focus on it for a while in your mind and then write about it in as much detail as you can.
- Look around your home and find a few objects that have a special meaning for you. Write a piece which is divided up into sections in which you talk about each of these objects as touchstones into your memories.
- Make a 'timeline' of interesting/important events for each year of your life.

- Write a summary for each year of your life.
- Think about when you have experienced something for the first time. It might be your first day in the Infants/Juniors or at Secondary school, your first attempt at swimming or learning to ride a bicycle. Try and remember one of these as vividly as you can and then write about it.
- Imagine a photograph album in which there is a picture of each member of your family. Begin with a description of each imaginary photograph, and then move on to talking more generally about that person. This could even become a poem if you wish.
- Another way of doing an imaginary photograph album is to have photographs of special memories throughout your life. So you could start each imaginary photograph with, 'This is me and my sister on the beach at . . .' or 'This was the day we went to . . .'
- One way of preserving the memory of a family member or perhaps even a pet that has died is to write about them. Write about that person or animal in a positive way that celebrates their life.

(See also 'Travel writing' worksheet, p. 186.)

Auto/biography: interview yourself

In the opening chapter of Jamila Gavin's autobiography, *Out of India*, Jamila answers questions that children used to ask her at school when she first arrived in England. Write your own autobiography in which you interview yourself. First, imagine the type of questions that you might ask someone new in your class, such as:

- When and where were you born?
- How many people are there in your family?
- What's the funniest/scariest thing that has ever happened to you?
- Have you ever had any pets?
- What is your earliest memory?
- What makes you happy/annoyed?
- What is the nicest thing anyone has ever said about you?

Draw up a list and then answer them yourself. Make your answers of interest to a reader.

Or, write a biography of someone that you know. Interview them. Work out your questions beforehand and record your conversation. Include photographs and pictures and do a timeline of their life. (See 'Interviews and questionnaires', p. 158.)

Book reviews

Pick a book that you have recently read. It does not have to be a favourite book necessarily, but one that you can say some interesting things about. Aim for two main paragraphs in your review:

> *Paragraph 1*: Give an overview of the plot. In a few sentences, talk about the main events of the book. Don't give too much away – especially the ending!

> *Paragraph 2*: Give your overall responses to the book – with a mixture of personal feedback and factual details. Respond to some of these:

- Did you enjoy the book? Why?
- Did your opinion of the book change as you read it?

- How did the book make you feel?
- What were the book's strengths and weaknesses?
- What are the themes of the book?
- What are your responses to the main character(s)?
- What style of book is it? Have you read any others like it or by the same author?
- If you have read other books by that author, how does this compare?
- Were the characters realistic?
- If there were illustrations in the book, how would you describe them? Did they complement the text?
- Opinions on the title, cover and design.
- What age group is this for?
- Would you recommend it to others?
- Five-star rating.

Try not to make your response too personal – consider what other people might think of the book too.

Historical fiction

See 'Historical fiction' worksheet on pp. 181–2.

Interviews

Have you ever interviewed anyone? You could approach your own interviews in one of two ways:

- Either think about who would make an interesting person to interview, e.g. someone in your school or local community. Has someone you know achieved something special or done something unusual? Has anyone been famous for anything?
- Or think about what subject you would you like to learn more about. Do you know someone who is an expert in that subject, someone you could talk to?

(For advice on conducting interviews, see 'Interviews and questionnaires', p. 58.)

Invention

Invent your own product. It can be anything at all: a type of food or drink, a special domestic appliance such as a cooker or vacuum cleaner, a music-playing machine, a pair of trainers, a form of transport, a musical instrument – anything at all. First, brainstorm your ideas. You could present your product in a variety of ways:

- draw a diagram
- produce a pamphlet explaining the purpose(s) and benefit(s) of your product
- do an advert to go in a magazine or newspaper
- write a jingle for the radio
- write a storyboard for a TV advertisement.

Journalism

See 'Journalism' worksheet later in this section.

Letters from soldiers

See 'Letter writing' worksheet later in this section.

The 1940/2100 house

A television series on Channel 4 entitled *The 1900 House* featured a family who were invited to live as Victorians in London in a terraced house which had been redecorated and re-equipped using only the household objects and technology that were used in the year 1900. There was no modern equipment whatsoever – no TV, video, microwave, washing mashine or even an electric kettle – as in most houses there was no electricity then.

Think back to the year 1940 – the time of the Second World War. What would it have been like living in a terraced house in a major city? Research that period and then write about a 1940 house. What would each room contain? What technology did people have then? Also think about how a family would have spent their evenings. To research the year 1940, use reference books and even interview people who you know were alive at that time. To develop this further, why not write about how your own family would cope with living in a 1940 house.

An alternative would be to write about a 2100 house – a house 100 years in the future. Imagine how people will be living then, and what technology there will be in homes. Do a plan of a 2100 house and write about an average day in 100 years' time.

Painting animals with words

See 'Painting animals with words' worksheet later in this section.

Pick a star: picture books

In his books *Picasso and the Girl with the Ponytail*, *Camille and the Sunflowers*, *Degas and the Little Dancer* and *Leonardo and the Flying Boy*, Laurence Anholt has written about four artists and how they came to produce some of their most famous paintings and sculptures. Rather than just telling the stories in words, he has told each of these stories in words and pictures. Each story is seen through the eyes of a real child who knew the artist. Here Laurence talks about the background to these four texts:

LAURENCE ANHOLT: When I was a small boy, I lived in Holland. One day I was taken to the Vincent van Gogh Museum in Amsterdam. I can still remember the excitement – it was like being sucked into a rushing, swirling, multicoloured snowstorm. The place made me as dizzy as a fairground and from then on, whenever anyone asked me what I wanted to be, I said, 'I want to be an *artist*'. That's why I went to art school when I was older, that's why I taught art for many years and that's why I made this series of books about great artists. I wanted everyone to get excited about art, but I also wanted to tell stories about real people with real feelings. These books take a very long time – about two years for each book. First I have to do a lot of research – so I use libraries, the Internet, museums and galleries. I can always find plenty of information about the artists, but the tricky bit is finding out about the real children who met the artists – children like Camille [in *Camille and the Sunflowers*] who was the son of the postman and became van Gogh's friend, or Zoro [in *Leonardo and the Flying Boy*] who tested Leonardo's flying machine. When I decided to write about Picasso, I began a long hunt, to track down the real 'Girl with a Ponytail' whom Picasso painted in 1954; eventually, by an amazing coincidence, I bumped into her at a dinner party and she told me the story herself!

When I have finished the research, I begin the process of putting the book together; although the events were real, I have to invent conversations and other details. Most importantly, I have to make it all into a really good story. All of that involves using my imagination and trying to 'get into the skin' of these amazing people – a little like being an actor. At the same time, I am doing dozens of sketches and I surround myself with that artist's pictures. In the end I only use a tiny part of all the writing and drawing I have done because I want the books to be very simple. Do I enjoy writing and illustrating? You bet I do! It's not easy but it's the most satisfying job in the world, especially when I receive so many drawings and letters from readers all over the world – I opened one the other day which said, '*When I grow up, I want to be an artist . . .*'

What famous people do you admire? Is there a sports person, an actor or actress, a pop star, a film star or someone in the media? Pick one person and do some research. Find out about their background, how they became famous and what they have done in their life. Pick one aspect of their personal history and write about it – and, like Laurence Anholt in his books – use pictures and words. Do not be afraid to invent some of the details – such as conversations – and to be creative with the facts. Perhaps you could even write it as a picture book or as a comic strip for younger readers.

Research topics

Here is a list of further topics that you may wish to research and write about. Useful sources of information include encyclopedias, reference books, CD-ROMs, specialist magazines, libraries and the Internet.

- the origins of Guy Fawkes/Bonfire Night and Hallowe'en
- religious festivals – such as Diwali, Holi, Ramadan, Eid, Hanukkah, Thanksgiving Day
- the history of Christmas/how other European countries celebrate Christmas
- life in your community 50, 75 or 100 years ago
- important scientific discoveries in the nineteenth and twentieth centuries
- a historical figure – Shakespeare, Elizabeth I, Charles Darwin, Anne Frank, Gandhi
- one important national or world event that happened in each year of your life
- the environment
- unexplained phenomena – UFOs, Atlantis, hauntings, the Loch Ness Monster.

There is advice on conducting research (including the Internet) at the beginning of this chapter.

Start with the facts

On the worksheets entitled 'Start with the facts' one contains information on space and the other has details on wolves. Think: how can you present these facts imaginatively? What could you do with these facts that would encourage people to want to read about them? Think of the *Horrible Science* and *Horrible Histories* series. These books have quizzes, comic strips, timelines, newspaper articles, poems, jokes, fact files, diagrams and illustrations and 'Did You Know?' and 'Ask Your Teacher' sections that make reading information fun.

Read through either Terry Deary's or Nick Arnold's section and then, using all or some of the information on one of the sheets, make the facts fun and entertaining. For example, you could set your teacher a quiz on wolves. Here's the first question for a quiz:

- How many wolves were destroyed by the white settlers when they took over North America? Was it approximately (a) 2,000, (b) 20,000 or (c) 2 million?

Travel writing

See the 'Travel writing' worksheet later in this section. In the Fiction chapter the 'Planning for fiction' and 'Places and descriptive writing' sections will also be useful (pp. 80–5 and 128–34).

START WITH THE FACTS: SPACE

- Space is made up of one huge universe — which itself is made up of many millions of galaxies — and is forever growing and expanding. Our solar system is part of the galaxy known as the Milky Way. Scientists believe that our solar system came about some 5 billion years ago and that the universe began with the 'Big Bang' some 12 billion years ago. Before that, space and time did not exist.

- There are nine planets in our solar system, which are in this order from the Sun: Mercury, Venus, Earth, Mars, Jupiter, Saturn, Uranus, Neptune, Pluto. Venus is about the same size as the Earth. Jupiter is the biggest, Pluto the smallest. Saturn is the planet surrounded by a series of rings and moons. The Sun is larger than all planets and the only star in our solar system. The Sun is a ball of burning gas and is the source of all our energy. The Sun has been burning for 4.6 billion years.

- Our Moon — one of over sixty in our solar system — is one-quarter the size of Earth. The Moon takes 27 days to orbit the Earth. The gravity of our Moon controls the tides of our oceans. The Moon is covered in craters and plains. The Earth revolves daily at a speed of 900 m.p.h. From space, the colours of Earth are blue and white. Earth is the only planet to have water as well as ice, oxygen and life. Over 10 per cent of the Earth's surface is covered in ice. The Earth is surrounded by an atmosphere, which protects us from space. Scientists believe that if one of the planets in our galaxy ever had any life, it was Mars.

- The two main nations that were most active in space in the twentieth century were the Soviet Union and the United States of America. The first journey into space was made by a Soviet Sputnik satellite in 1957. Satellites now orbit the earth for many different reasons — to observe and predict the weather, for military observation, to transmit television and Internet signals and for navigation of the seas and oceans.

- Over the years, various animals have been sent into space — dogs, fish, birds, honey bees, a rat and even a monkey called Ham. The first person to travel to space was the Soviet Yuri Gagarin on 12 April 1961. The first woman in space was Soviet Valentina Tereshkova in 1963. The first craft to land on the moon was the Soviet Luna 9 in 1966. The first landing on the Moon by humans was made by the Americans Neil Armstrong, Buzz Aldrin and Michael Collins in Apollo 11 on 24 July 1969. Armstrong and Aldrin walked on the Moon's surface for 2½ hours and collected rock and dust samples. When stepping onto the Moon for the first time, Neil Armstrong said the now famous words, 'That's one small step for a man, one giant leap for mankind'. As in space there is no air and less gravity than on Earth, rockets and space stations have to provide oxygen and compensate for weightlessness. About 50 per cent of astronauts experience space sickness.

continued over

- There are two types of eclipse. A lunar (Moon) eclipse is when the Moon passes into the shadow of the Earth; there can be as many as three of these a year. A solar (Sun) eclipse takes place when the Moon moves between the Earth and the Sun; this happens every one or two years.
- Space is never static. At any moment in time there are rocks moving through space at incredible speeds – meteors (known as 'shooting stars' made of rock and dust), comets (snow and dust) and asteroids (rocks). Their sizes vary: the biggest asteroid was 560 miles wide, the smallest ones are as small as dust. The two best nights of the year to see shooting stars are 10 and 11 December.
- The stars are huge globes made of hot gases. They give off energy such as heat and light and can exist for billions of years. Stars vary in colour according to their temperature. Scientists believe our Sun is now halfway through its life, and will exist for another 5 billion or so years. If you want to observe the night sky, you could use binoculars or a telescope and a star map. The best views of the night sky are away from the lights of a town or city, where on a dark and moonless night you should be able to see the Milky Way.

This information has been researched and adapted from a number of source books, including these titles:

Eyewitness Project Pack: Space (Dorling Kindersley)

Heather Couper and Nigel Henbest – *Space Encyclopedia* (Dorling Kindersley)

Carole Stott – *New Astronomer: The Practical Guide to the Skills and Techniques of Skywatching* (Dorling Kindersley)

Russell Stannard – *Ask Uncle Albert* and *Space, Time, Rhythm and Rhyme* (Faber & Faber)

- Once upon a time the wolf was the most common large mammal in Europe, and what's more, there were many millions of wolves all over the world. It is believed there are only 122,000 wolves worldwide today. So it is now a rare and endangered species. It has been extinct from the British Isles for over 200 years. The only wolves living in the UK are in places such as zoos. Some wolves can still be found living wild in Alaska, Canada, the United States, Mexico, Spain, Northern Italy, Eastern Europe, Russia, the Middle East, India and China.

- The war on wolves began about 8,000 years ago when humans started to cut down woods and forests and to build farms. This killed off many of the wolves' prey, and so they had little choice but to eat livestock from farms to survive. In return, humans then spread lies and rumours about wolves in the form of myths and fairy tales. The most common myth about the wolf is that it is a threat to humans. It is very rare indeed for wolves to attack people. Wolves may be carnivores – meat eaters – but they do not choose to eat humans. When we think of the wolf we think of an animal that is cruel, cunning, greedy, selfish, evil and ruthless – but really, these are human, not animal qualities. Wolves are known to be social, loyal, clever, intelligent, resourceful and hard-working.

- In the seventeenth and eighteenth centuries, the white settlers who came to North America slaughtered some 2 million wolves. But the native peoples of North America greatly respected the wolf and were very angry and upset that it was being destroyed. Nowadays, in Alaska, the wolf is still hunted for fur coats. It takes up to five wolves to make one single coat. Other than humans, the wolf's enemies include the bear in North America and the tiger in India.

- The wolf is a mammal and is most closely related to the domestic dog, dingo, coyote and jackal. The Latin name for the wolf family is *Canis lupus*. There are about twenty-three subspecies of wolf. Wolves are nomadic creatures that travel and hunt in packs. They spend eight to ten hours each day travelling. One-third of a wolf's life is spent in search of food. Between four and six wolf pups are born in each litter, and most die due to lack of food. The average life span of a wolf that reaches adulthood is nine years. Wolves eat mainly meat from deer, moose, elk, rabbit, sheep and beaver.

- Most people know about wolves from fairy tales such as 'Little Red Riding Hood', 'The Three Little Pigs' and 'The Wolf and the Seven Kids', the song 'Who's Afraid of the Big Bad Wolf?' and the musical *Peter and the Wolf* – which are not about real wolves at all. Aesop was a writer who lived some 2,500 years ago and he wrote fables in which the wolf often features, and always as a bad character. Yet there have been some stories about kind wolves too – in Rudyard Kipling's *The Jungle Book*, the boy Mowgli is raised by a pack of wolves. We often talk about the wolf without realising it, in sayings

continued over

such as: 'cry wolf', 'keep the wolf from the door', 'wolf down your food' and 'a wolf in sheep's clothing'. The French have a poetic saying, 'Entrée le chien et le loup' (between the dog and the wolf), which means early evening or dusk.

- Within the past few years, a number of books for children have tried to show a more positive image of the wolf: *Wolf* by Gillian Cross, *The True Story of the Three Little Pigs by A. Wolf* by Jon Sciezka, *The Small Good Wolf* by Mary Rayner and *Walk with a Wolf* by Janni Howker. So why are we afraid of wolves? Shouldn't wolves be afraid of us?

This information has been researched and adapted from these research sources:

Candace Savage – *Wolves* (Hale)
Barry Holstun Lopez – *Of Wolves and Men* (Dent)
BBC Wildlife magazine vol. 14, no. 3, March 1996
Magic Animals: Wolves – BBC2 television programme, broadcast 1 March 1995

Fictional books referred to:
Gillian Cross – *Wolf* (Puffin)
Janni Howker – *Walk with a Wolf* (Walker)
Rudyard Kipling – *The Jungle Book* (Puffin)
Mary Rayner – *The Small Good Wolf* (Walker)
Jon Sciezka – *The True Story of the Three Little Pigs by A. Wolf* (Viking)

HISTORICAL FICTION

Would you say that historical fiction is non-fiction or fiction? Really it is both, a hybrid of the two. Historical fiction is *based* on facts but written as fiction – with characters, dialogue and plots. Terry Deary has written a series of historical fiction books called *Tudor Terrors*. These are all stories based on real historical events. Here Terry Deary explains his ideas regarding writing in this genre:

TERRY DEARY: With my *Tudor Terrors* I wanted to create adventure stories about authentic historical characters who went through authentic historical incidents. Essentially what I'm doing is dramatising historical events. There's not a great deal of difference between writing historical fiction and normal fiction – in that you have to make the world of your story and your characters as vivid and realistic as possible. You have to have strong characters with whom you feel some sympathy. There have got to be good, clear issues. You have to feel comfortable with the period in which the story is set. So, when I wrote my *Tudor Terror* series I researched the Tudor period so deeply I could almost imagine stepping into that time. And my research brought some interesting things that influenced some of the actual stories in the series.

Below is the introduction to one of the four books from the *Tudor Terrors* series, *The Lady of Fire and Tears*. The chapter title is a quote from William Shakespeare's play *King Henry IV Part 2*. Notice how vividly Terry Deary portrays the setting in this passage. It is clear that he wants his reader to experience what it would have actually felt like to have been in that room. He talks about the draught from the windows and also the warmth and the light generated by the fire. By telling the story in the first person, the reader is given an intimate, first-hand account of life in the Tudor period:

Chapter One
'Barren winter, with
his wrathful nipping cold'

When winter came to Marsden Hall we would huddle round the fire and tell tales. The fire roared in the huge stone hearth of the main hall and lit the faces of the family. The draught from the windows and the doors made the tapestries on the walls ripple. The bright embroidered figures seemed to come alive then and walk across the fields of green silk. They were ghosts that had come to listen to our stories.

The Marsden family stories were not like the stories your family tell. Our stories were true. The laughter and the tears, the mysteries and the fears, were real. When I was a boy I listened to those stories and they haunted my dreams. Even now, years later, as I write them down I can see the family gathered there in the flickering amber light. I can feel the warmth of the fire on my face and the cold of the winter air on my

continued over

back. And I can feel the chill of fear that ran down my spine as I listened to some of those sad stories.

I can see the flowing white beard of Great-Uncle George as he roared out the tales of ancient battles the Marsden family had fought through the years. I can hear Grandmother's creaking voice chilling us with her memories of the murderous Henry VIII. Grandfather thrilled us with stories of his adventures in the lawless wilderness that was the border with Scotland. Father boasted about his travels and bored us with his battles against the miserable criminals who lived their secret lives in our part of Durham County in the north east of England. He was the magistrate who brought them to justice – when he could catch them.

'They respect me,' he said.

'They hate him,' our orphaned serving girl, Meg, used to say.

But most of all I remember my mother's stories. She was the quietest of the storytellers, yet some of her stories were so terrifying that they froze my blood.

Activity

Pick any period from history that interests you. It could be the First or Second World War, the Victorian age or even before that. Read about that period in the books in your library or classroom or on the Internet. Make notes on the way people lived, the clothes they wore, the food they ate and their lifestyles. Instead of writing about famous people from that time – such as kings and queens – write about everyday people such as farm workers, maids, servants, trades people, crafts people or musicians. If you are picking an era from the early to mid-twentieth century, perhaps you could trace and interview some people who lived through that time. Work hard on developing your character(s) for your story. You could tell a story about an incident that happened in the life of your character. Or, you could write a monologue in which your character talks about events in her or his life.

Have a look at some of your local newspapers. Find out what types of news they cover – such as key local events, business news, sports, weddings, concerts. Look at the style of writing and see how a lot of information can be put across in just a few short paragraphs.

Here is one example:

'Festival of Light is Shining Glory for Hindus' (Reading Chronicle – 12 November 99)

More than 300 members of the Hindu community gathered on Saturday to celebrate Diwali, the Festival of Light.

The Festival dates back to when Lord Rama and his family returned to his kingdom after 14 years in exile.

His people celebrated the homecoming by lighting their houses, holding street parties and distributing sweets and the Hindu community has celebrated the same way ever since.

Last Saturday the Festival at Reading's Hindu Temple was divided into two halves.

Part of the programme was held in the middle hall at the Whitley Street Temple and concentrated on prayers and the religious aspects of the occasion.

Festivities then moved on to the main hall for the cultural element with the evening's singing and dancing, finishing with a meal for all the guests.

Paul Gupta, chairman for the Reading Hindu Temple's Educational and Cultural Community Centre said, 'It was very well received. The children who took part have been practising for the past few weeks and it was marvellous to see them on the stage.

'The actual date of the festival was on Sunday but we decided to hold it on the Saturday evening because the families would hold celebrations in their own homes the following day.'

Activity

Choose an event in your local area. It could be a forthcoming football match, a school concert/play/performance, the hundredth birthday of a local person, a village fair, a writer visiting your school, a shop being opened by a celebrity or even a protest against a new car park being built. Do as much research as you can, and if possible, include quotes from people involved. Write a piece informing people of the event. As with the piece above, aim to give an overview of what happened without going into too much detail.

LETTER WRITING

Below is an extract from a piece entitled 'Letter from a Roman Soldier' by Brian Moses. It is a fictional letter sent by a Roman soldier stationed at Hadrian's Wall to his beloved in Colchester.

> *My Darling Flavia, we have been parted for too long now. I grow bitter at the delays and false news that greet my every enquiry as to when I can expect a transfer south. I know that I am voicing the feelings of many when I say that I hate this posting. If it isn't the ceaseless rain or the sleet that penetrates even my thickest tunic, it is the boredom of sentry duty that drives me to despair. Occasionally we see action when rebellious northern tribes fling themselves at the wall, but more often than not our days are filled with patrols and fatigues. Of these, changing the toilets is by far the worst duty. Maximus, our officer, he doesn't get his hands dirty, he just barks out the orders. Three times a month we have to strap on full kit – armour, weapons, cooking pots, camp building equipment – and march for thirty kilometres. If our feet are blistered or attacked by frostbite, this can be agony . . .*
>
> *One day, when I complete my twenty-five year service, we will be married and I will take you to Rome. I shall buy some land with my pension and our sons will farm the soil and have no need to follow their father's footsteps.*
>
> *Until that day, my dearest Flavia, I must content myself with thoughts of you, our children and home.*
> *Tiberius*

Activity

Choose a war in history – even recent history: Bosnia, the Falklands, the Gulf War or the First or Second World Wars. Write a letter from a soldier or a nurse to their loved one(s)/family at home, in which they tell of the conditions in which they are living. Research the war you have chosen first of all.

Or, you could pick an important figure from history talking about a significant moment in their life. Write a letter from that person to their wife/husband, relation or friend. Here are some examples:

- Alexander Graham Bell at the time he invented the telephone.
- Emily Pankhurst talking about being arrested for tying herself to the railings.
- William the Conqueror when arriving at the English coast in 1066.
- Joan of Arc shortly before she was burnt at the stake in 1431.

Before you write your letter, research some information on that person.

PAINTING ANIMALS WITH WORDS

This passage, taken from Janni Howker's fictional short story *Badger on the Barge*, contains a description of a badger. Notice how the author paints a very striking picture of the animal. Much of her description is based on sound – such as the noise the badger makes when it is eating, its whinny and the sound the animal's claws create on the wooden floor of the barge. Notice too how she uses such devices as simile (including 'like a grey shadow' and 'noisy as a pig') and metaphor ('skirting-board of his body'), alliteration ('claws clicked'), assonance ('planks, making a chickering') and many colourful, expressive verbs, such as 'rippling', 'thumping', 'chickering', 'snuffling' and 'guzzled'.

> *Helen peered through the crack. Beside her, the smell of damp earth rose from the bucket of worms she had left on the deck. For the first time ever, she saw a badger. The black and grey striped head poked through the door, and then came the fat rippling skirting-board of his body. Like a grey shadow, he moved out of the far cabin – then he was like a fat bear, bouncing along, thumping the planks, making a chickering snuffling whinny, like a tiny horse.*
>
> *His claws clicked and scratched on the wood. He lifted his striped snout towards the old woman, as if he was looking at her from out of his black nose, then he buried his face in the milk, and slurped and guzzled, noisy as a pig.*

(Janni Howker – *Badger on the Barge*: Walker Books)

Activity

Think of an animal. Write a short piece in which you describe this animal doing a number of things (depending on what type of animal it is) – such as moving, eating, sleeping, swimming, hunting for or catching food, wriggling or flying. As in Janni Howker's piece, make your language colourful and expressive.

TRAVEL WRITING

See how in this short extract from her childhood autobiography, *Out of India*, Jamila Gavin creates a vivid and lively picture of a railway station:

> *More travel; tongas, trains, busy Indian railway stations; more excitement.*
>
> *An Indian railway platform is a composite of all life in India: animal and human. As you stand there waiting, at any time of night or day, for a train which could be hours late, the vendors are cooking any number of delicious dishes. Everywhere are groups of people or families, crouched in initimate circles, or wrapped in shroud-like coverings, grabbing sleep whenever possible. And watching, scurrying, poised, coveting, are the rats and cockroaches and ants and dogs and crows and monkeys, all waiting to pounce on any morsel which falls their way. Sometimes, they take things into their own hands – or claws! Once, when the train had pulled into a station, I got off to go and buy a dry banana leaf of vegetable curry from a platform vendor. Little did I know what other eyes were on my food. As I returned with the banana leaf cupped in my hands, a huge crow flew down. It grabbed the edge of the leaf in its beak and pulled it from my hands. All my curry went spilling down on to the platform as the crow flew away. But there wasn't a mess for long. Immediately, the hungry station dogs leapt forward, as did the monkeys, cockroaches and all kinds of other creatures, to consume my meal. As for me, I was forced to go back and start all over again.*

Activity

Think of a memorable place you have been to or a special journey that you have made. It could be a holiday abroad, a trip to London or another city, a visit to a museum or a day at the seaside. Brainstorm as much as you can remember about the day/holiday/journey. Before writing your piece, consider the following issues:

- Have an opening sentence/paragraph that will grab your reader's attention.
- Give short but detailed descriptions of the places to let your reader know what it is like to actually be there.
- If the holiday was abroad, try to use some of the language from that country in your own writing.
- Tell your reader how you felt about being there. Were you excited, frightened, fascinated?
- Use dialogue – conversations between you and other people – as if it was a story. Speech can make the piece more lively.
- Do you have any photographs or postcards you could put in your piece? Could you refer to part of a postcard or letter that you sent someone?

Make your travel writing as stimulating and entertaining as you would a piece of fiction.

NON-FICTION GLOSSARY

alliteration Where words begin with the same letters or sounds: 'table top', 'car keys', 'green grass'.

appendix A section at the back of a non-fiction book or project that contains extra information such as research notes, interview transcripts or questionnaires.

assonance Where words have the same sounds – 'green bean', 'new view'.

autobiography A piece of writing in which one person writes the story of her or his own life.

bibliography A section at the back of a non-fiction book or project which lists all of the books (and all other sources of research from newspapers to videos to CD-ROMs) mentioned or used for research.

biography A piece of writing in which one person tells the story of another person's life.

book review A report of a book, often a new book.

contents page A page at the front of a book that lists the various chapters and sections.

drafting and editing Drafting is doing different versions to improve and develop a piece of writing. Editing is checking a piece for spelling, grammar and punctuation.

index The last part of a non-fiction book, the index lists all the different subjects, themes and topics covered in the book with page reference numbers.

interview A meeting in which one person asks another a set of prepared questions.

genre The type of non-fiction, for example, biography, travel writing and journalism.

glossary A section in a book where technical words and phrases are explained in everyday language.

journalism Reporting on and writing about real events and news stories.

non-fiction Writing based on facts and real events.

metaphor and simile Simile is when you say one thing is *like* something else: 'he eats like a horse', 'her hands are as cold as ice'. Metaphor is when you say one thing actually *is* something else: 'it's raining nails', 'the city is a jungle tonight'.

research Finding out information on a subject, for example, from books, CD-ROMs, libraries, the Internet or by interviewing people.

structure How a piece of writing is set out, with a beginning, middle and an end.

theme The subject of a piece of writing.

transcript An interview in written form.

travel writing Autobiographical writing about journeys and places.

Part Two
Author Visit Guide

5 Author case studies

Malorie Blackman
(Novelist and screenwriter)

Figure 5.1 Malorie Blackman

Visits to schools, libraries and bookshops

MALORIE BLACKMAN: I do love meeting children and getting feedback on my books. Though I just like talking to children, anyway. On average I do three school visits a month. Schools either get hold of me via my publishers – Transworld or Scholastic – or contact me at my email address: malorie.b@ukgateway.net. I generally work on a first-come, first-serve basis, and as I can't travel too far in a day, because of my young daughter, I tend to do one-off visits rather than residencies. I often do many visits and events around the time of Children's Book Week.

I do a lot of preparation for each event – such as choosing passages from my books to read that are appropriate to the age range I'll be meeting. I also show children the stages involved in producing a book – and again, the demonstration materials I choose will depend on the age of my audience. What I do is to show children the various drafts that a book goes through, how illustrations are produced to interact with the text as well as how a book is edited and assembled. For my talks I don't have a script as such, though I do follow a set structure.

Recently I've started doing writing workshops in schools. They're such fun! I begin with some warm-up exercises first, and these always go down really well. One easy exercise I start off with is asking the children to pick their favourite sport, and then I ask them what that sport would be if it was an animal. Then, I ask what that sport would be if it was a colour. And then I might ask what the sport might be if it was a food. I tell the children that the point of this exercise is to get them thinking of everyday things but in a different way, and to come at things from different angles. A variation of this is picking a favourite food, and imagining what type of weather it would be. One child once chose spaghetti – he said it would be like a sea bubbling and boiling! You get some amazing responses like that. When children read these out, they're not allowed to say what the food or the sport is, because we have to guess what it is. Ultimately what I'm trying to do with this activity is to give children different images to think about.

From there we'll go on to another activity. One I do is to give the children an opening paragraph of a story and they have to continue with it. It's a piece that I wrote myself. It's in the first person, and it's an atmospheric piece set at midnight in which the narrator of the story goes out into a garden:

> *I crept down the stairs, wincing each time the floorboards groaned under my feet. The house was night-time dark, but I knew the way by heart. Through the hall, through the kitchen, open the door and out into the garden. The moon was hiding behind a cloud. But at last the clouds drifted out of the way. The garden filled with moonlight, bathing me in its silver glow. And slowly, I turned into a . . .*

I ask the children to describe in great detail what they turned into – how it felt and what it made them feel like.

Another activity is one in which I'll give them an opening phrase which they have to continue with two or more lines:

> Above the shining clouds . . .
> Beneath the sparkling ripples . . .
> Beyond the distant stars . . .
> Behind the TV/computer screen . . .
> Under my bed . . .

There was one 12-year-old boy at an all-boys school I visited who wrote the most incredible piece for this exercise. I told his teacher that he was a born writer – the things he came up with were marvellous and very mature. Yet another exercise I do is to get the class to write a conversation between the following:

> Fire and water
> Black and white
> Day and night
> Earth and air

As I go around schools it's really satisfying when a teacher comes up to me afterwards and tells me that they didn't know that certain pupils were capable of the standard of writing that they achieved in my workshop – or that a certain pupil has never shown any interest in writing stories before. There was one school where I'd set the children a writing exercise. I asked volunteers to read out what they'd written. The children put their hands up and the teacher whispered to me to choose one specific girl who had her hand up. And this girl came out with some absolutely wonderful writing. Later the teacher told me that this girl never volunteers to do anything, and that she usually hates reading and writing. It's so nice to hear that you can spark off an interest in these workshops. It's really rewarding. I often get sent pieces and projects by classes after a workshop. I do love reading children's writing.

Overall, what I try to do in my workshops is to show children that writing fiction doesn't have to be like writing an essay, and that it can actually be great fun. I don't know how creative writing is taught in schools nowadays, but when I was at secondary school the joy of writing was taken out of us because all we ever seemed to do was to analyse fiction rather than write it. English was all about giving critical appraisals of novels and poetry, and we were only encouraged to use the logical part of the brain – never the emotional or creative part.

I'm soon going to Michael Faraday Primary School in London. The Year 6 pupils there have done a whole project on me, and apparently the children's reviews and drawings of my books are all displayed out in the hall. They've been making up quizzes about my books as well as doing artwork and embroidery and tea towels and all kinds of things! They've also used my novel *Thief!* as a starting point to write their own stories. It's so flattering – I can't wait to do that visit. I'm quite amused that I've been the topic for the children's homework!

Ampthill Library, Bedfordshire: one-day visit

Malorie Blackman's visit to Ampthill Library was part of a short tour to promote her novel *Dangerous Reality* and was attended by Year 5 pupils from Alameda Middle School in Ampthill. The event was organised by the library services in Bedfordshire and Buckinghamshire and featured as part of *Buzzwords*, the region's highly successful and innovative Children's Literature festival. For 1999, the festival took the theme of the sea, and there were many exciting and eclectic events such as a book character parade, an official opening by poet and broadcaster Michael Rosen, a chance to meet authors and illustrators discussing their work – Keith Brumpton, Julia Jarman, Frank Rodgers and Ted Dewan, readings by Tony Bradman, Colin Hawkins, Laurence Anholt and Margaret Nash, Mr Willy Wonka reading from Roald Dahl's *Charlie and the Chocolate Factory*, storytelling from Gabamouche, Word of Mouth, Us Two and Margie Barbour.

The visit to Ampthill Library – the first author event to be held at this part-time branch library – took place on 23 February 1999. It was co-ordinated by Naomi Cooper, Transworld publicity manager, and Vicky Fox, Schools Co-ordinator for Bedfordshire. Prior to the event, Naomi had sent publicity materials out to the teachers at Alameda Middle School.

On the day, Malorie undertook one morning and one afternoon presentation. Each session was attended by two Year 5 classes. As Malorie set up her display materials for her first talk, Vicky Fox spoke briefly to the expectant audience. From this short exchange it was evident that the children were very familiar with Malorie's work and also that they had been attending and thoroughly enjoying other author events in the *Buzzwords* festival.

MALORIE BLACKMAN: So – what books do you like to read?

With this very first question, Malorie's talk began as it continued – as an interactive, lively and highly engaging celebration of reading, and not only of her own work, but of books in general. Malorie's humour, her effervescent personality and her passionate delivery were highly infectious, and so much so that for the duration of her talk, the sixty children in attendance sat open-eyed and enraptured. It was clear throughout not only that Malorie was keen for her audience to take an active role in this event themselves, but also that she was genuinely interested and concerned with what the children had to say.

MALORIE BLACKMAN: And what do I read? I love thrillers and mysteries and whodunnits, and because I love reading them, these are the types of books I like to write. And what I'm going to do today is talk about the books I write – how I write them, why I write them, and, if you're lucky, I might tell you how much I get paid for writing them!! I hope you've all come with lots of questions to ask me, as I love answering questions – it's my favourite part of these talks.

From here, Malorie covered a great breadth of material, including:

- how she came to be published
- the origins and evolutions of the titles *Dangerous Reality*, *Hacker*, *Operation Gadgetman*, *A.N.T.I.D.O.T.E*, *Pig-heart Boy* and *Not So Stupid!*
- the role of editors in the writing and publishing process
- her books that have been adapted for television
- readings of passages from *Pig-heart Boy* and *Dangerous Reality*
- children's own writing and the *Young Writer* journal
- planning a novel and doing chapter breakdowns
- drafting and reworking a text
- where her ideas come from, such as listening in to conversations!

Frequently Malorie stopped to ask the children a question in order that they would be able to relate their own ideas and experiences to those of the characters in her novels:

Have any of you ever been accused of something that you didn't do? (*Thief!*)
How would you all feel about having a transplant from an animal? (*Pig-heart Boy*)

One boy responded to the latter with his own rhetorical and yet most insightful question: 'How would you feel about your kidneys being given to a pig?'

The talk was finally rounded off with an extended question and answer session, to which Malorie responded to the following questions:

Do you know the end of a book when you start writing it?

Do you ever get ideas from the books you read?

Did you enjoy being on 'Live and Kicking'?

Do you have a mascot like Jacqueline Wilson does?

Have you written any non-fiction books?

Do you ever read the last page of a book first to find out what's going to happen?

Do you get annoyed if your editor tells you to change something in a book?

Malorie's final comment to the children was:

If anyone ever tells me that they don't like reading, I say, there are so many brilliant books out there, so it's clear to me that they just haven't found the right book yet!

To conclude the session, Malorie happily engaged in book signing, conversations and photo-opportunities with the children. As the two Year 5 classes filed out of the library to return to school, one 10-year-old boy obviously could not wait until later to enjoy his signed copy of *Thief!* He was reading the book as he walked out of the door.

Vicky Fox, organiser of the event, was clearly delighted with the day:

The visit was a resounding success. The school promoted Malorie's books, the children read them with enthusiasm, using the class packs and coming into Ampthill Library to borrow books. In fact, the demand for books after Malorie's sessions was so great we ran out of books very early on. Fortunately, Naomi

Cooper had brought quite a number of Malorie's books with her so we were able to satisfy the children.

Malorie is a wonderful speaker. The children's attention was caught instantly and her obvious enthusiasm for books and writing was transmitted to and received by them with gusto! The teachers were very happy with the visit and they have since commented that Malorie Blackman is an excellent speaker and a great champion of books and reading.

Anthony Masters

(Novelist and screenwriter)

Figure 5.2 Anthony Masters

Visits to schools

ANTHONY MASTERS: Some years ago, one of the chief librarians at Kent County Council asked if I could inject some excitement into their creative writing sessions. A residency was set up on the Kent coast and my Book Explosions came about as a result. Essentially, they're two-hour drama simulations in which the children get emotionally and physically involved in a fictional world. It's physically challenging as it involves ropes and nets and adventure training equipment. Originally, I used Conan Doyle's *Lost Valley* as a focus, though I tend to change the focus of the Book Explosions around as I like to keep the workshops fresh. The activities are designed to give a whole experience to the children – in which they will go through a series of realistic and stressful sequences, and as a result, they will produce a great deal of adrenalin for creative writing. I've never done normal school visits, just to read my work or to do a writing activity – that doesn't really interest me. The work I do now in schools comes either through repeat visits or personal recommendations. I occasionally work on an Arts Council project and with some library events or literacy groups.

It would be true to say that I'm fairly choosy about the schools I go to as my workshops are quite draining. I probably do about 20 per cent of the invitations I receive. Book Explosions tend to be very popular and the danger would be to do too many. The ideal year groups for the workshops are Years 5, 6, 7 and 8. As a rule, I don't work with teenagers over the age of 13 as you need to have total suspension of disbelief. Ideally, a Book Explosion will be done in a drama studio, if a school has one. Assembly halls are too big as I need a venue that is fairly contained. We have fifty children at a time – fifty in the morning and fifty in the afternoon.

In a Book Explosion the pupils go through what one reviewer from the *Times Educational Supplement* referred to as a form of 'safe danger' – which will give them confidence and will empower them to go on and create some powerful and evocative writing. The writing that the pupils produce is like my own first draft 'splurge' writing – and will need further work and development. I do encourage the children to be quite dark in their writing, but I won't allow any crude violence or blood and guts. I'm terribly directive about what I want them to produce. I try to open up the children's latent imaginations that have been battered by television and soap operas.

Some children might feel threatened about the writing aspect, so I try to reassure them and I say that I'll give them some ideas if they can't think of anything to write. If some don't want to write – or can't write – they can draw or do a strip cartoon. At this point of the Book Explosion, some children will work on the floor in the foetal position. They'll actually curl up on the floor. It's as if they're recovering from the stress of the activities.

If I'm doing a residency, I'll run something I call 'Critics' Forum'. This is when volunteers get to read out the first draft of their pieces. Often, they'll just read out the beginning of the piece, perhaps two or three paragraphs. The rest of the class have to respond constructively, and pick out elements that they like. I won't allow them to say that the writing is rubbish, they have to be positive. I'll go around the class asking them for their opinions. It's a potentially volatile situation as some children can get quite upset. And I'll do all kinds of work during a residency, in addition to Book Explosions – such as writing on location, Critics' Forums and book review panels. As a result of one recent residency, a class produced an anthology of their work.

A residency ultimately needs a goal, a focus. I like to be really energetic during a residency, and do lots of assemblies. I'll discuss the Book Explosions and I'll ask the children to read out their work, or I'll read out their work myself. I like to invite the parents in one evening as well – and I'll do a writing workshop with them too. I get them to do something safe, like emotive childhood experiences. And I'll do a workshop with the teachers too. All these different activities will be organised from the outset, in agreement between myself and the school.

I must have total teacher involvement. For a start, I ask that teachers not only oversee a second draft of the children's writing after my visit, but also that they write during my visit too. If I see a teacher marking books during one of my workshops, I instantly remark upon it! I can usually tell if a school is suitable for one of my Book Explosions because the teachers will be wanting a visit to help inspire creative writing in their school, and they'll feel that as a result of a partnership with me something positive could be achieved. Also, such schools will ask me what kind of atmosphere or environment I need to work in, and how they as teachers can get involved with my visit. I tend to avoid straight requests from teachers as I want my visits to derive from a whole school need for assistance with reluctant writers and readers. And I don't appreciate being asked when I do my visits if I'm having fun. Usually, I'll reply with a glib remark like, 'No. We're working hard, because writing is serious business.'

I've been writer in residence at Barnardo's, and at schools with severe behavioural problems. My two-year Barnardo's residency was deeply rewarding. Barnardo's take on statemented children with behavioural difficulties. The teachers there are highly vocational and they genuinely like the children. It's a potentially volatile environment, though I very much liked working there. In general, I would say that I like going into schools and environments where help is really needed.

The Weald Community School and Sixth Form, Billingshurst, Sussex: one-day visit

The Weald is a large community comprehensive school with 1,500 pupils on register. Set on a 25-acre site, the school offers a range of academic and vocational courses for all ages.

Anthony Masters' visit to The Weald on 7 July 1999 – his fourth visit in four consecutive years – contributed to the school's annual Year 8 Reading Festival. The festival is considered a key event in The Weald calendar and is organised by a committee chaired by the Head of Learning Support, Angie Burroughs. Here she outlines the background and aims of the festival as well as the activities for the 1999 event:

ANGIE BURROUGHS: The Reading Festival began four years ago with the aim of fostering a love and appreciation of reading in the school. Each festival, the Year 8 English groups are retitled as celebrated authors for the three days: Shakespeare, Dickens, Brontë, Gaskell, Rossetti, Wordsworth, Hardy and Austen.

Our aim with the festival is to give the children as wide a viewpoint on reading as possible. To this end, we always invite a whole range of professionals connected with reading – authors, poets, illustrators, paper engineers, actors and drama specialists. This year we have a cartoonist, which will bring another completely different dimension. On top of this, we're having one group using IT to write their own cartoons.

At the end of every festival the committee discusses which visitors ran successful sessions – as ultimately what we need are people that can hold and sustain the children's attention whilst giving them an insight into their specialism. Those that have gone down well and have produced good results are always invited back. And generally speaking, we go by recommendations. If we hear of someone doing good work in schools, we'll invite them in ourselves.

Part of the Year 8 English syllabus in the summer term is for each pupil to design and write a book specifically for the junior age range. The Year 8 pupils have been working on their books for the last three weeks. The books are judged and awards will be given at a presentation ceremony. Edward Enfield – Harry Enfield's father – will be coming in to present the awards. During the festival, the pupils will go out to various local Junior schools to read their books to small groups of Junior children. Everyone really enjoys it. And what's more, it gives their writing a great sense of purpose – having a real audience to write for.

The Festival Committee works very closely with the English faculty and this year we're going to fully evaluate the Reading Festival afterwards. We're going to interview the children and ask what they feel they have got out of it. We need to discover if the festival does truly justify coming off the regular school timetable for three days as well as all the time and energy that go into setting it up. Running a festival like this is very hard work – it takes a whole year of planning. What's more, it's a difficult logistical exercise – organising the 240 pupils in Year 8 and organising a three-day timetable for them.

Funding this year comes from £2 pupil donations as well as our local sponsors – Royal Sun Alliance, Horsham District Council and also The Weald PTA. Our sponsors have been very generous to us over the years.

As regards Anthony Masters' workshops, I've seen pupils produce the most amazing writing that we wouldn't have thought they were capable of. The children themselves are often surprised by what they find they can do. What Anthony does is to take them into another world. And in just two hours he's able to recognise and utilise special skills and qualities in pupils that we don't always get to see as teachers. He enables us to see the pupils in a very different situation, and we see leaders emerging. I really admire him for that. When I've told some of the Year 8 groups in assemblies in the past that Anthony Masters is coming in to do these workshops, perhaps half would be enthusiastic, the other half not. Afterwards, every single child is very positive about them, and that makes it so worthwhile. His workshops are hard graft – and really, the results speak for themselves.

In addition to Anthony Masters' Book Explosions, the activities during The Weald's three-day Reading Festival included:

- 'Desert Island Books' with senior members of staff
- Poetry workshops with Emma Greengrass
- Cartoon workshops with Griselda
- Play reading with John and Rene Humphreys
- Visits to junior schools for Year 8 pupils to read their own books
- Storytelling with Linda Cotterell
- Illustration workshops with Alan Baker
- Pop-up book workshops with members of the English faculty
- Award ceremony with Edward Enfield
- Bookshop.

Anthony Masters' 'Book Explosion' workshop

For this visit Anthony chose the fictional contexts of his own novel *The Dark Tower* and Arthur Conan Doyle's *Lost World* for the Book Explosions, the first of which is reported in detail below. Both workshops were held in the school's octagonal-shaped library – a large, bright and airy room, highly suitable for such an event.

Throughout the Book Explosions, Anthony's manner was strict – vital for these activities – yet tempered with much compassion towards the groups. He regularly gave genuine praise and merit where it was due and was swift to eradicate any inappropriate behaviour. He maintained a momentum over the two hours that succeeded not only in keeping the interest and motivation of the participants, but also in creating and sustaining a self-contained fictional world. At the start of each workshop he warmly reassured the groups, 'It doesn't matter if you fail, what really matters is that you try'.

What characterises Anthony's approach to school visits is his genuine concern for interacting with and inspiring young writers, and it was apparent that publicity of his own work does not feature anywhere on his agenda. He talked openly about his writing in the question and answer session at the end of each workshop; however, this was not to talk about specific titles, more to enlighten young people as to how writers work. At lunch, Anthony was approached by a pupil who had been in a Book Explosion during a previous Reading Festival. Anthony took time from his meal to discuss various matters with this young fan, and together they agreed that Anthony would swop some of his latest novels for a copy of the boy's latest poem. Anthony continued to spend the remainder of his short break giving advice and guidance to a visiting teacher from Paris who was conducting postgraduate research into French translations of classic English children's novels.

When observing a Book Explosion one could be forgiven for forgetting that Anthony – a most charismatic and dynamic workshop leader – is principally a novelist and screenwriter, as during the first hour or so issues such as books and writing are not addressed. It is not until the creative writing part of the workshop that Anthony begins to discuss writing, and then only in the context of the pupils' own work.

'You won't have seen anything like a Book Explosion!' Angie Burroughs declared as she introduced Anthony to the fifty Year 8 pupils sitting expectantly on the library floor. Unlike more traditional author visits, Anthony did not begin by giving an amusing anecdote, summarising his writing career or bursting into a poem or a spot of storytelling. Having made the announcement – 'I want you to take risks with your minds and bodies, I want you to build up your confidence and I want you to prepare yourselves for the teamwork ahead' – he guided the group through a series of skills-based warm-up activities:

- '*Numbers*' – Anthony called out a series of random numbers between two and twenty and the pupils had to form themselves into groups of that number. This activity enabled Anthony to select two individuals who had both been displaying strong leadership skills – Sarah and James – to head up the teams for the activities that followed later.
- '*Falling Backwards*' – performed in pairs, this activity involved catching your partner as he or she fell backwards.
- '*The Executioner*' – a volunteer is blindfolded and placed between two chairs and is given a rolled-up newspaper with which to swipe at the rest of the group as they attempt to pass between the chairs.
- '*Blind Courage*' – the group formed a wide circle; another volunteer, again blindfolded, had to run as fast as they could from one side of the circle to the other, to be caught by a wall of people on the other side.
- '*Mirror Language*' – performed in pairs, one person moved their hands and arms around in the air and their partner had to follow the movements as closely as possible.

Anthony Masters next introduced the fictional context:

> You have been in a passenger aircraft and have crashlanded in a particularly hostile part of South America. There are rumours that somewhere in this wilderness is a tower of dark, smoked glass which climbs up out of the mists of a valley. It is rumoured that some people have disappeared into this place. So our proximity to the Dark Tower is unfortunate. We have no food. We have no water. We can survive for maybe ten days without food, but only two or three days without water. In a moment we're going to cross the mountains . . .

Anthony divided the group into two teams, now led by Sarah and James. In turn, each team was roped together and had to move swiftly around the room as one unit, whilst keeping their rope slack at all times. As each team completed their tasks, the two leaders were instructed to choose a deputy leader – someone, as Anthony suggested, who they might not get on with in usual circumstances, but someone that they would trust and respect in a crisis.

From here, the teams had to cross a salt lake represented by a cargo net. In turn, the two teams manoeuvred under the cargo net as they were timed with a stopwatch. For 'Russian Roulette' – an exercise in which volunteers from both teams race each other – Anthony informed the group:

> Now my friends, imagine this. You are standing on top of a mountain and you are looking down into the valley below. You can see in front of you the Dark Tower, looming up out of the mists. It has a door at the bottom with a faded sign saying 'Danger'. Someone is walking up and down in front of the door. It is the Blind Hunter, the guardian of the Dark Tower. Strangely and

suspiciously, you find a key on top of a stone table. It looks as if the key would fit the door of the tower – yet you know that some people die if they enter the tower . . .

For 'The Blind Hunter', the whole group again sat in a circle and the team leaders chose a volunteer each. A member of one team was blindfolded and had to lash out with a rolled-up newspaper at a member of the opposing team. For the creative writing segment that followed, Anthony informed the group:

With your writing I want you to be original as well as atmospheric. You've got to totally and utterly believe in the world of your story. You're going to write what we call a 'splurge' – which is writing without giving any attention to spelling or punctuation or grammar, all of which you can do in your second draft in class. I want you to get your pen and paper and to go off somewhere in this room to work. And while you are doing this, two judges are going to come around to read your work and they will choose one beginning each that really makes them want to read on.

The background for your writing is as follows. You have now got the key to the Dark Tower. You open the door. What is behind the door? What is behind the door that would make the most atmospheric and original story? What can you write that will make your reader want to read on?

Anthony spent the following twenty minutes walking around the whole group, giving help and advice to various individuals. Finally, the judges – teachers observing the workshop – chose these two introductions:

> *Inside the rotten old door was a giant, green, slimy dragon which breathed yellow and orange flames from its mouth. Sam's expedition fled for their lives. Some of the members of the expedition ran as fast as cheetahs.*

(Sean Gibson)

> *My heart was pounding in my chest. My body trembled and the adrenalin raced in my veins. I pushed the door open with my shaking hands and inched my way in. What lay behind the door? As I entered the room my heart skipped a beat. Before me lay a marbled staircase which swirled up towards the ceiling.*

(Karla Pett)

The group were given the opportunity to vote for their own favourite of the two introductions. Various pupils spoke of why they chose their specific piece:

I wanted to know what happened next . . .
It really moves you along . . .
I liked the descriptions and the atmosphere . . .

Anthony oversaw the final activity, 'Mind Blow' – a timed race in which team members had to retrieve the key to get out of the Dark Tower. Afterwards, he thanked and praised the two teams for their commitment and enthusiasm. Finally, he responded to questions from the group on issues such as writing novels and writing for television. Angie Burroughs thanked Anthony for his workshop, and received a most affirmative response to her final question – 'Anthony, will you come back for your fifth visit next year?'

Anthony Masters can be contacted for school visits via the publicity departments of any of his publishers, including Egmont, Puffin, Orchard and Scholastic.

Brian Moses

(Poet)

Figure 5.3 Brian Moses

Three-day residency at St John's C.E. Primary School, Tunbridge Wells, Kent

St John's is a Church of England controlled primary school made up of separate Infant and Junior departments. It is now the largest primary school in West Kent, with 620 pupils on roll.

Brian Moses is a most active and popular visitor to primary schools. He conducts a wide range of visits from one-off, single-day visits to short residencies and also accompanies classes on a variety of school trips. Brian gives talks and performances to parents, teachers and children. His recent residencies have included Castle Cornet on Guernsey and a book bus tour of schools in the Highlands of Scotland.

Brian was poet-in-residence at St Johns for three days during the Junior Department's Community Arts Week 8–12 February 1999. The themed week is now an established and popular feature of the St John's calendar; previous weeks have had a humanities and an information technology focus.

As a general policy, St John's is keen to invite children's authors to meet the pupils and to conduct readings, performances and workshops. Other recent visitors have included Nigel Hinton and David and Rhoda Armitage. The Arts Week was co-ordinated by Graham McArthur, deputy headteacher, who steered the two working parties responsible for arranging the timetable. Junior teacher Christine Morton organised Brian's residency; she had set up Brian's previous visit to St John's some four years before.

The focus for the Junior Department's Arts Week was taken from one of the themes of the National Year of Reading – that of stories and storytelling – and the cross-curricular events for the week were partly chosen to reflect this focus, as well as to 'celebrate achievement and diversity in the arts'. These events included jazz and folk music workshops, dance, African masks and jewellery workshops, a Foyle's book fair, art and design projects set up by students from West Kent College and Greenwich and Christ Church universities, reading and writing competitions and a fancy dress day.

Many of the staff fondly remembered Brian's first visit to the school four years before. The teachers' enthusiasm for Brian's work was evident throughout the residency, and this had a very positive impact upon the children, who resultingly treated Brian as something of a celebrity. During Brian's performance to the lower Junior school on the first morning, one teacher leaned over to her colleague and whispered, 'Ooh great! I really love this poem!' Indeed, Brian was met with great warmth and interest wherever he went in the school. The children were all familiar with Brian's work, having spent time prior to the visit reading his poetry.

During the three-day residency, Brian conducted two poetry performances for the pupils (one for upper Juniors, the other for lower Juniors) as well as individual workshops for all the Junior year groups. On the evening of the second day, Brian gave a poetry performance especially for parents and staff. For the first half of the performance, twenty pupils from across the year groups were invited to read the poems that they had created during Brian's poetry writing workshops.

Empowerment very much underpinned the residency. Brian not only was willing to share and discuss his own work, but also was keen to promote and nurture the poetic skills and talents of the children too. The poems written throughout the residency – of which only a few are reproduced in this case study – bear testament to this.

Brian Moses in performance

> **BRIAN MOSES:** In this session this morning I'm going to read you some of my poetry. I hope you're going to hear something to make you *smile*, something to make you *laugh*, something to make you *think*. And I'm hoping that I can show you that poetry isn't just something that sits inside books, but that it can brought to life . . .

Thus Brian announced at the start of his first performance at the school. And really, for the following fifty minutes he continued to do just that – spellbinding two hundred children and ten teachers in the process, all with his invigorating and energetic mix of performance poetry, raps, chants and percussion. But Brian didn't simply bring poetry to life, he made it fun, physical, interactive, vital and wonderfully dynamic. And energetic is the operative word – as Brian is not one to keep still and remain at the front – he paces around the hall and chases in and out of his audience.

Participation was a central theme for the performance and the children were only too willing to enjoy whatever Brian had to offer. With his percussion accompaniment, Brian highlighted the musical and rhythmic elements of his poetry. Brian's percussion repertoire featured hand drums, claves, tambourines, maracas and even a glass washboard.

Although the majority of the poems performed were lively and humorous, there were a number of reflective and thoughtful pieces such as the eco-poem 'Make Friends with a Tree' and the mystical pieces 'The Lost Angels' and 'Dragon's Wood'. Over the course of the performance, Brian's subject matters ranged from the Loch Ness monster to teenage romance and from aliens to urban crocodiles.

Many of the pieces were introduced with short anecdotes which revealed that inspiration and material for poems can come from observing everyday events and occurrences.

BRIAN MOSES: What do you think about mobile phones? For someone like me, someone who likes watching people and listening into their conversations, they're wonderful. I was at Gatwick Airport the other day, going off to the Channel Islands. I was following this guy who was obviously very pleased with his new mobile phone. He was going, 'It's me! I'm at the airport! I'm walking down this really long corridor – and there are windows here – and they've got green carpet! And there's the plane – and it's got two wings!!' And from then I very happily spent the whole plane journey – all three-quarters of an hour – writing this next poem, which is called 'Mobile Phone'. It's got a chorus and you can all join in:

> Mobile phone, mobile phone
> Wherever I go I take my mobile phone!

Further such anecdotes included the origins of other poems, such as observing his neighbour's cat trying to catch fish in his garden pond, a trip to London Zoo, shopping in supermarkets and also a newspaper article on alligators that lived in the sewers of New York. The latter introduced a participation piece entitled 'Croc City':

> Beneath the streets of New York
> There are sewers that stretch for miles
> They say the sewers of New York
> Are filled with crocodiles . . .

Some of the favourite poems for this audience were from Brian's anthology *The Secret Lives of Teachers*:

Have you ever wondered what your teachers get up to behind the staffroom door? Or what they do at the weekend, or what they do on holiday, or if they fall in love? I got the idea for the anthology *The Secret Lives of Teachers* when I was sitting in a staffroom and there were six teachers there and they were all telling each other what they wore in bed at night!

Throughout the session, children were invited to clap, chant and even perform 'tree aerobics'. The performance built up to a grand finale for which Brian called for volunteers to play percussion instruments. The final piece was a rap based upon 'The Pied Piper of Hamelin'. Having assembled his group of percussionists, Brian careered around the hall performing 'Rat Rap':

> We're the rats – we strut through the kitchen
> And sniff for cheese – and we turn around – and chase our fleas . . .
> We're the rats!!

Brian Moses' workshops

On the first day of the residency, Brian conducted three poetry workshops with Year 4 classes, two of which are detailed below. At the beginning of each workshop, Brian would read some of his more recent work and then demonstrate how his poems are shaped and crafted.

Workshop 1: 'The Magical Cat'

This workshop is based upon the poem 'The Magical Mouse' by the American poet Kenneth Patchen and began with Brian having a discussion with the class:

Tell me something that a cat does.

Eats . . . sleeps . . . hisses . . .

If we wanted, we could write a poem about the everyday things that cats do – like eating and sleeping and so on – but today we're going to stretch our imaginations and take an ordinary cat and make it into a magical cat. And first we're going to give this cat a voice.

From here, Brian composed a poem on the board with the class:

I am the magical cat
I don't eat . . .

What do cats eat?

Fish . . . meat . . .

I don't eat fish or meat
I eat . . .

Kit-E-Kat . . .

There's nothing magical about that!

Leaves . . . stars . . . sunbeams . . . rainbows

I eat rainbows and sunbeams
and the crunchy tips of stars

We could have just put 'stars', but don't you think that 'the crunchy tips of stars' makes it sound even more magical and interesting?

I don't drink milk or water
I drink . . .

Coke . . . rain . . . moonlight

I drink moonlight, cobra spit and red wine
I don't sleep on your bed
I sleep . . .

In the sky . . . in the clouds . . . on the moon . . . on top of a rainbow . . . on Jupiter

I sleep in the clouds on the dark side of Jupiter
I don't chase mice or birds
I chase . . .

Elephants . . . dogs . . . the wind . . . comets . . . leopards

I chase comets, elephants and fast sports cars!

Having completed this communal poem the children were set the task of writing a poem in the voice of their own magical creature. Brian informed the class that they would not have to begin with 'I am the magical . . .' but that they could begin however they chose, and gave other examples: 'I am the fantastic frog' and 'I am the wonderful wood louse'. In addition, the children did not have to stick to what their imaginary creature ate or drank, but they could cover their own details, such as 'I am the fantastic frog, I don't croak like other frogs, I sing like Pavarotti!'

Next, Brian highlighted the fact that their communal poem of the magical cat did not rhyme, but that it had a rhythm, a pattern which came from the repetition of the lines:

I don't . . .

I . . .

Finally, Brian asked the children to find their first line and then to establish a similar such pattern throughout.

Brian and the host teacher moved around the classroom, observing the ideas that were being generated, providing support and advice as required. When supporting the children, Brian had high but realistic expectations of these young writers. He would give praise but also be critical in a positive manner. When reading a child's evolving poem, he would first of all highlight something that he liked, and then home in on an area that needed further developing. Brian listened to this working draft of the following poem by Stuart Smith (aged 8):

> I am the luxurious lion
>
> I don't eat meat or deer
> I eat starlight and rainbows
>
> I have the best coat of all the land
>
> I don't drink water or red wine
> I drink sun rays and blood
>
> I am the God of all the universe
> I am the King of all lions
> I am the light of the morning sun

Brian responded with:

> You've got a lovely ending there, with those last three lines. They're super. But I think you need to get a few more lines into the poem before you finish off with those last three. Think about what this lion chases and what it might do instead of roaring – things like that. But you've got the makings of something really good there. Well done!

Brian concluded the session with a message to the class:

> Don't forget that all you've done so far are the first drafts of your poems. And well done, there's some great ideas coming out. I hope you've all found something that you've enjoyed in this session.

The following piece by 8-year-old Tamsin Prideaux is another poem that began in this workshop and was redrafted and completed in a later class:

I am the Miraculous Puppy

I don't run after rabbits,
I run after powerful whirlwinds.

I don't eat meaty, marble white bones,
I eat spicy starlight.

I don't drink crystal clear water,
I drink the beat of horses' hooves.

I don't fight with fierce dogs like normal dogs do,
I fight with swirling, rushing whirlpools.

I don't sleep curled up in a dog basket,
I sleep on fluffy white clouds.

I don't guard my owner's house,
I guard courageous, flying cats and silvery rain.

I don't play with balls,
I play with the golden sunset and the sunrise on a cold winter's day.

I don't growl or bark like any dog,
I screech and moan.

I am the King of all puppies.

Workshop 2: 'Oath of Friendship'

The final workshop for the day was based upon an idea from the American book *Rose, Where Did You Get That Red?* by Kenneth Koch. To introduce the session, Brian talked about the theme of friendship and he told of the friendship rituals of the Native Americans and the Chinese. As with the previous workshop, he wrote a poem with the class at the blackboard. Brian started off by writing the title 'Oath of Friendship' and then the line:

I want to be friends with you until –

Brian took suggestions from the class:

The end of Christmas . . . when the world ends . . . the end of our lives

From there he wrote another line:

If we are friends I will give you –

Some money . . . a star . . . a gift

And the final line was:

My friend I will like you more than –

Some money . . . a chest of gold . . . a violin made of gold . . .

The children were asked to write their own poems using these three lines as a structure. At the end of the session, volunteers were asked to read out their creations. To finish off, Brian asked the children to go back to their poems the following day to see how their ideas could be improved upon and to read their own work critically. He encouraged the children to consider such questions as 'Is this the best idea here?' and 'Could I make this line longer?' and 'Could I give the reader a better picture with my words?' Finally, Brian suggested that the children illustrate their poems and that they spend time thinking of the best way that they could present their poems to their friends.

Of the pieces produced during this workshop, the following two are final drafts completed the following day:

Oath of Friendship

I want to be friends with you until
The stars and moon go down
Until the seas fade away
Or until the hottest part of the Sun stops shining.

If we are friends I will give you
The greatest glitter of a crystal,
And a grand piano full of gold and silver,
Or the world with God.

My friend, I will like you more than
All of the angels in heaven,
More than a cave full of diamonds
Or all of the stars in the universe.

Rebecca Perkins (aged 8)

Oath of Friendship

I want to be friends with you until
The last cry of the last eagle
Or 'til the water of the sea runs out
Or 'til the shine of the last star fades away

If we are friends I will give you
The shiniest part of a star
Or the flame of the Sun in a wooden box
I will give you
The golden egg of a crystal-winged swan

My friend, I will like you more than
The last and most precious crystal
Or a magical gold fish
I will like you more than
The last chant of an ancient wizard

Naomi Ellis (aged 8)

The poems that follow were written in other poetry workshops during Brian's residency. These and the other poems above were published on the children's poetry website Poetryzone: www.poetryzone.ndirect.co.uk. Throughout 1999, Brian Moses was the guest poet at this website, and he regularly contributed children's own poems to the site that had been written during his school visits.

A Spirit of Mystic Lake

She appeared when the full moon was bright,
Peeping round the tree.
Her silver wings glistened on the surface of the lake,
Moving like a shadow, a mystery to see.

Her white face was beautiful but fairylike,
Kind and gentle.
Her golden dress tinkled like a hundred bells.
Her dark black hair fell over her shoulders
Dark and curly like wool.

Her appearance was not menacing,
Nor her departure.
But she danced until the Sun broke the silver sky.
She danced on her dainty feet
In miniature ballet shoes.
At the sound of feet, turning sharply
As the noise hits her pixie ears.

She hides until all noise vanishes,
Before returning.
She plucks a reed and makes a hole,
And pushes a flower through.

She ties her curly hair
Sitting on a stool,
Takes out her flute and plays a tune,
Until dawn breaks the peace.

She disappeared for ever,
But for one day she came back to sit on the dune.
Where is the spirit?
Where did she go?
She came at twilight to sing to the deer.

Now where is she whose singing
Ravaged the ears of the cruellest human?

Alyss Barnes (aged 9)

Shark's Complaint

I am the Great White Shark,
Like ammunition in the water
Helping dolphins get free.
All I earn is a bad reputation,
Humans and fish alike hate me!
What did I do to earn this?
I just attack people who annoy me.
Is that not normal?

I think I'm very attractive,
Leathery skin and fin.
Ocean-living is not easy –
There's the colossal whales that will eat me.
And the dolphins who hit me hard on the belly.

It's not my fault I get angry,
I'm hunted as well.
So many things out to get me.
But I'll get even!

Kate Smith (aged 9)

The Bee

I am the Bonkers Bee.

I don't dance like other bees,
I dance like a drunken Celine Dion.

I don't collect honey,
I watch the Bee Gees on tour.

I don't sting people when they tease me,
I charm them with my impression of Cher.

I don't bow down to my queen,
I drive the ants up the wall.

I don't suck pollen,
I drink electricity.

I don't want to live in a hive,
I would rather live in Kate Winslet's wardrobe.

I am the Bonkers Bee, you can see.

Edward Atkins (aged 8)

Outcomes of the residency

It was evident from staff, parents and pupils alike that Brian's residency and indeed the Arts Week had been most rewarding. Graham McArthur, deputy headteacher at St John's, comments:

> *The Arts Week as a whole was a great success, and certainly vindicated the time spent planning and co-ordinating activities across both the Infant and Junior departments. Feedback from the children and the many guests that we accommodated has been extremely encouraging, and many new parent faces were attracted into school – how the message spread!*
>
> *Brian Moses' evening performance was delightful. Brian involved children from across the school in presenting their ideas, and the poems produced during his residency show that hidden depths were plumbed and extraordinary creativity captured.*

Brian Moses can be contacted for visits at 11 Barrow Rise, St Leonards-on-Sea, East Sussex TN37 7ST. Email: redsea@freeserve.co.uk

Andrew Fusek Peters
(Poet)

Figure 5.4 Andrew Fusek Peters

Visits to schools

ANDREW FUSEK PETERS: I visit schools for many reasons, one of which is that I like surprising teachers by showing them what children are capable of in terms of writing poetry. I love turning kids on to poetry, and it's so reassuring to hear comments like 'We've never had interesting poetry before' or 'We didn't know you could write poems about such and such'. When I leave a school at 3.30 p.m. I feel that I've done something positive. I've had so many children tell me that they didn't like poetry before my visit – and that's why I'm still visiting schools after thirteen years. My performances involve poetry and storytelling and I also play the didgeridoo and jew's harp and I even juggle too! I set out to be interactive and lyrical and to move people and to make them laugh.

What makes for a good visit? Preparation, preparation, preparation. Before you go in, the children need to know who you are, and they need to have read your work in advance. I don't see my visits as a 'treat' or as a 'reward'. I do get a bit annoyed when I come across the attitude that what I do isn't work for the children – what I do is *real* work. A good visit is when a school follows up what I do in the workshops, and they develop it. My best visits are to schools where the teachers care passionately about the arts.

I tend to do less preparation myself nowadays for individual visits as I have various routines I've established over the years, but I'm always including new material. Prior to going into a school, I liaise with the teachers over the phone and we arrange the structure of the day. I will often prepare work specifically for the current topic, and I might even do some research. I did a whole day in a school recently where the topic was dragons. So I did some research on dragons on the Internet beforehand.

I like to explore the many different forms of poetry with children in schools. I do a lot of work in secondary schools on teaching various poetic forms. I've taught sonnets to Years 9 and 10, and syllabic poems to Year 7 – and proper syllabic pieces that rhyme. And it's a delight. They love it. They're up for it if you give them a chance. I tend to capture their interest with the funny poems first, and, once they're into it, I'll move on to more serious subject matters. Some of the sonnets I've done with Years 9 and 10 over the years have been about grief and death, and the results have been excellent. There was one particular Year 10 group I worked with, and I think this particular boy had lost his mum.

One Last Look Before You Go

Is it you or is it me? I'm not sure.
All I know is that you're not meant to be here,
Up the stairs to afterlife,
I know that you're
Not coming back. My mind a Mecca of fears,
Never knowing what's behind my next thought
The pain and suffering that you have fought
is gone. Now you are in the place so high,
One last look before you go, Why? I sigh,

And there's this incredible line:

Never knowing why God must have been short
On angels. Something tells me I ought
To have been better and more caring to
You. If God was the defense, I would sue;

That's a phenomenal metaphor.

With the money I would buy something new –
Life, Love, Soul, Shape and Dreams come true.
One last look before you go . . .

Andrew Jackson (Lord Silkin School, Telford)

That's what interests me in working with young people – it's that they're actually very capable. I've seen results of teachers working and developing poetry with children and the results are amazing.

I was recently Poet-in-Residence in Warwickshire for the year, and the resulting book, *A Pint of Unleaded Please*, was very well received. The wonderful review we had in the *Times Educational Supplement*, the double page write-up in the Young Writer magazine, the foreword by Michael Rosen – all vindicate that children really can produce great sonnets, conceits, syllabic poems, ballads and other forms.

With residencies there's more time to develop ideas and build up relationships with the pupils. I really enjoy that. What I don't like so much is when a local education authority will send me to two schools a day, and I'm just a slot, fitting into criteria just to secure funding. It makes me feel like a product. However, I've had some single days in schools which have had incredible fruition. And all because the schools have been prepared – they've written to me beforehand, the children have already read and worked on my poems. And afterwards, the children have sent me their own work, which I've read and then responded to.

With a residency you can take it even further – writing sonnets and syllabic poems and you can work towards an anthology and a performance. During one two-week residency at Maidenhill Secondary School, I did poetry workshops based upon the local woods and the work of the nature sculptor, Andy Galsworthy. We did all kinds of things like building sculptures in the woods out of leaves and trees and rubbish, and we wrote poems. We did a final group performance, in which we filled the school hall with leaves and did a fantastic costumed performance of poetry and storytelling. This is what you can do if you've got time. This was a big, co-ordinated and cross-curricular project between the Music, Art and English departments. I believe that with every residency you need to show that process and product are equally important, and that you need to have something to work towards – a finale, a celebration – to which the parents come. But ultimately, and most importantly, it means that the children's work and creativity are recognised and validated.

Another memorable residency was at Ercallwood School in Telford, Shropshire. It was soon after my brother died, and our collection *May the Angels Be With Us* had just been published. The final performance was immensely powerful. It was a cold, January night. It was a mixed media event – the pupils did choreographed dramatisations of the poems from the collection, and some of it was set to live flamenco guitar music. In my early, more radical days, I did a term's residency at Broadoak Secondary School in Weston-super-Mare. For the final performance I had Year 7 pupils improvising rap on stage. Improvising rhyme – it was wonderful! The audience were falling on the floor with laughter! The energy was fantastic. It's moments like those that make it so worthwhile.

I always try to get the teachers writing during my workshops. Before I go in to any school, I ask that the teachers are encouraging, that they support the pupils and that they join in the exercises. A few teachers are resistant to writing themselves, but most are really enthusiastic.

Stoke Park Secondary School and Community Technology College, Coventry: one-day visit

Stoke Park is an inner city multicultural school with 1,100 pupils on roll. The school specialises in maths, science, technology and information technology and gives high priority to extra-curricular activities such as music, drama, sports and residential trips.

Andrew Fusek Peters – alongside Roi Kwabena and Kevin O'Sullivan – was one of three visiting poets to the Year 8 Poetry Day at Stoke Park on 9 March 1999. Andrew's visit to the school on the previous Poetry Day had been so popular that he had been invited back to conduct another performance as well as a series of poetry writing workshops.

The 1999 Poetry Day was initiated and co-ordinated by English teacher Maggie Moorhouse. Maggie explained that the previous year's event had necessitated much more preparation, as it had been the first event of its kind in the school. Funding for the 1998 event had derived from the English Department budget, whereas the 1999 Poetry Day received funds from the central school budget.

Andrew was originally chosen as a result of a recommendation from Warwick University, and Maggie contacted Andrew through the Poetry Society in London. Kevin O'Sullivan is a local poet and a disc-jockey at a Coventry radio station. Kevin had made himself known to the school by sending advertising flyers directly to the English Department. Roi Kwabena, as well as being a musician and poet, is the Literature Development Officer for Coventry. Maggie invited Roi to participate having seen an article on his work in a local newspaper.

Maggie Moorhouse says that poetry plays a significant role in the Stoke Park Year 8 curriculum. All of the Year 8 English classes have poetry boxes from which pupils can borrow collections and anthologies. There is a pre-twentieth-century poetry unit in Year 8 which covers texts as wide as *Beowulf*, Chaucer, Milton, Clare, Wordsworth and Tennyson. In Year 7 there is a poetry writing unit which gives pupils the opportunity to express themselves in a wide variety of poetic forms, ranging from free verse to haiku. Although no other year group has a Poetry Day equivalent, the school's commitment to literature and creative writing extends to running extra-curricular book clubs, celebrating National Poetry Day, holding 'Readathon®' events and entering national poetry competitions.

Prior to the 1999 event, Maggie discussed the forthcoming event with all three of the poets, though she chose not to stipulate the nature of the material that they should include in their performances and workshops. Maggie explains:

> *I'd rather people come in and do what they're best at rather than come in thinking that they've got to cover certain topics. Last year, the theme for the day was 'Poems about People', though we didn't stick to that rigidly. It gave the children a focus for a subject to write about, but it wasn't compulsory. However, it did give them a good starting point. Our 1998 Poetry Day was a great success. In fact, a few weeks ago one Year 9 pupil went up to our Head of Supportive Studies and showed her some of her poems. She said 'I write poems all the time now. It was last year's Poetry Day that started me off.' Overall, that event really put poetry on the map as far as that year group was concerned. However, everything we do in the English Department here is to raise the profile of reading. And this year, the National Year of Reading has backed us up in doing just that.*

Maggie's aims for the 1999 Poetry Day were

> *for everybody to express themselves poetically, and, just as important, for them to enjoy not only these published writers' work, but also each other's work. I think that it's important for the pupils to listen to poets perform their work as it helps them to see that poetry doesn't just happen on the page. I want them to see real people performing their poetry and bringing it to life.*

In preparation, Maggie ensured that collections of Andrew's poetry were read throughout all of the Year 8 English classes in the weeks leading up to the event. The collections, she reports, were very well received. In addition, and having consulted Andrew previously, Maggie prepared small booklets of Andrew's poetry for the pupils to buy for a nominal price.

The programme for the event was as follows:

9.30–10.30:	Andrew Fusek Peters – reading/performance in hall
11.15–12.15:	Poetry workshops – Andrew Fusek Peters / Roi Kwabena / Kevin O'Sullivan
	Drama workshops based upon Andrew Fusek Peters' poetry
12.15–1.15:	Lunch and book signing (Andrew Fusek Peters)
1.15–2.15:	Roi Kwabena – reading/performance (poetry and music)
2.15–3.15:	Poetry workshops – Andrew Fusek Peters / Roi Kwabena / Kevin O'Sullivan
	Drama workshops (as above)
3.15–3.45:	Drama performances

From the excitement and enthusiasm of those gathering in the school hall at the start of the day it was evident that the Poetry Day has fast become a very popular feature of the Stoke Park calendar for both staff and pupils alike. Throughout his visit, Andrew Fusek Peters himself was keen to meet with and talk to pupils about poetry. During the lunch break when he was signing books, one sixth former came to him for some advice on her own poems – which Andrew was more than happy to provide.

Before leaving for the day, Andrew returned to the school hall to observe and delight in some highly charged and inspirational dance and drama realisations of his poems 'Rush Hour' and 'The Bully' from two exceptionally talented Year 8 groups.

Andrew Fusek Peters in performance

It would be easy to forget that Andrew is known primarily as a poet in performance: he is a versatile and all-round consummate entertainer. He takes his audience on what might be described as an emotional rollercoaster – for his set had equal and abundant measures of humour, pathos and thought-provoking material. Andrew performed pieces on issues as diverse as humanitarianism, bullying, romance, sexism, Aboriginal land rights and even the harmful effects of smoking and drug-taking – all in a vibrant mix of poetry, music and storytelling.

Andrew's performance in the main school hall was attended by all six of the Year 8 English groups – some 180 pupils in all. Andrew's thirteen years' experience of visiting primary and secondary schools was evident from the outset of his lively and charismatic performance. This first piece had the hall laughing within moments. 'A true story to start with':

My First Girlfriend

Her boyfriend had broken his leg
It was time to get rid of him
She asked if I would be the one for her
I lied about my age
I was over the moon
In fact I was over the whole planetary system
And now I had to kiss her . . .

Then Andrew gave a performance on the didgeridoo and told of the cultural significance of the instrument: it has been used for many thousands of years and it is connected with the aspect of Aboriginal mythology known as the Dreaming. After some fine playing on this sonorous and hypnotic instrument, Andrew demonstrated how the didgeridoo is played, explaining that it involves a technique known as circular breathing. Volunteer members of the audience were invited to attempt the technique on a piece of plastic tubing.

From here, Andrew asked the audience 'Does bullying still exist?', to which he received a resounding and affirmative response. Andrew confessed that he himself had been bullied at school because of his sensitivity and his height – Andrew is 6ft 8in. This served as the introduction to an a capella version of a piece entitled 'What shall we do with Duncan Taylor?', a reworking of the popular sea shanty:

> What shall we do with Duncan Taylor?
> What shall we do with Duncan Taylor?
> What shall we do with Duncan Taylor –
> Early in the morning?
>
> *Hoo-ray and up he rises!*
> *Life is full of cruel surprises!*
> *And we're several sizes*
> *Bigger than him this morning! . . .*

Later in his set, Andrew read a poignant and moving piece entitled 'A Child's Poem'. He led into this piece by explaining that his brother Mark, who had been a poet himself, had died of AIDS in 1993. This poem clearly moved the audience and moved one teacher present to tears:

> Why is there rain, and where does it come from mum?
> And how come clouds live up in the sky?
> And why did my brother get ill and die?
>
> *The rain is a river of tears, my dear,*
> *For every cloud sees how sad we are here.*
> *Yet I don't know why your brother should die . . .*

The Aboriginal theme resurfaced later in a bathetic piece which involved Andrew telling the story of the British invasion of Australia in the eighteenth century. This may not seem particulaly unusual, except that Andrew was juggling apples throughout his narration!

Finally, Andrew conducted a question and answer session, and he awarded postcards of his poems to the best questions raised. When Maggie Moorhouse thanked Andrew publicly she said to the audience: 'One of you asked why Andrew chose poetry, well, I think poetry probably chose Andrew.'

Andrew Fusek Peters' poetry workshops

Andrew conducted poetry workshops with two different Year 8 English classes. Before starting these sessions, Andrew talked about his own writing and engaged in discussions with the pupils about their perceptions of poetry. Throughout the workshops, Andrew sat with his laptop computer and printer at a desk in a prominent position in the class, typing in the many wonderful ideas and suggestions that abounded.

Workshop 1: The Natural World

To open the session with English group 8L, Andrew asked the group for their ingredients for a good poem, to which they responded:

> *Rhythm . . . Rhyme . . . Something different . . . Humour*

Andrew asked the class what they felt was the difference between a poem and a story:

> *A poem rhymes . . . A poem doesn't have to make sense all of the time*

Next he asked the group to write at the top of their pages: 'Poem – bringing words to life' and invited the class to look out of the window and to write down something that is natural and to describe it in terms of the senses – be it smell, colour or feel. He reassured the class by saying that there is no such thing as an incorrect response. A few minutes later, he listened to the resulting ideas:

> *Bare trees . . . Green grass . . . Bushes . . . Clouds . . . Birds . . . Light . . . The sun*

Can you actually see the sun?

> *No, it's hidden.*

Okay, let's try something interesting. The sun is hidden. Tell me something else that is hidden.

> *Keys!*

Lovely! What are keys like?

> *Shiny.*

Where do you lose your keys?

> *In the settee.*

Fantastic! Okay, how about 'Sun is hidden like shiny keys in the settee of clouds'?

Andrew told the class to describe the clouds, but without resorting to clichés such as 'grey like elephants', 'puffy like candy floss' or 'white as cotton wool'. This resulted in the line 'Laptop-grey clouds type hailstones'. He further explained that he wanted them to invent new colours, and he gave specific examples of the type of imaginative and metaphoric descriptions that he was after, such as 'crumpled paper-clouds' 'leaves that are burnt toast-brown'. Andrew listened to the pupils' ideas that followed:

> *Squirrel-grey . . . Mashed potato-white . . . Dust-grey*

Heather Sutherland, the class teacher, provided her own line for the evolving poem:

> *Lonely branches crave luscious fresh beds*

This exchange continued – with Andrew typing the pupils' ideas into his laptop computer – until the following poem was created:

Spring: An Instant Class Poem

Sun is hidden like shiny keys in the settee of clouds.
Laptop-grey clouds type hailstones;
Squirrel-grey, they bury the nut sun;
Mashed potato-white, gobbling up water;

Pale-faced, coughing over phlegm-green grass.
Yolk-yellow sun dips into rainbows.
Custard-yellow daffodils pour out over bottle-green grass;
Lonely branches crave luscious fresh beds.
Lime green ivy makes the walls bitter with life.
Trees wear twig wigs;
Get drunk on Budweiser
And snog the birds.

While Andrew edited the class poem above, the pupils, including the teacher, set to work on their own poems on the topic of the natural world. Andrew stipulated that everyone wrote free verse as he wanted them to concentrate on imagery rather than rhyme, which, he said, would take much longer. He actively encouraged the class to use figurative devices such as metaphor, simile and personification, and to consider what various aspects of nature might say, wear, eat, do or dream of if they were human. He read out a line from a poem from a previous workshop to exemplify the sort of figurative imagery that he was after: 'Winter is Jack Frost riding his icicle'. Andrew promoted the use of puns, and gave comic examples in the context of trees, such as 'Leaf me alone', 'You don't tree-t me very well', 'Trees that are unhappy with their bank might go to another branch'.

Before leaving the class, Andrew listened to volunteers reading out their creations, and offered support and suggestions. By the end of this hour-long workshop, each pupil had written a first draft of a poem and had been given a photocopy of the instant group poem produced on Andrew's laptop. Andrew encouraged the class to develop their poems further and requested that the final drafts be sent to him. His final question to the class – 'Okay, so what have you learnt?' – stimulated a variety of very positive responses, such as:

You can change words around
You can invent your own colours
You can describe things in really interesting ways

Workshop 2: The Outsider
The afternoon workshop was with 8S. After an introductory discussion on the group's experiences of poetry, Andrew asked the class to write 'The Outsider' at the top of their pages and then to brainstorm the qualities of people who are outsider figures:

Not listening . . . Getting into trouble . . . Being a brainbox . . . Bullying . . .
Wearing different clothes . . . Having different hair cuts

Andrew discussed the issue of difference as a positive concept and asked the class to write down the word 'Exaggeration' and the phrase 'Things come to life'. He then informed the class that they were going to create a fictional outsider figure and gave examples of the type of ideas that he was looking for:

He was such a saddo that even the pavements could trip him up
He was so lonely even the wind wouldn't talk to him

Various ideas followed:

He is such a saddo even the lampposts laugh at him . . . He stinks so much even the cars hold their breath

Andrew highlighted the effective use of unusual collective nouns in poetry, and gave initial examples such as 'a herd of fears' and 'a flock of tears'. Again he stressed that with this form of creativity all ideas are valid:

> *A flood of tears . . . A tea bag of tears . . . A cloud of tears . . . A sponge full of tears . . . A kettle of tears . . . A spoon of fears . . . A school of fears . . . A shoal of fears . . . A lorry load of fears . . . A dictionary of frowns . . . A platoon of frowns*

Andrew, who was by now typing the class's ideas into his laptop, took just one of the suggested images and developed it:

A kettle of tears. What do you do with a kettle?

> *You pour it . . . It pours out of his eyes*

Great! How about 'A kettle of tears pours from the spout of his eyes'. Okay, somebody said 'Tea bag of tears'. What do you do with a tea bag?

> *Drain it . . . Dunk it*

Brilliant! 'A tea bag of tears dunked in my –'

> *Tea pot . . . Sadness . . . Heart . . . Depression*

Yes! 'A tea bag of tears dunked in my depression'! Now, someone else said 'A box of fears'? What do you do with a box?

> *You open it . . . Inside your friend . . . A bully . . . Your enemy*

How about – 'A box of fears opens inside his enemy'?

The next brainstorm was of different types of leaders:

> *Queen . . . Avatar . . . Shah . . . Prince . . . Ayatollah . . . Commander . . . Sultan . . . Captain . . . Principal . . . Prime minister . . . Messiah . . . Viceroy . . . Sheikh*

So perhaps this outsider we're creating, this person could be a 'messiah of moodiness'. Notice the alliteration in that phrase, with the two 'm's? See if you can discover other alliterative ones. Another might be the 'pharaoh of fear'.

> *The queen of quarrels . . . The sultan of sadness . . . The manager of mayhem*

Wow! These are really good! Now try playing cards too. You could use the ace, jack, queen and so on.

> *The ace of anger . . . The jack of jokes*

This activity resulted in the class poem reproduced below, which Andrew constructed and edited on his laptop. As with the previous group, the poem was printed and distributed to every class member at the end of the session. For the duration of the workshop, Andrew encouraged the group to be highly imaginative, to take risks with their ideas and to continually refine their language and their imagery.

For the final half-hour the class wrote their own free verse 'Outsider' poems – which were to be entitled 'He' or 'She'. These were to incorporate the concepts that Andrew had discussed with the group – such as collective nouns, hyperboles and types of leaders. Throughout, Andrew and the host teacher, Kim Hopper, offered advice to individuals around the class. To round off the workshop, Andrew listened and responded to the early drafts of the poems written in the session. Always supportive, Andrew provided positive criticisms and offered the class various ways of developing their pieces.

He – An Instant Class Poem
He is such a saddo even the lampposts laugh at him.
He stinks so much, cars hold their breath
He is so ugly, onions cry.
He is such a tramp, dustbins walk away
He is so unpopular, doors close on him
He is so lonely that the sun turns away from him
And he is the sheikh of shadow.
A kettle of tears pours from the spout of his eyes
A box of fears opens inside his enemy
A dictionary of frowns looks up to God
This viceroy of victims,
Sultan of sadness,
Jack of all jokes.

These are final drafts of pieces that began in the workshop:

He
He is the star of sunlight
He is so intelligent that books run away from him
He is the sheikh of saints
He is such a mastermind that monks can't question him
When you see him a box of tears come out of you
He is so great that gurus come to imbibe from him
He is the master of magnanimous
He is the player of players
He is the protector of the poor
He is the doctor of dignity
His brain is the encyclopaedia of Lord Buddha
His eyes are like two flashing light bulbs
He is so brainy that teachers learn from him
His heart is so hungry that he would give his life for world hunger to end
He is the god of generosity.

Mithilesh Joshi

Me!!!!!
I am the mighty God of war, with my sword of death, and muscles of steel
I am a mighty God, that is the real deal,
I am the God who kills those that have done wrong,
I am the strength that kills those who do not belong,
I have an intellectual mind that works overtime,
To protect the innocent and put an end to crime,
I am the crusader that lurks in the night,
To fight this everlasting evil fight,

I am the mighty God of war, with a sword of death and my muscles of steel,
I am a mighty God that is the real deal,
I must not let anyone know about my undercover mission,
So Shhhh!! It's a secret.

Kulwinder Toor

Andrew Fusek Peters can be contacted for visits at The Old Chapel, Lydbury North, Shropshire SY7 8AU. Email tallpoet@compuserve.com

Celia Rees
(Novelist)

Figure 5.5 Celia Rees

Farmor's School, Fairford, Gloucestershire: one-day visit

Farmor's School was founded in 1738 and became a comprehensive school in 1966. There are 870 pupils on roll, of whom 150 are in the sixth form. The school serves a predominantly rural area in the Cotswolds and has 18 acres of school grounds and sports fields.

The Farmor's School Book Week – the first of its kind at the school – took place 27–30 September 1999 and was co-ordinated by Anne Newman, School Librarian. The Book Week was for pupils of all year groups, though Celia Rees' visit on 28 September was exclusively for pupils from Year 8. Other highlights of the week included a book fair, Roald Dahl and Harry Potter book quizzes, teaching staff giving readings from their favourite books, talks from authors Judith Hann and Jane Greenoff, and an evening performance of poetry from John Foster with music and drama from students.

Anne Newman had a number of objectives for the week:

> *After the National Year of Reading I wanted to maintain everybody's interest in books. There had been such a focus on books throughout that year that I felt it was vital to keep it going. And really, every year should be a year of reading. Above all, I wanted everyone in the school to be touched by a book of some sort.*

We chose authors that the pupils could relate to, authors that worked with teenagers and authors that the pupils knew already. I had heard Celia Rees give a talk to the School Library Association and I knew of two other schools that have had Celia in – and they'd been really pleased with the work she'd done. Also, I've seen John Foster before and his poetry is very popular at the school. We started planning the Book Week last February, when a small committee was set up to organise the events.

Now a full-time writer for children, Celia previously worked as an English teacher. She currently runs a course in Writing for Children and has been a regular visitor to secondary schools for a number of years, conducting one-day visits and residencies, and giving talks and workshops on genre writing. She gave three one-hour workshops during her visit to Farmor's School, the first of which is reported below.

Celia Rees' writing workshop

This, the first of Celia's three workshops for the day, took place in the school's drama studio. Some fifty pupils from two Year 8 English classes attended the session. For the duration of the hour Celia gave an intriguing insight into her work and her research methods. She talked passionately about her philosophies on creating fiction, writing within various genres and the writing process in general. Throughout, she was keen on conducting a two-way communication with her audience, and responded with great enthusiasm to the ideas and feedback from her captive audience.

From the start, Celia emphasised that this was a workshop requiring involvement from everyone, and her first questions received unanimously positive responses:

How many of you like reading horror stories? How many of you enjoy frightening each other by telling each other scary stories – like when you're having a sleepover, or you're camping? Well that's what I do when I write horror stories – so it's my job to scare people!

From the group's responses, it became apparent very quickly that the group wanted to create their own stories, and Celia promised them that they would have the opportunity to write either a horror, ghost or supernatural story or a tale of the unexpected.

Celia began by giving an overview of her published works – describing her 'Point Horror' titles – *The Vanished* and *Blood Sinister* – her thrillers such as *Midnight Hour* and *Every Step You Take* – and her supernatural series for primary-age readers, *H.A.U.N.T.S.* She explained that however different her books seem, they all had one common element, namely that every story is set in a real place, a place that she has actually researched and visited. She admitted that sometimes it is impossible to visit the exact site. For example, instead of visiting Highgate Cemetery in North London when writing her novel *Blood Sinister*, Celia visited a cemetery in Coventry instead, where she conducted research and took photographs. She showed the group a photograph of the mausoleum that inspired the place inhabited by the vampire character in *Blood Sinister*. The advantage of taking photographs, Celia added, is that it can greatly help when writing a detailed description of a specific setting. She further stressed that atmosphere is vital for such a novel, and she read a passage from the first chapter of *Blood Sinister* which features Highgate Cemetery.

The group were asked to reflect upon times when they had been frightened, how they had actually felt, and to think of the scariest place they had ever visited. Celia claimed that as a writer she could make anywhere frightening. She challenged the audience to think of a setting that could not be made frightening, to which one volunteer offered the setting of a school. A school, Celia laughed, was only too easy – and she demonstrated how it could be done. With feedback from the audience, she assembled a list of ideas on a flip chart to prove that anywhere – even a drama studio in a school – could be an ideal location for a ghost or horror story:

1 Choose a SETTING.
2 Choose an unusual TIME of day to be at that place, such as early morning or evening or night time.
3 Choose your CHARACTERS – you and one other person – as having two people can be more frightening.
4 Find your REASON for being at that place; this must be a genuine reason – such as you are meeting someone there, someone has left something there or even a dare.
5 Consider the TIME of year – the weather/temperature may have an impact upon your story.
6 How do you FEEL about being there? Are you anxious or nervous? Are you feeling cold or hot?
7 Imagine and then DESCRIBE the place as clearly and in as much detail as you can. Think:
   What can you SEE?
   What can you HEAR?
   What can you SMELL?
   What can you TOUCH?
   Write with as much ATMOSPHERE as you can.
8 Something tells you that THINGS ARE NOT RIGHT. What is it?
9 You REMEMBER something that happened here – something you read about or overheard about this place. You may well have laughed about it previously but, now that you are here, it does not seem quite so amusing. When Celia asked if Farmor's School had any ghost stories, one pupil told of a local myth that on the school site there had once been a large house in which a nun had been killed and that her body had been cemented into a wall. Celia highlighted that this would make a perfect background scenario for the writing activity that was to follow.

At Celia's request, each member of the group wrote down a list of three everyday places, which they had to swop with a partner. Each pupil had to choose one of the three locations written down and, using Celia's advice, had to use that as a setting for their story. After ten minutes, Celia listened with great interest to the settings and scenarios offered by the group:

A church – the organ seems to be playing on its own

A cinema – after the last film at night

A cottage – something happened there in the past

Celia emphasised the need to create an atmosphere of fear and to make the situation as believable and as vivid as possible. Writers have, Celia said, to call upon their own experiences of fear to make other people frightened – as what scares them will also scare others.

She revealed that with writing ghost or horror stories it is often the minor details – and often something quite familiar – that can be the most frightening thing of all, and she gave examples from her own experience. One was of the time that she had been alone in the house and had heard the alarm of a digital watch go off in a wardrobe, and had thought that an intruder was in the room. The next morning she discovered that the watch was a future

Christmas present from her husband! Another anecdote involved a radio being left on that was again mistaken for an unwanted intruder. Celia encouraged the group to consider including such devices in their writing – digital watch alarms, radios – as well as televisions, flapping letter boxes, jammed doors, children's toys that make sounds, noises from pets – to mislead and terrify their readers.

Celia recapped on the nine-point story structure and demonstrated to the group how they could develop their ideas. Their stories, Celia suggested, could begin at the moment when their two characters enter the location. The workshop concluded with Celia encouraging the group to write out their stories in full during their next English class. To finish off, Celia responded to questions from her audience.

It was only too evident not only from the rapturous applause but also from Celia's queue of autograph hunters at the end of the session that the group had thoroughly enjoyed the workshop and were now keen to continue their scenarios for their own stories.

The two following pieces originated in Celia's workshops. The first is the opening to a story written by Clare Chadwick. Her story goes on to tell of a disused house, a murder story and a dare:

A Scary Story
Prologue

It was night. Summer had passed into early autumn and through the still, warm night a faint chill nipped the air. Soon the seasons would paint the leaves brown and frosts would crisp the grass. Above, the sky was a smooth, velvety dark blue, dotted with stars. Below, streetlights cast a sickly orange glare over the cement pavements. Trees waved shadows. Houses were blacked out, curtains drawn. People slept peacefully, oblivious of what was about to happen.

One light.
One light was still on at number four. A glow seeped through the thin curtains.
A rattle . . .
A crash. A scream. A thud.
Then silence . . .
And, a few minutes later, the wail of a siren.
Just too late . . .

And this is the original brainstorm of notes completed by Kerry Gibson during Celia's workshop:

Why – A dare.
Where – A supermarket.
Time – Present, at night on Xmas Eve.
Hear – Fridges humming and mysterious footsteps.
See – Lots of fridges and shelves, but out of the corner of my eye I can see toys moving and jumping back to their places when I look at them.
Feeling – Curious and scared. Like I've been there before. Something's wrong.
Smell – Smell of foods mixed together – musty smell like of something rotting.
Stories – Someone froze to death in a freezer. There was a ghost with pale blue lips and grey skin.
Title – Pale Lips / Frozen Heart / The Dare.

The first book week at Farmor's School proved to be a great success, as Anne Newman's responses indicate:

> *Our first Book Week was very exciting; both students and staff agreed it was a good focus for books, reading and the Library. The evening performance was very much enjoyed, although several of the children later admitted they had to be 'encouraged' by their parents to come and were surprised to really enjoy it – particularly John Foster's poetry readings. John brought with him a selection of books for sale during the interval and these sold out almost immediately. The main focus for the week was Celia Rees' visit and this was very popular with the students. They thought it great fun to meet a real author and it certainly promoted reading as every student wanted to read one of her books – the Library was a very busy place for horror stories that week!*
>
> *My impression is that the whole school found it an exciting and fun week. We hope to make it an annual event from now on.*

Celia Rees can be contacted for school visits at 195 Rugby Road, Milverton, Leamington Spa, Warwickshire CV32 6DX or via her publishers Macmillan, Scholastic or Hodder Headline.

Jacqueline Wilson
(Novelist)

Figure 5.6 Jacqueline Wilson

School of Education, University of Reading, half-day visit

Jacqueline Wilson came to the University of Reading on the afternoon of 18 May 1999 to give a talk to a group of trainee primary teachers – Year 1 undergraduates on the BA.Ed degree. The students were English specialists, and the visit featured as part of the Year 1 English Craft of Writing course. Previous visitors to the course have included Philip Pullman, Norman Silver, Jan Mark and John Foster.

In the transcript that follows – which features edited highlights from her talk – Jacqueline provides an overview of her writing career and discusses the nature of her work in schools and libraries. At the end of the session, she invited questions from the group, a few of which are reproduced at the end of this section. Jacqueline was keen to hear about the students' own writing and their experiences in primary schools. The group themselves responded most positively to the visit, and later, on completion of the Craft of Writing course, many students commented that the visit had been invaluable and had directly informed their own writing for children.

On becoming a writer

JACQUELINE WILSON: I was an only child and I was left by myself a lot. This was splendid for me because what I liked to do most of all was to read, to make up stories in my head and to play imaginary games. And really, from as far back as I can remember, what I always wanted to do most of all was to write. From about the age of 6 I started writing down stories in notebooks. It was a lovely ritual for me on Saturdays – spending my pocket money in Woolworths on a brand new exercise book. I'd write a bit of a story, get fed up with it and then wait until the next Saturday to buy a new book and start all over again. The only story I still have from then is called *The Maggots* – which I wrote when I was 9. *The Maggots* is about a poor, dysfunctional family – very much the same sort of people as in my current books. I don't know whether that says that I haven't developed as a writer, or that I've remained true to myself!

By the age of 17 I was working for the publisher DC Thompson in Scotland. Although they named their magazine *Jackie* after me, I mainly worked on their women's magazines. It was wonderful to see my work in print every week. As a writer I learnt a number of things by doing journalism. It taught me not to get above myself as a writer as my work was constantly being edited. It was brilliant training as I had to write every single day. I learnt that you can't sit about and worry about writer's block, you've just got to get on with it and put words down on the page. It also encouraged me to be versatile in that I had to do all kinds of things for the magazines. I had to write the readers' letters page, and I was often a Mrs. So-and-so from Wrexham! I even wrote the horoscope page once – with no knowledge of astrology whatsoever. So journalism taught me how to write in different styles. It was good training for novel writing as I had to adopt different styles and different readers' voices.

Eventually I came back to London, got married and had my daughter, Emma. Somehow, despite having a small baby in the house, I wrote two novels in those early family days. Both of those were turned down by publishers. I also wrote many articles that were published – articles for mother and baby magazines as well as romantic stories for women's magazines. But I knew that what I really wanted to do was to write for children.

I came across a series of books for children that were edited by Leila Berg. They were published by Macmillan. The series was called 'Nippers' and these were the first books specifically for and about children from working-class backgrounds. By now, my daughter was coming up to three and we loved reading together. I liked this series and I wrote my own story in this style. It was called *Ricky's Birthday*. I sent it off, and amazingly, it was published! I continued to write pieces for magazines and I even wrote a number of crime novels that were published for adults. At this time teenage novels were starting to take off in a big way. I saw that they were mainly American, and frequently written in the first person. I took a number out of the library. I had a go at writing one. It was called *Nobody's Perfect*. I sent it to various publishers and finally Oxford University Press accepted it. I wrote about seven or eight teenage novels for girls for Oxford. The books became more and more complex and literary. They all had these obscure literary references and various themes running through them.

At this point I started visiting secondary schools. I noticed that only a few of the very literary children were fully appreciating my books. Many children seemed to get bogged down with all the dense text. I started to realise as I spoke to Year 9 pupils that although they were often very capable, imaginative and intelligent, they thought that many of the books they were reading were boring. As a result of this, I decided to change my writing style. I wanted to discover a style that I liked myself and that children would want to read too.

My editor at that time, David Fickling, had moved to Transworld, and he invited me to do a new book for him. The book that resulted was *The Story of Tracy Beaker*. We went for a book with bigger print, so it looked as if it would be easier to read. I wanted lots of illustrations – and with illustrations even telling parts of the story. I had no idea who Transworld would choose as the illustrator for the book. David Fickling knew Nick Sharratt's work and he sent me some samples of his illustrations. I very much liked what I saw. When I got to see what he'd done for *Tracy Beaker* I was absolutely thrilled to bits.

It means all the world to me having Nick Sharratt illustrate my books as his wonderful covers and illustrations immediately give my books eye appeal. I know that I'm already half-way there at reaching the reader even before they've read a single word. And now although I've been writing for years and years, I feel that my writing career only really started properly from *Tracy Beaker* onwards.

It often seems strange to me that my books are popular now as when I was at school I was a bit of an odd one out. I didn't feel part of or in touch with my own peer group at all. Some children write to me now as if we're best friends – so obviously I'm creating characters and situations in my books that children can identify with – and that's lovely for me.

On visiting schools

I do three visits a week. I go to schools and libraries and bookshops all over Britain and Ireland. I must go to more schools than Ofsted inspectors! Recently, I was lucky enough to give talks to children in Australia and New Zealand. Though wherever I go, and however different children may seem, and whether they're from a rural school or an inner city school, generally speaking children seem to respond to the same things in my talks, which is nice, as it gives you the idea that there's a universality about the experience of childhood. Usually, when I go in to a school or library I'll talk for three-quarters of an hour and then we'll have questions.

I talk about my book *The Suitcase Kid* for a variety of reasons. One of these reasons is that Andy, the central character – like many of the children I meet in schools and libraries – has divorced parents. When I talk about this book you can tell immediately by the looks on the children's faces which ones have parents that have split up. I try not to encourage too much eye contact at that point as I don't necessarily feel it's appropriate for children to put their hands up and disclose all sorts of personal and private information that they might later regret telling. If there's a child that looks like they've got a lot of emotions bottled up I might linger around after my talk so that the child and I can have a private chat if necessary. Some children write to me about these kinds of issues. It was quite difficult for me a couple of years ago when my own marriage ended as children often ask me 'Are you married?' or 'Has your marriage split up?'. It really gave me an added insight into how painful it is for children, as they're expected to go into school and perform and cope with everything when all these upsetting emotions are exploding inside them.

In *The Suitcase Kid*, the central character, Andy, has a toy Sylvanian Family rabbit called

Radish. Andy has had Radish ever since she was a baby. It's her way of coping. She talks to Radish as if he's real – he's both her comfort blanket and imaginary friend. For me as an author, the light-hearted moments with Radish stop the novel from becoming too depressing a read and provide comic relief. It was also a useful plot device, as I could let the inevitable happen, which was that Radish could go missing!

Illustrators and artists in schools have the advantage that they have something to show the children during their talks. At times during a talk you need to hold the children's attention by showing them things. What I do is to show the children my own Radish – she used to belong to my daughter. I like to tell children that writing can be hard for professional writers too and at difficult moments I'll fidget around at my desk and I'll do daft things like tricks with Radish in which I make her do bunny bungee-jumping with a pencil and some long rubber bands!

When I go around schools I take in *The Maggots,* a story that I wrote when I was 9. My purpose in showing this to children is to demonstrate that even though I wrote it day after day – thinking I was writing a whole book – it's only about twelve sides of paper. I meet children who desperately want to write but they find that after two and a half pages their story fizzles out. I try to reassure them that you really do have to wait until you're an adult to have the stamina and ability to sustain a novel of two hundred or so pages.

No matter what school I'm visiting, there's always a forest of hands that goes up at the end of my talk. Children always have questions that they want to ask. Teachers generally talk with the children beforehand about the sort of things that they might like to ask. Often, in the excitement of the moment, the 'Where do you get your ideas from?' type of questions get brushed aside and inevitably – and most naturally – children ask me why I wear so many rings or how old I am or exactly how much money I earn – so I'm used to any kind of question!

Occasionally schools will ask for a writing workshop, which can be quite difficult sometimes as you don't know the children at all or maybe they don't even enjoy writing very much. I find *The Story of Tracy Beaker* a very useful book to talk about during my visits, and particularly if I'm asked to do a writing workshop. In one part of the book, Tracy gets advertised in the newspaper. As I was writing the book I came across various adverts in newspapers of children that were available for adoption. The adverts would say things like 'Are you special enough for two lively brothers?' Of course, 'lively' is an understatement, and it really means naughty or difficult. To begin the workshop I will read out some of these descriptions to the children and I'll ask them how they would feel if they were advertised themselves. We discuss issues such as the fact that the younger, cuter children would find it easier to find homes, but the older ones – who might have various problems – may find it harder to be adopted. I talk to the children about Tracy's advert, and the fact that she is a very streetwise and determined child, and that in the book when she does her own advert she exaggerates and goes completely over the top.

In the book we then see Tracy's real advert, with a photograph of her looking very angry. The advert tells the truth about Tracy, saying how difficult her life has been. So, I show the children one positive and ideal advert with exaggerations, and the other, more low key advert that tells the truth. Then I get children to do their own versions – one ideal and one truthful. This always seems to work, no matter what age the children are – from 7 year olds up to Year 8 children in secondary schools. I do my own versions too, and we all read them out at the end. This initial exercise is very useful as quickly I can glean those children who have real ability as well as those whose literacy skills are not so developed. It also gives me an idea as to what sort of children they are. And when you do a writing workshop like this you're going into a classroom completely cold. Sometimes I find I can't go by what the teachers have told me about their pupils beforehand. For example, the difficult, more disruptive ones can at times be the ones that will come up with the interesting ideas in their writing.

Next, I might show the class the section in the 'All About Me' booklet that all children in care are given to complete. It's the section in which children are asked to write down their favourite things – such as animals, games and so on. Then I get the class to make up their own character and actually write a profile on the character based upon this list of questions. From there I tell the children that their fictional characters are going to be the new kid in the children's home where Tracy Beaker lives. I ask the children to consider how their character will feel about moving in and whether they'll have a good or bad time initially, and how they would get on with Tracy. I find this is a good exercise because the children are doing character studies without even realising it.

For this part of the workshop I give a story structure. I get every child to write down 'In the middle of the night . . .' and they have to write from there. By the end of the session we have a finished piece of work, which is great. And some teachers are very particular about this – they want a completed piece by the end of the workshop.

I've been on visits when teachers have said to me, 'The children are having difficulties with punctuation. Will you stress to them how important punctuation is?'. I feel that if you're telling somebody that's just set out to write a story that they've got to have speech marks here and a comma there, you'll kill their story stone dead. Surely it's best to write the story and to imagine it as hard as you can first, and then you can go back and do an exercise on how to punctuate it.

Children who've read quite a few of my books – because they're generally written in the first person – are surprised to see that I'm old enough to be their grandmother! But they seem to relate to the 10 year old inside me. They ask me if I have any pets or which football team I support. One boy recently asked me how late I'm allowed to stay up – which was very sweet! But generally, both children and adults ask me how I got started writing, whether I always wanted to be a writer and what gave me the idea for such-and-such a book.

Do children ever get upset by the issues in your books?

It doesn't bother me quite so much if adults get upset – but it certainly does concern me if children do. Most children know that though there might be worrying things in my books, by the end – although there won't always be a completely happy ending – the situations will more or less be resolved. My latest book is *The Illustrated Mum*. This is perhaps a more worrying book than my others as the mother is a manic depressive. I've had lots of letters about *The Illustrated Mum* – and I'm thrilled, because they're wonderfully positive and many children insist it's their favourite book.

People often ask me about tackling difficult issues in my books. Theoretically, there are no subjects that are considered taboos in children's books any more, you just have to apply common sense when writing about them though, and obviously try not to upset your readers too much. I try to inject humour into my books to counterbalance the more serious themes and issues. People often come up to me and say that they've got a great idea for one of my books – that is, an issue. But you can't just have a book about an issue, it can be part of a plot, but it won't be the whole thing.

What advice do you have regarding writing fiction for children?

It can be difficult getting into children's publishing now as it is so commercially orientated. As a result, it's hard to get one-off books published – so look to see what series are being published, who is publishing them, and what age groups they are for. And personally, first person is the best form of narration for me as it cuts out the issue of whether children will understand the language I'm using or not. If you're writing in the voice of either a 9-year-old boy or an

11-year-old girl you will only use the words that they would use, and you'll see the world from their point of view. These days, children as readers like lots to be happening in a story. And they want to get right into the story from the very first page.

6 Arranging an author visit

Author visits to schools

As schools across the United Kingdom will testify, young writers can gain a great deal from direct contact with authors – fiction or non-fiction writers, poets or illustrators. Author events have repeatedly proved to inspire and motivate young writers, to help develop and extend literacy skills, and to nurture a passion for literature and performance. Graham McArthur, deputy headteacher of St John's Primary School in Tunbridge Wells, talks about some of the further benefits of author visits:

> First, an author brings in their own experiences. Second, a visit shows that authors are real people, they're not just a name that appears on a book. Third, visits help to generate excitement, to develop children's interest in and enthusiasm for books. Writers have that ability to motivate children as writers themselves. Also, visits bring about a team spirit for writing.

There are three fundamental stages in the organisation of an author event:

- before
- during
- after.

Considering the visit in these terms enables teachers or librarians preparing for the event to gain an overview of the administration entailed and to give time and thought to the many significant aspects of the organisation process. This chapter provides a comprehensive guide to setting up an author event; it may be photocopied and used as a checklist if required.

This chapter has a number of key functions, and hopes to ensure that:

- an excessive amount of time is not spent on organisation and administration
- the right author is chosen for the visit
- the visit is positive, meaningful and enjoyable for all concerned
- funds are spent appropriately
- the event is well organised and runs smoothly
- the author is properly looked after and is made to feel welcome
- the visit is linked to ongoing curricular activities before and afterwards so that it does not become a one-off event that is soon forgotten.

Please note that throughout this section the term 'visit' here is used in a generic sense and can imply anything from a half-day or one-day event to a book week or a whole term residency. (Please note that half-day visits in isolation are rare and are generally discouraged.) Also, the generic term 'author' signifies any form of literary visitor.

Funding and costs

At the time of publication, the rate for an author visit is £100 for half a day, £150 for a whole day. Travel expenses will need to be paid in addition to the author's fee. Please contact the Poetry Society or the Arts Council to check current standard rates (details below).

Some authors may be prepared to negotiate their fee if they are being asked to do a half-week, whole-week or term residency. It is necessary to calculate exactly what funds can be made available before an author is contacted.

Funds can derive from a number of sources:

- central school budgets
- curriculum-led budgets
- donations from parents
- fundraising events
- sponsorship from local companies, charities and organisations
- local education authority English advisors may know of sources of funding
- if a member of the Poetry Society, the school will be able to make application for funding for a poet for three days (funding cannot be guaranteed – details provided on p. 234)
- Arts Council grants may be sourced from the Arts Council and Regional Arts Boards.

Forms of events and visitors

Some schools and libraries will have events that take place over a number of days, weeks or even months. Additional factors are involved when setting up a book or poetry event or a book week or residency rather than a single day visit from an author. Clearly, these forms of events will require much more time and administration and would ideally be organised by a team or committee to share the responsibilities.

Book weeks (either half-week or whole-week events) tend to involve a variety of visitors and can be a celebration of text and literature in the widest sense:

- novelists and prose writers
- picture book writers
- poets and performance poets
- playwrights
- oral storytellers
- illustrators or cartoonists
- librarians with subject specialisms
- songwriters or composers
- book designers
- book, magazine or newspaper printers
- editors, publishers and specialists from publishing companies
- book consultants
- literary critics
- journalists from local newspapers, radio and TV
- actors or Theatre-in-Education groups
- directors and producers of film or theatre.

Some schools will widen the focus beyond reading and writing to include other media, art forms and events:

- dance or drama workshops
- music workshops
- instrument-making workshops
- book-making workshops
- puppet shows
- a Readathon® (Readathon, Swerford, Chipping Norton, Oxon OX7 4BG tel/fax: 01608-730335; website: http://www.readathon.org; e-mail: reading@readathon.org)
- visit to a local library, bookshop, publisher or newspaper.

Extra activities

Many of the text-related activities below can be included as part of an author visit, residency or book week:

- publishing anthologies and creating displays of work produced in workshops
- competitions and quizzes based on popular books and authors
- friezes of scenes from books
- special features in school magazine
- class displays featuring pupils' profiles on visiting authors – including students' own book reviews, biographies and illustrations
- Secondary pupils visit Junior schools to read their own writing specifically produced for the Junior age range; Junior pupils visit Infant schools or departments to read their own writing specifically produced for the Infant age range
- staff and pupils discuss 'Desert Island Books' or produce lists of 'Top Ten' authors
- designing book event posters and programmes
- a literary theme – some schools will celebrate the works of a single author; Helen Cresswell and Malorie Blackman have visited schools in recent years where their books have been the focus for a class or school topic; other schools will have a fancy dress day in which staff and/or pupils will dress up as favourite characters from books, nursery rhymes or fairy tales
- some authors will accompany a class on a school visit – to a farm, zoo, museum, art gallery, field trip – to produce writing on location.

Special events in the calendar

Some schools and libraries organise events specifically to coincide with a special day in the calendar, such as

- International Children's Book Day: Hans Christian Andersen's birthday, 2 April
- World Book Day: Shakespeare's birthday, 23 April
- Anne Frank Day: 12 June
- National Poetry Day: usually the first Thursday in October
- Children's Book Week: one week in early October.

Preparations before the visit

Time scales and responsibilities

The organisation and responsibility of any author event needs to be shared between members of staff. Larger events such as book weeks or festivals need to be set up by a committee with designated roles. On average, a single author visit is planned at least a term in advance; larger events tend to be organised over an academic year.

Choosing the right author

- It is worthwhile taking time to consider exactly what type of author you need. Do you want a novelist, picture book writer, poet, illustrator, storyteller or playwright? Or would someone connected with publishing be more appropriate – an editor, book designer, critic or journalist? (See 'Forms of events and visitors' on pp. 231–2.)
- Consider:
  (a) Which author might complement your current literacy activities?
  (b) Who would the pupils respond well to?
  (c) Do you want a local or a famous author?
  (d) Do you want someone whose work you have been reading in class?
  (e) Do you want an author visit to coincide with a specific event?
  (f) What do you want to achieve from this?
  (g) Which year group(s) do you need the author for? Will you be needing a writer who can do workshops with Infants as well as Juniors?
- A one-day visit will probably entail a maximum of one performance or reading and workshops in three single classes or four single workshops.
- A series of visits or a residency from one author will allow the author to meet more classes or even do an extended project with one or two classes. This will give the author time to address such issues as drafting and research, to explore further the nature and forms of poetry or narrative, conduct a variety of workshops and to work towards a performance of the pupils' own writing.
- Go to a library or bookshop or read a current magazine such as *Books for Keeps*, *Carousel*, *Young Writer* or *School Librarian* to see which authors are currently being published.
- Different authors do different things. Some poets will do only workshops and some novelists will give only talks. Spend time thinking about whether you want workshops and/or performances.
- Some authors will also do performances and/or talks for parents and staff after school hours. This may increase the fee, but an entrance fee could be charged.
- National Poetry Day – in early October – is a popular day for poets to visit schools; either book a poet a term or two in advance or invite a poet immediately before or after the day; the Poetry Society (details below) can provide practical advice on celebrating the day and contacting poets.
- Try not to be too specific from the outset – 'I want so-and-so for my book week and s/he must do three workshops and then a performance and . . .'. There is a tendency for the more established the author, the fewer visits they tend to do, so do not set your heart on acquiring an award-winning or best-selling author – it could be that they do not do visits any more.
- Being published does not necessarily guarantee a successful visit. Many excellent and memorable visits are conducted by writers who do not produce books at all, but by

individuals who have a natural gift for performing, running workshops and inspiring young writers.

Sources of information and advice

Advice on which authors are available and what they do can be obtained from a wide variety of sources. Contact your Regional Arts Board or these national organisations:

The Poetry Society
Education Department
22 Betterton Street
London WC2H 9BU
Tel: 020-7420-9880
Fax: 020-7240-4818
Email: info@poetrysoc.com
Website: http://www.poetrysoc.com
Education Officer direct line: 020-7420-9894
(The Poetry Society keeps a database of poets available for visits all over the UK)

The Arts Council of Great Britain
14 Great Peter Street
London SW1P 3NQ
Tel: 020-7333-0100

National Association of Writers in Education (NAWE)
PO Box 1
Sheriff Hutton
York YO6 7YU
Tel/fax: 01653-618429
Website: http://www.nawe.co.uk
(NAWE keeps a database of authors available for visits all over the UK)

Young Book Trust
Book House
45 East Hill
London SW18 2QZ
Tel: 020-8516-2977

Young Book Trust Scotland
137 Dundee Street
Edinburgh EH11 1BG
Tel: 0131-229-3663

Speaking of Books
Tel/fax: 020-8692-4704

> *At last! Here's an easy way to arrange just the right visitor for a school or reading-group – also to guarantee back-up information together with a book supply on a*

sale-or-return basis. Since January 1998, 'Speaking of Books' has been backed by Puffin, Orchard, Random House, HarperCollins, Walker and other leading publishers. Jan Powling hopes that:

> *I'm not just solving the problems teachers or book group organisers have in finding an author, illustrator, poet or storyteller to meet their particular needs . . . I'm also helping the speakers themselves by making sure visits are less of a hit-or-miss affair. Basically what we offer is the equivalent of one-stop shopping – a call to us and we'll organise the rest.*

Personal recommendations

Further advice can come from recommendations – so talk to colleagues, contact other schools and visit your local main library or bookshops.

Publishers

The publicity/marketing departments of these publishers will discuss which of their authors are available and will also provide advice on preparing for the event and will send schools, libraries and bookshops publicity materials such as posters and author information packs.

- Transworld – 020-7579-2652
- Puffin – 020-7416-3000
- Scholastic – 020-7421-9000
- Hodder – 020-7873-6000
- Faber & Faber 020-7465-0045
- For further publishers see the *Writers' and Artists' Yearbook* (A & C Black) or *The Writers' Handbook* (Macmillan) – both updated annually.

Publications

Looking for an Author is a most comprehensive author directory published by the Reading and Language Centre at Reading University (0118-931-8820) and Young Book Trust, London (0208-516-2977). Highly recommended.

What to discuss with the author prior to the event

- Does the author do performances or talks or writing workshops?
- Does the author offer anything else – INSET, talks to parents, staff, and so on?
- What would you like her/him to do on the day?
- Which year groups will the author be with? Authors may well need to tailor their material or even generate new material depending on the age group(s).
- How many sessions is the author prepared to do in one day? (Absolute maximum of four one-hour sessions.)
- Negotiate and talk through a timetable or schedule that you and the author are happy with.
- Does the author prefer that the pupils are familiar with her/his work beforehand?
- Ask directly what the author needs from a school during a visit.
- Does the author have any specific dietary or medical requirements?
- When does the author require payment – on the day or afterwards?
- Do you have all the contact numbers and addresses for the author?
- How will s/he be travelling to the school? Will s/he need a lift from a bus stop or railway station from a member of staff?

- Does the author wish to eat at the school at lunchtime or does s/he prefer to go out for the lunch break, for a quiet period before the afternoon?
- What are the author's current publications? How can publicity materials be obtained?
- Ask the author's permission if you wish to take photographs or make video or tape recordings.

Confirmation in writing

Issues to cover in a letter of confirmation:

- date and time of forthcoming visit
- fee and expenses as arranged
- map of school/area – details of how to find school
- copy of schedule for the day
- recap on any other issues raised in telephone conversations – age groups, size of classes, requirements for performances etc.
- if the visit is part of the school book week, inform author of the other events taking place
- school prospectus
- telephone numbers – home and work numbers for event co-ordinator(s).

Preparation and the author's needs for the day

Find out if the author needs any of the following and ensure they are provided in advance:

- chair(s)
- suitable room with good acoustics (with no possibility of any interruptions)
- certain amount of physical space to set up equipment or to perform
- overhead projector and/or a paper board
- power socket or PA system
- glass or bottle of water
- somewhere to store coat, hand luggage, resources and books
- pens and paper to give out to pupils; space for pupils to write.

PLEASE NOTE: pupils should not have to write whilst sitting on the floor – it is not conducive to creativity; if there is no other option, the children will need to be provided with clipboards.

Also ensure that all rooms are booked or reserved well in advance. Layout of the room is also a major consideration – how should chairs and desks be set out?

Preparation – the pupils

Clearly, if a class have already read the author's work, the visit will be met with greater enthusiasm. Ensure that the classes who are to meet the author have read at least one book or a selection of poems beforehand. Many teachers prepare for the visit by discussing with the class what they think an author actually does, and this type of discussion invariably leads to insightful and intelligent questions being asked of the author during the visit.

Sizes of groups

Although classes may be brought together for an author talk or performance, writing workshops should only be with one class at a time.

Publicity

Considering the amount of time and effort you will be putting into the event, why not make the most of it and invite the local media – newspaper or radio or television – to cover the event? If they are to report on the author and would like a brief interview, discuss this with the author before the day. This type of activity would ideally not be in one of the author's breaks but at the very beginning or end of the day. Such coverage will also help to boost the profile of the school in the local community.

Displays

Some classes do displays of authors' books in corridors and classrooms. These can be decorated with publicity materials – photos, biographies, posters and book covers. All UK children's book publishers can be found in *The Writers' Handbook* (Macmillan) and the *Writers' and Artists' Yearbook* (Black). Alternatively, classes can make their own displays comprising book reviews by the pupils, illustrations of scenes from the authors' books and photocopies of book covers.

Organising books for sale

Some authors, particularly poets, bring in their own books to sell. Alternatively, local bookshops and book fairs (see *The Writers' Handbook* or *Writers' and Artists' Yearbook*) are often keen to come in to schools. If books are to be brought in by an outside organisation, make sure that they know of the author(s) coming into the school, so that they can order copies of their current titles. Ensure that pupils have brought sufficient money, parents are informed well in advance and pupils have plenty of time to browse and select books.

Informing parents, governors and staff

- Parents and governors may wish to be involved with the day.
- Some parents may wish to volunteer a financial contribution.
- Parents need to be aware if their child will need to bring in extra money to buy a book.
- All staff need to be informed of visitors.

Above all

- Be well prepared so that it is an enjoyable, meaningful and rewarding experience for pupils and staff alike.

Arrangements during the visit

Welcoming the author

- Notify all pupils and members of staff well in advance of the visit.
- Put up a welcome board or poster in the main entrance – for example, 'St Trinians welcomes Charles Dickens . . .'
- Have a prominent display of the author's work in the classroom, hall or entrance.
- Ensure that someone is waiting to greet the author on arrival.

- Ensure that the author knows where all amenities are – such as toilets, eating area, staff room – a brief tour of these areas is usually conducted on the author's arrival.
- Ask the author if s/he has any questions regarding the timetable.

Throughout the day

- Ensure that there is someone to escort the author at all times.
- Ensure that the author has breaks between sessions.
- Make the author feel welcome during breaks in the staff room.
- Ensure that the author is NEVER left on her/his own in a classroom or hall with pupils – writers are *not* supply teachers and are *not* insured.
- Allocate time for book signing.

Recording the event

- Many schools take photographs or videos or make tape recordings of author talks. Clear this with the author in advance.

During the performances and workshops

- A minimum of one adult should be present at all times – one of these *must* be a teacher.
- Be attentive and responsive.
- Be prepared to write alongside the pupils, if possible.
- Arrange for pupils with special needs to be catered for.
- Authors are adamant that teachers should not mark work or prepare for other lessons; authors find this most insulting. In addition, it communicates to the pupils that the staff are not interested and the visit means nothing to them.

Above all

- Generate enthusiasm throughout the event.

Activities after the visit

Contact with the author

- Some authors will actively encourage pupils to send completed stories or poems that originated in their workshop. Ask the author if they are happy to do this. Those authors who do encourage letters will tend – due to many other commitments – to produce a generic response to the class as a whole.
- Send letters from the pupils thanking the author.
- Ensure that payment was either sent or given on the day.

Follow-on activities

- If the author initiated some writing, ensure that the children develop and complete this.
- If the author wrote a story or poem during the visit, ensure that this is displayed.
- When writing has been completed, produce a class anthology.

- Celebrate the event with a display in the hall or corridor; use photographs and writing produced in the workshops; add to the display any further correspondence from the author in which they discuss how much they enjoyed the visit and their responses to any writing sent.
- Discuss with the class what they thought of the visit, what they enjoyed and what they feel they gained from the experience; recap on issues that the author raised.
- Return to the author's work: reread her/his novels, stories or poems, which will be viewed differently now that the author has given an added insight into her/his work.
- Put into practice any useful advice that the author may have given – such as methods of brainstorming, ways into writing poetry, things to look out for when drafting stories, or general writing methodologies – and ensure that you take time to share these approaches with other members of staff.

School magazine

Organise someone to write a report of the event for the school magazine.

External publication

Some schools regularly send their pupils' writing to publications such as *Young Writer* (Kate Jones, Glebe House, Weobley, Herefordshire HR4 8SD Tel: 01544-318901, website: www.mystworld.com/youngwriter), to the 'Young Poet of the Week' column in the *Times Educational Supplement* and to the Poetryzone website: www.poetryzone.ndirect.co.uk.

Spread the word

Tell teachers, librarians and book retailers at other schools about your successful visit.

A return visit

Why not? Authors can become part of some schools' calendars.

Above all

- Don't just forget about the visit; let it be a vital and positive part of a continuum of literacy activities.

ARRANGING AN AUTHOR VISIT: CHECKLIST

BEFORE

DURING

AFTER

USEFUL TELEPHONE NUMBERS

Appendix
Further information on creative writing

Competitions: children's own writing

Apple Tree Award
Closing date by end of Spring term. A writing competition for children who have difficulties with reading, writing and communication. There are three sections: 5–7, 8–11 and 12–16 years. Entries can be submitted in the following formats: handwritten, typed, computer generated, sound tape, signed video, braille, rubus, Blissymbols. Any non-print format must be accompanied by a written script.
National Library for the Handicapped Child
Reach Resource Centre
Wellington House, Wellington Road, Wokingham, Berks RG40 2AG

BBC Radio 4 Young Poetry Competition (8–21 years)
BBC Broadcasting House
Whiteladies Road, Bristol BS8 2LR

Roald Dahl Foundation Poetry Competition (7–17 years)
PO Box 1375
20 Vauxhall Bridge Road
London SW1V 2SA
Tel: 020-7824-5463

Simon Elvin Young Poet of the Year Awards
The Poetry Society
22 Betterton Street, London WC2H 9BU
Any writer between the ages of 11 and 18 can enter the Simon Elvin Young Poet Awards. Simply send your poem or poems on A4 paper with your name, address and date of birth written clearly on every sheet.

WH Smith Young Writers Competition (up to 16 years)
Strand House
7 Holbein Place, Sloane Square, London SW1W 8NR

Welsh Academy Young Writers Competition (up to 18 years – closing date July)
PO Box 328, Cardiff CF2 4XL

Write Away
A competition for pupils aged 7 to 11. It is a chance for Juniors to find an audience for their writing, to explore new styles and voices – and to win cash prizes. A competition organised by

the *Times Educational Supplement,* the National Association for the Teaching of English and McDonald's Restaurants Ltd to give young writers the opportunity to reflect on their lives.
National Association for the Teaching of English
50 Broadfield Road, Sheffield S8 0XJ

Contact the publicity departments of the following publishers for details:
A&C Black competition
Tel: 020-7242-0946
Puffin Wondercrump competition
Tel: 020-8899-4000

Reference texts and further reading

The following publications provide useful introductions and insights into various aspects of creative writing. Some of these are intended for adult writers, but still contain a number of activities relevant to the classroom and writing workshops in general.

Peter Abbs and John Richardson – *The Forms of Narrative* and *The Forms of Poetry* (Cambridge University Press)

Julian Birkett – *Word Power: A Guide to Creative Writing* (Black)

Sandy Brownjohn – *To Rhyme or Not to Rhyme?* (Hodder & Stoughton)

James Carter – *Talking Books: Children's Authors Talk about the Craft, Creativity and Process of Writing for Children* – interviews with children's authors including Ian Beck, Terry Deary, Berlie Doherty, Philip Pullman, Celia Rees, Jacqueline Wilson (Routledge)

James Carter – *rap it up: reading, writing and performing raps in the classroom* – rap poetry anthology, teacher's guide and accompanying CD of rap poetry/music (Questions Publishing)

Pie Corbett and Brian Moses: *Catapults and Kingfishers* (poetry) and *My Grandmother's Motorbike* (fiction) (Oxford University Press)

Dianne Doubtfire – *Teach Yourself Creative Writing* (Hodder & Stoughton)

Kate Jones – *Writing* (Hodder & Stoughton, super.activ series)

Michael Rosen – *Rosen's Poetry Attic – Book Box Teacher's Guide* (Channel 4) and *Did I Hear You Write?* (André Deutsch).

Anthony Wilson with Sian Hughes – *The Poetry Book for Primary Schools* (Poetry Society)

Cliff Yates – *Jumpstart: Poetry in the Secondary School* (Poetry Society)

Writers' and Artists' Yearbook (A & C Black) – updated annually

The Writers' Handbook (Macmillan) – updated annually

Bibliography

Books cited that are not listed in 'Selected current titles'

Fiction
Charles Ashton – *Billy's Drift* (Walker)
Paula Danzinger and Ann M. Martin – *P.S. Longer Letter Later: A Novel in Letters* and *Snailmail No More: A Novel by E-Mail* (Hodder)
Goscinny and Uderzo – *Asterix* series
Kenneth Grahame – *The Wind in the Willows* (Puffin)
Hergé – *Tintin* series (Methuen)
Simon James – *Dear Greenpeace* (Walker)
Rudyard Kipling – *The Jungle Book* (Puffin)
Mary Rayner – *The Small Good Wolf* (Walker)
Jon Sciezka – *The True Story of the Three Little Pigs by A. Wolf* (Viking)

Non-Fiction
Heather Couper and Nigel Henbest – *Space Encyclopedia* (Dorling Kindersley)
Barry Holstun Lopez – *Of Wolves and Men* (Dent)
Candace Savage – *Wolves* (Hale)
Russell Stannard – *Ask Uncle Albert* and *Space* and *Time, Rhythm and Rhyme* (Faber & Faber)
Carole Stott – *New Astronomer: The Practical Guide to the Skills and Techniques of Skywatching* (Dorling Kindersley)
BBC Wildlife magazine vol. 14 no. 3 – March 1996
Eyewitness Project Pack: Space (Dorling Kindersley)

Television documentary
Magic Animals: Wolves – BBC2 television programme, broadcast 1 March 1995

Selected current titles from all featured authors

Please note that although a number of the authors featured in this book write for adults as well as children, only current children's titles are listed below.

David Almond

Hodder Headline
Skellig
Kit's Wilderness
(both available as talking book audio cassettes read by the author)
Heaven Eyes
Counting Stars and Other Stories

Laurence and Catherine Anholt

Laurence and Catherine Anholt are one of the UK's leading author/illustrator teams who have produced more than sixty books in seventeen languages.

Frances Lincoln
Laurence Anholt's titles include:
Picasso and the Girl with the Ponytail

Camille and the Sunflowers
Degas and the Little Dancer
Leonardo and the Flying Boy

Picture Mammoth
Laurence and Catherine Anholt's titles include:
Look What I Can Do
Animals Animals All Around
Ton's Rainbow Walk
When I Was a Baby

Laurence and Catherine can be contacted via www.anholt.co.uk

Neil Ardley

Dorling Kindersley
101 Great Science Experiments
A Young Person's Guide to Music (with music by Poul Ruders)
Dictionary of Science
Eyewitness Guide No 12: Music
How Things Work (Eyewitness Science Guide)
My Science (15 volume series)

With David Macaulay:
The New Way Things Work (also on CD-ROM)

Nick Arnold

Horrible Science series (Scholastic)
Blood, Bones and Body Bits (winner of the Rhône-Poulenc Junior Science book prize)
Bulging Brains
Chemical Chaos
Deadly Diseases
Disgusting Digestion
Fatal Forces
Frightening Light
Nasty Nature
Shocking Electricity
Sounds Dreadful
Suffering Scientists Special
Ugly Bugs (winner of the Rhône-Poulenc Junior Science book prize)
Vicious Veg

Funfax
The Action Man File

Wayland
Volcanoes and Earthquakes
Voyages of Exploration

Peter Bailey

A Scary Story (André Deutsch – Scholastic)

Recent texts illustrated by Peter Bailey include:
Tony Mitton – *Red and White Spotted Handkerchief* and *Plum* (Scholastic)
Philip Pullman – *I Was a Rat* and *Clockwork* (Transworld)
Dick King-Smith – *The Crowstarrer* (Transworld)

Ian Beck

Picture Corgi
Noah and the Ark – text by Antonia Barber
The Teddy Robber

Doubleday
Emily and the Golden Acorn
The Owl and the Pussycat
Peter and the Wolf – and music/narration cassette
Puss in Boots – text by Philip Pullman
Teddy Tales – Cinderella
Teddy Tales – Hansel and Gretel
Tom and the Island of Dinosaurs

Scholastic
Alone in the Woods
Home Before Dark
Lost in the Snow
Ian Beck's Picture Book
Ian Beck's Red Book, Green Book, Blue Book, Yellow Book – board format
Poems for Christmas – compiled by Gill Bennett

Orchard
Five Little Ducks – board book and large book format
Little Angel – text by Geraldine McGaughrean
The Orchard ABC
The Orchard Book of Fairy Tales – text by Rose Impey
Peter Pan and Wendy – text by Rose Impey
The Ugly Duckling – board book and large book format

Oxford University Press
Little Miss Muffet
Oranges and Lemons – text by Karen King
The Oxford Nursery Book

The Oxford Nursery Story Book
The Oxford Nursery Treasury
Round and Round the Garden – text by Sarah Williams

Malorie Blackman

Corgi – Yearling
A.N.T.I.D.O.T.E.
Dangerous Reality
Hacker
Noughts and Crosses
Operation Gadgetman
Pig-heart Boy
Snow Dog
Space Race
Thief!

Hippo
Computer Ghost
Deadly Dare
Lie Detectives
My Friend's a Gris-Quok

Puffin
Forbidden Game
Girl Wonder and the Terrible Twins
Girl Wonder to the Rescue
Girl Wonder's Winter Adventures
Jack Sweettooth the 73rd
Whizziwig / Whizziwig Returns

Hodder
Jessica Strange

Egmont – Mammoth
Animal Avengers
Betsey Biggalow titles
Words Last Forever

Macmillan
Tell Me No Lies

Andersen
Mrs. Spoon's Family

Orchard
Elaine, You're a Brat!
Fangs

Puzzle Adventures series
Where's My Cuddle?

Tamarind
Dizzy's Walk
Marty Monster

The Women's Press – 'Livewire Books for Teenagers'
Not So Stupid!
Trust Me

Valerie Bloom

Valerie Bloom writes and performs for children and adults. These are her current children's titles:

Ackee Breadfruit and Callaloo (Bougle L'Ouverture)
Fruits (Macmillan picture book)
Let Me Touch the Sky (Macmillan)
New Baby (Macmillan)
The World is Sweet (Bloomsbury)
Yuh Hear Bout? (cassette featuring readings of her poetry) (57 Productions)

Valerie Bloom can be contacted for performances or workshops via Macmillan publicity department or Bougle L'Ouverture.

Melvin Burgess

Andersen Press and Puffin
An Angel for May
The Baby and Fly Pie
Bloodtide (not Puffin)
The Cry of the Wolf
The Earth Giant
Junk
Kite
Loving April
Tiger Tiger

Hodder
Burning Issy

Helen Cresswell

Oxford University Press
The Bongleweed
The Piemakers

Kingfisher
Book of Mystery Stories (editor)

Puffin
Lizzie Dripping
Moondial
The Phoenix and the Carpet – novelisation of TV series
Stonestruck

Hodder & Stoughton
Bag of Bones
The Night-Watchmen
Snatchers
The Bagthorpes Saga:
      Ordinary Jack
      Absolute Zero
      Bagthorpes Unlimited
      Bagthorpes v. the World
      Bagthorpes Abroad
      Bagthorpes Haunted
      Bagthorpes Liberated

For younger readers (Hodder & Stoughton)
A Gift from Winklesea
The Little Grey Donkey
The Little Sea Horse
The Seapiper
Sophie and the Sea Wolf
Whatever Happened in Winklesea

Gillian Cross

Chartbreak (Puffin)
The Dark Behind the Curtain (Point – Scholastic)
The Demon Headmaster (Puffin)
The Demon Headmaster Strikes Again (Puffin)
The Demon Headmaster Takes Over (Puffin)
The Great Elephant Chase (Puffin)
The Iron Way (Oxford University Press)
Map of Nowhere (Mammoth)
New World (Puffin)
On the Edge (Puffin)
Pictures in the Dark (Oxford University Press)
Prime Minister's Brain (Puffin)
Revenge of the Demon Headmaster (Puffin)
Roscoe's Leap (Puffin)
Tightrope (Oxford University Press)
Wolf (Puffin)

For younger readers
Beware Olga! (Walker)
Gobbo the Great (Mammoth)
The Goose Girl – retelling of the fairy tale (Scholastic)
Mintyglo Kid (Mammoth)
Posh Watson (Walker)
Rent a Genius (Puffin)
Roman Beanfeast (Antelope Books)
Swimathon! (Mammoth)
The Tree House (Mammoth)
What Will Emily Do? (Mammoth)

Jan Dean

Fiction
Me, Duncan and the Great Hippopotamus Scandal (Oxford University Press)
The Fight For Barrowby Hill (Puffin)
Harry and the Megabyte Brain (Cambridge University Press)
Shakespeare's Stories (MacDonald Young Books)
    Much Ado About Nothing
    Twelfth Night

'Cheesy and Zoom' series (MacDonald Young Books)
The Claygate Hound
Frogsnot Ate My Goldfish
Babysitting Jellyflob
Craxis and the Cow-Juice Soup
Neddlebelly and the Bullyboy

Poetry
A Mean Fish Smile: Sandwich Poets Volume 4 (Macmillan)

Terry Deary

Fiction:
Tudor Terror Series (Orion) including:
    The Lady of Fire and Tears
    The King in Blood Red and Gold

The Spark Files series (Faber & Faber) including:
    Over the Moon
    Chop and Change

Diary of a Murder (Ginn)
Ghost Town (Black)
The Joke Factory (Black)

Shadow Play (André Deutsch)
Time Detectives series (Faber & Faber)
The Treasure of Crazy Horse (Black)

Non-fiction
Horrible Histories series (Scholastic) including:
>   *The Blitzed Brits*
>   *The Incredible Incas*
>   *Mad Millennium* (play script)
>   *The Massive Millennium Quiz Book*
>   *The Nasty Normans*
>   *The Savage Stone Age*
>   *The Sensational Saxons*
>   *The Vile Victorians*
>   *The Woeful Second World War*

Wild Words – a series for learning English – includes a set of CD-ROMs (Letts)

Top Ten (Scholastic) including:
>   *Top Ten Shakespeare Stories*
>   *Top Ten Greek Legends*

The Knowledge – Potty Politics (Scholastic)

True Stories (Scholastic) including:
>   *True Detective Stories*
>   *True UFO Stories*

Shivers series (Franklin Watts) including:
>   *Mystery*
>   *Spooks*

Berlie Doherty

Children of Winter (Mammoth)
Daughter of the Sea (Puffin)
Dear Nobody (Lions Tracks)
Granny was a Buffer Girl (Mammoth)
How Green You Are! (Mammoth)
The Making of Fingers Finnigan (Mammoth)
Midnight Man (Walker)
The Sailing Ship Tree (Puffin)
The Snake-stone (Collins Tracks)
Spellhorn (Collins Tracks)
Street Child (Collins Tracks)
Tough Luck (Collins Tracks)
White Peak Farm (Mammoth)

Poetry
Walking on Air (Hodder)

Short stories
Running on Ice (Mammoth)

For younger readers
Bella's Den (Yellow Bananas – Mammoth)
Fairy Tales – illustrations by Jane Ray (Walker)
The Famous Adventures of Jack (Hodder)
The Golden Bird (Heinemann Young)
The Snow Queen (Scholastic)
Tilly Mint and the Dodo (Mammoth)
Tilly Mint Tales (Mammoth)
Willa and Old Miss Annie (Walker)

Picture books
The Magical Bicycle – illustrated by Christian Birmingham (Picture Lions)
Midnight Man (Walker)
Paddiwack and Cosy (Hodder)
Snowy (Picture Lions)

Collections
The Forsaken Merman and Other Story Poems – selected by Berlie Doherty (Hodder)
Tales of Wonder and Magic – collected by Berlie Doherty (Walker)
Trickster Tales (Walker)

Plays (Collins Education)
Dear Nobody
Morgan's Field
Street Child

Alan Durant

Creepe Hall (Walker)
Creepe Hall For Ever! (Walker)
Happy Birthday Spider McDrew (Collins)
Jake's Magic (Walker)
Leggs United – football series of eight books (Macmillan)
Little Troll (Collins)
Little Troll and the Big Present (Collins)
Return to Creepe Hall (Walker)
Spider McDrew (Collins)
Star Quest: Voyage to the Greylon Galaxy (Walker)

Picture books
Angus Rides the Goods Train (Viking)
Big Bad Bunny (Orchard)
Big Fish, Little Fish (Macmillan)
Mouse Party (Walker)
Snake Supper (Picture Lions)

Anthologies
Short story in *Centuries of Stories* (HarperCollins)
Short story in *Gary Lineker's Favourite Football Stories* (Macmillan)
Short story in *Same Difference* (Mammoth)
Vampire and Werewolf Stories – anthology edited by Alan Durant (Kingfisher)

For older readers
Blood (Bodley Head)
The Good Book (Bodley Head)
Publish or Die! – a Point Crime novel (Scholastic)
A Short Stay in Purgatory – short stories (Bodley Head)

Anne Fine

For older readers
The Book of the Banshee (Puffin)
Flour Babies (Puffin)
Goggle Eyes (Puffin)
The Granny Project (Mammoth)
Madame Doubtfire (Puffin Modern Classic)
The Other, Darker Ned (Mammoth)
Round Behind the Icehouse (Puffin)
Step by Wicked Step (Puffin)
The Stone Menagerie (Mammoth)
The Summer House Loon (Mammoth)
The Tulip Touch (Puffin)

For middle readers
The Angel of Nitshill Road (Mammoth)
Anneli the Art Hater (Mammoth)
Bad Dreams (Doubleday)
Bill's New Frock (Mammoth)
Charm School (Corgi Yearling)
The Chicken Gave it to Me (Mammoth)
The Country Pancake (Mammoth)
Crummy Mummy and Me (Puffin)
How to Write Really Badly (Mammoth)
Loudmouth Louis (Puffin)
A Pack of Liars (Puffin)
A Sudden Glow of Gold (Mammoth)

A Sudden Puff of Glittering Smoke (Mammoth)
A Sudden Swirl of Icy Wind (Mammoth)
Telling Tales – interview/biography (Mammoth)

For younger readers
Care of Henry (Walker)
Countdown (Heinemann Banana)
Design a Pram (Mammoth)
The Diary of a Killer Cat (Puffin)
The Haunting of Pip Parker (Walker)
Jennifer's Diary (Puffin)
Only a Show (Young Puffin)
Poor Monty – picture book (Mammoth)
Press Play (Mammoth)
Roll Over Roly (Puffin)
The Same Old Story Every Year (Young Puffin)
Stranger Danger (Young Puffin)
The Worst Child I Ever Had (Young Puffin)

Educational titles:
Bill's New Frock – playscript (Longman Educational)
The Country Pancake – playscript (Ginn)

John Foster

All of these poetry titles published by Oxford University Press

Poetry Collections
Four O'Clock Friday
Making Waves
Standing on the Sidelines

Poetry – 'Lollipop' series for younger readers
Bare Bear
Bouncing Ben
Doctor Proctor
My Magic Anorak
You Little Monkey!

Anthologies
Crack Another Yolk and Other Word Play Poems
Dinosaur Poems
Dragon Poems
Excuses, Excuses
First Verses (action rhymes, counting rhymes etc.)
Let's Celebrate – festival poems
Never Say Boo To a Ghost!

Poetry Paintbox titles and anthologies
Twinkle Twinkle Chocolate Bar
A Very First Poetry Book (series)
Word Whirls (shape poems)

Jamila Gavin

Out of India – childhood autobiography (Pavilion)
The Surya Trilogy – including *The Wheel of Surya* (Mammoth – Egmont)
The Wormholers (Mammoth – Egmont)

Morris Gleitzman

Penguin
Bumface
The Other Facts of Life
Second Childhood
Toad Rage
Two Weeks with the Queen

'Rowena Batts' trilogy (Penguin)
Blabber Mouth
Gift of the Gab
Sticky Beak

Macmillan
Belly Flop
Misery Guts
Puppy Fat
Water Wings
Worry Warts

With Paul Jennings (Macmillan)
Wicked series

Russell Hoban

The Battle of Zormla (Walker)
The Court of the Winged Serpent (Jonathan Cape)
The Flight of Bembel Rudzuk (Walker)
Frances series (Picture Puffins, London)
How Tom Beat Captain Najork and his Hired Sportsmen (Jonathan Cape)
Jim Hedgehog and the Lonesome Tower (Hamish Hamilton)
Marzipan Pig (Puffin)
M.O.L.E. (Jonathan Cape)
Monster Film (MacDonald Young)
The Mouse and his Child (Faber & Faber)
The Sea-Thing Child (Walker Books)
They Came from Aargh! (Walker)

The Trokeville Way (Jonathan Cape)
Trouble on Thunder Mountain (Faber & Faber)

Poetry
The Last of the Wallendas (Jonathan Cape)
The Pedalling Man (Mammoth)

Janni Howker

Walker Books
Badger on the Barge (short stories)
Isaac Campion
The Nature of the Beast
Walk with a Wolf (picture book)

Colin Macfarlane

Colin Macfarlane is a widely anthologised poet. He is a popular visitor to schools – where he gives poetry workshops and undertakes residencies. He can be contacted at:

Railway Cottage
Hardington Marsh
Yeovil
Somerset
BA22 9QF
Website: http://tellingtales.web-page.net

Roger McGough

All titles Penguin unless indicated

Poetry
Bad, Bad Cats
Helen Highwater
An Imaginary Menagerie
Lucky
My Dad's a Fireater
Nailing the Shadow
Pillow Talk
Puffin Portable Poets (with Brian Patten and Kit Wright)
Sky in the Pie
You Tell Me (with Michael Rosen)

Poetry for older readers
The Kingfisher Book of Comic Verse (editor) (Kingfisher)
The Kingfisher Book of Poems About Love (editor) (Kingfisher)
The Ring of Words (editor) (Faber & Faber)
Strictly Private (editor)
You at the Back

Fiction
The Great Smile Robbery
Stinkers Ahoy!
The Stowaways

Anthony Masters

Bloomsbury
Bypass
Police Dog series
Roadkill series
Weird World series

Ginn
The Black Dog
Dead Man's Fingers
Ivy
Lights Out
Sinking Sands
Watersnake

Mammoth (Egmont)
Badger
Badger Boy
Ghost Blades

Macdonald Young
The Curse of the Ghost Horse
The Ghost Bus
The Haunted Lighthouse
The Marlow House Mystery series
Phantoms in the Fog
The Seahorse

Orchard
Dancing with the Dead
Dark Tower
Day of the Dead
Deadly Games
The Drop
Ghosthunter series
Haunted School
Poltergeist
Possessed
Spinner
Wicked

Puffin
Bullies Don't Hurt
Dead Man at the Door
Ghost Stories to Tell in the Dark
Horror Stories to Tell in the Dark
Scary Stories to Tell in the Dark
Vampire Stories to Tell in the Dark
Werewolf Stories to Tell in the Dark

Scholastic
Finding Joe

Tony Mitton

All poetry

Scholastic
Once Upon a Tide
Pip
Plum
The Red and White Spotted Handkerchief
Riddledy Piggledy
The Seal Hunter

Orchard
Big Bad Raps
Fang-tastic Raps
Monster Raps
Robin Hood Raps
Royal Raps
Scary Raps

Kingfisher (for younger readers)
Dazzling Diggers
Flashing Fire Engines
Roaring Rockets
Terrific Trains

Walker
Goldilocks
Little Red Riding Hood
Spooky Hoo-Hah!
What's the Time, Mr. Wolf?
Where's My Egg?

Cambridge University Press
A Door to Secrets: Riddles in Rhyme

Brian Moses

Poetry

Barking Back at Dogs! (Macmillan)
Croc City (Victoria Press)
Don't Look at Me in that Tone of Voice (Macmillan)
Hippopotamus Dancing and Other Poems (Cambridge University Press)
I Wish I Could Dine with a Porcupine (Hodder Wayland)
Knock Down Ginger and Other Poems (Cambridge University Press)
An Odd Kettle of Fish – with John Rice and Pie Corbett (Macmillan)

Poetry anthologies

Aliens Stole My Underpants and Other Intergalactic Poems (Macmillan)
Hysterical Historical series (Macmillan)
I'm Telling on You! – poems about brothers and sisters (Macmillan)
Minibeasts (Macmillan)
Poems about – Me / Me and You / School / Food (Wayland)
School Trips (Macmillan)
A Sea Creature Ate My Teacher (Macmillan)
Secret Lives of Teachers / More Secret Lives of Teachers (Macmillan)
Welcome to the Snake Hotel (Macmillan)
We Three Kings – Christmas poems (Macmillan)

Picture books

The Dragons Are Coming (Ginn)
Play With Me (Ginn)
Shoo Fly Shoo (Ladybird)
Ten Tall Giraffes (Ladybird)

Books for teachers

Catapults and Kingfishers: Teaching Poetry in Primary Schools – with Pie Corbett (Oxford University Press)
My Grandmother's Motorbike – Story Writing in Primary Schools – with Pie Corbett (Oxford University Press)
Stories from the Past (Scholastic)

Literacy hour books

Bubble (All Aboard, Ginn)
Character Portraits (BG Pelican Book, Longman)
Classic Poems – Books 1–3 – co-edited with David Orme, Collins
Essential Texts Books 1–4 (Literacy World, Heinemann)
Follow Me (All Aboard, Ginn)
Hop to the Sky (All Aboard, Ginn)
Poems from Around the World – Books 1–3 co-edited with David Orme (Collins)
Poems to Compare and Contrast (BG Pelican Book, Longman)
School Time, Play Time (All Aboard, Ginn)
Sugarcake (All Aboard, Ginn)
What Kind of Poems? Books 1–3 – co-edited with David Orme (Collins)

Andrew Fusek Peters

Poetry
May the Angels Be With Us (Shropshire County Council)
The Moon is on the Microphone (Sherbourne Publications)
Poems with Attitude – with Polly Peters (Hodder Wayland)
When I Come to the Dark Country (Abbotsford)

Editor of poetry anthologies
On Great Form – form poems (Hodder Wayland)
Poems about Festivals (Wayland)
Poems about Seasons (Wayland)
Sheep Don't Go to School – collection of East European children's poetry (Bloodaxe)
The Upside Down Frown – shape poems (Wayland)

Prose
Barefoot Book of Strange and Spooky Stories (Barefoot)
The Goat Eared King and other Czech Tales (Collins Educational)
The House that Learned to Swim (Ginn)
Salt is Sweeter than Gold (Barefoot)

Philip Pullman

Point-Scholastic
Dark Materials trilogy
    Northern Lights
    The Subtle Knife
    The Amber Spy Glass
Sally Lockhart novels
    Ruby in the Smoke
    The Shadow in the North
    The Tiger in the Well
    The Tin Princess

Other novels
Clockwork or All Wound Up (Corgi Yearling)
Count Karlstein (Corgi Yearling)
The Firework Maker's Daughter (Corgi Yearling)
I Was a Rat (Doubleday)
The New Cut Gang: Thunderbolt's Waxwork (Puffin)
The New Cut Gang: The Gas-Fitters Ball (Puffin)
Spring-Heeled Jack (Transworld)

Fairy tale retellings
Mossycoat – illustrations by Peter Bailey (Scholastic)
The Wonderful World of Aladdin and the Enchanted Lamp (Scholastic)
Puss-in-Boots – illustrations by Ian Beck (Transworld)

For teenage readers
The Broken Bridge (Macmillan)
The Butterfly Tattoo – previously *The White Mercedes* (Macmillan)

Celia Rees

Scholastic
Point Horror Unleashed:
    Blood Sinister
    The Vanished
    The Cunning Man

Bloomsbury
The Witch Child

Macmillan
Colour Her Dead
Every Step You Take
Midnight Hour
Truth or Dare

Hodder & Stoughton
Ghost Chamber
H.A.U.N.T.S. series
Soul Taker

Norman Silver

Fiction
South African Quartet – for teenage readers (Faber & Faber):
    No Tigers in Africa
    An Eye for Colour
    Python Dance
    A Monkey's Wedding

The Blue Horse (Faber & Faber)

Poetry collections
Choose Your Superhero (Hodder & Stoughton)
The Comic Shop (Faber & Faber)
The Walkman Have Landed (Faber & Faber)
Words on a Faded T-shirt (Faber & Faber)

Picture books
Cloud Nine (Bodley Head)
Temper-Temper (MacDonald Young Books)

Website: http://www.storybook.demon.co.uk

Matthew Sweeney

Poetry (Faber & Faber)
Faber Book of Children's Verse (editor) (spring 2001)
Fatso in the Red Suit
The Flying Spring Onion
The Snow Vulture (novel)

Jacqueline Wilson

Transworld
Bad Girls
The Bed and Breakfast Star
Buried Alive!
The Cat Mummy
Cliffhanger
The Dare Game
Double Act
Girls in Love
Girls Out Late
Girls Under Pressure
Glubbslyme
The Illustrated Mum
Jacqueline Wilson's Diary 2001
Lizzie Zip-Mouth
The Lottie Project
The Monster Story-Teller
The Mum-Minder
The Story of Tracy Beaker
The Suitcase Kid
Vicky Angel

Puffin titles for younger readers
Mark Spark in the Dark
Video Rose
The Werepuppy
The Werepuppy on Holiday

Oxford University Press
How To Survive Summer Camp

Barn Owl
Jimmy Jelly

Benjamin Zephaniah

Face – novel (Bloomsbury)
Funky Chickens (Puffin)
School's Out (AK Press)

Talking Turkeys (Puffin)
Wicked World (Puffin)

Audio cassettes
Adult Fun for Kids (Benjamin Zephaniah Associates)
Funky Turkeys (Audio Book and Music Company)

Website: http://www.oneworld.org/zephaniah/